Palaces
for the
People

HOW SOCIAL INFRASTRUCTURE
CAN HELP FIGHT INEQUALITY,
POLARIZATION, AND THE
DECLINE OF CIVIC LIFE

Eric Klinenberg

CROWN
NEW YORK

Published in the United States by Crown, an imprint of the
Crown Publishing Group, a division of Penguin Random
House LLC, New York.
crownpublishing.com

CROWN and the Crown colophon are registered trademarks
of Penguin Random House LLC.

Portions of this book first appeared in *The New Yorker*
("Adaptation," January 7, 2013) and *Wired* ("Want to
Survive Climate Change? You'll Need a Good Community,"
November, 2016).

Library of Congress Cataloging-in-Publication Data
Names: Klinenberg, Eric, author.
Title: Palaces for the people : how social infrastructure can
    help fight inequality, polarization, and the decline of civic
    life / Eric Klinenberg.
Description: First Edition. | New York : Crown, 2018.
Identifiers: LCCN 2018002837 | ISBN 9781524761165
    (hardback) | ISBN 9781524761172 (paperback) |
    ISBN 9781524761189 (ebook)
Subjects: LCSH: Infrastructure (Economics)—United
    States. | City planning—United States. | Equality—
    United States. | Quality of life—United States. | BISAC:
    SOCIAL SCIENCE / Sociology / Urban. | POLITICAL
    SCIENCE / Public Policy / City Planning & Urban
    Development. | ARCHITECTURE / Urban & Land Use
    Planning.
Classification: LCC HC79.C3 .K55 2018 |
    DDC 307.760973—dc23 LC record available at
    https://lccn.loc.gov/2018002837

ISBN 978-1-5247-6116-5
Ebook ISBN 978-1-5247-6118-9

Printed in the United States of America

Jacket design by Lucas Heinrich
Jacket illustration by Felix Sockwell

10 9 8 7 6 5 4 3 2 1

First Edition

For Lila and Cyrus

CONTENTS

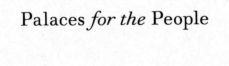

Palaces *for the* People

The Social Infrastructure

On July 12, 1995, a tropical air mass with searing heat and high humidity settled over Chicago, making it feel like Jakarta or Kuala Lumpur. On July 13, the temperature hit 106 degrees and the heat index, which measures how a typical person experiences the weather, reached 126. Local newspapers and television stations announced that the heat wave could be dangerous, but they didn't recognize its severity. Along with basic health warnings and meteorological reports, they also ran humorous stories about how to "ward off wardrobe wilt and makeup meltdown" and shop for air conditioners. "This is the kind of weather we pray for," said a spokesperson for one regional supplier. The *Chicago Tribune* advised readers to "slow down" and "think cool thoughts."

Chicago broke its record for energy consumption that day, and the surge in demand overwhelmed the electrical grid, causing outages in more than two hundred thousand homes, some lasting for days. Water pumps failed, leaving units on high floors dry. Across the city, buildings baked like ovens, roads and railways buckled, thousands of cars and buses overheated. Children riding school buses to camp got stuck in gridlocked traffic and had to be hosed off by public health crews to avoid heat stroke. Despite the mounting problems, Chicago's city government neglected to declare a state of emergency. The mayor, along with leaders of several key city agencies, was out of the city, vacationing in a cooler spot. But millions of residents were stuck in the heat.

Like all cities, Chicago is a heat island, with paved roads and metallic buildings that attract the sun's warmth and heavy pollution that traps it. While the verdant suburbs surrounding Chicago cooled down at night, urban neighborhoods continued to broil. So many people called 911 that paramedics had to put some of them on hold. Thousands rushed to emergency rooms with heat-related illnesses, and nearly half of the city's hospitals refused to admit new patients because they had no more space. A line of trucks formed outside the Cook County Medical Examiner's Office, waiting to unload dead bodies. There were 222 bays at the morgue, all of them filled. The owner of a meatpacking company offered to bring a forty-eight-foot-long refrigerated truck. When it was fully loaded, he brought another, and another, until nine trucks holding hundreds of bodies were jammed into the parking lot. "I've never seen anything like this in my life," said the medical examiner. "We're overwhelmed."

During the week between July 14 and July 20, 739 people in excess of the norm died in Chicago, roughly seven times the toll from Superstorm Sandy and more than twice as many as in the Great Chicago Fire. Before all the bodies had been buried, scientists began to look for patterns behind the deaths. The US Centers for Disease Control and Prevention (CDC) sent a team of researchers from Atlanta and recruited dozens more in Chicago to investigate. Interviewers visited the homes of more than 700 people, creating "matched pairs" of victims and surviving neighbors and compiling demographic information that they used for comparison. Some of the results were unsurprising: Having a working air conditioner reduced the risk of death by 80 percent. Social isolation increased the risk. Living alone was particularly dangerous, because people often fail to recognize the symptoms and the severity of heat-related illnesses. A close connection to another person, even to a pet, made people far more likely to survive.

But fascinating patterns did emerge. Women fared far better than men, because they have stronger ties to friends and family. Despite high levels of poverty, Latinos had an easier time than other ethnic groups in Chicago, simply because in Chicago they tend to live in crowded apartments and densely packed neighborhoods, places where dying alone is nearly impossible.

For the most part, heat wave mortality was strongly correlated with segregation and inequality: eight of the ten community areas with the highest death rates were virtually all African American, with pockets of concentrated poverty and violent crime. These were places where old or sick people were at risk of hunkering down at home and dying alone during the heat wave. At the same time, three of the ten neighborhoods with the *lowest* heat wave death rates were also poor, violent, and predominantly African American, while another was poor, violent, and predominantly Latino. On paper, these neighborhoods looked like they should have fared badly in the heat wave. In fact, they were more resilient than Chicago's most affluent areas. Why?

I grew up in Chicago, and when the heat wave hit I was about to move to California for graduate school. I had no plans to return to my home city. I hadn't thought much about neighborhoods, natural disasters, or the climate. But I couldn't stop thinking about the heat wave, and the puzzle of why some people and places that seemed fated for disaster managed to avoid it. Although I did move to California, I scrapped my plan to study the drug business and started digging into the disaster. I came back to Chicago whenever I could and eventually moved there to conduct fieldwork, turning my family's basement into an operations center and making the heat wave the subject of my dissertation.

Like the CDC, I conducted my own comparison of "matched pairs," only I was looking at how the heat wave affected entire neighborhoods, not just individuals. To get oriented, I found a map of heat deaths and laid it over various maps of poverty, violence, segregation, and aging in Chicago neighborhoods. I identified adjacent communities that had similar demographic profiles yet sharply different rates of heat wave mortality. I ran the numbers, analyzing all the neighborhood data that social scientists ordinarily use, but none of the standard variables could explain the divergent outcomes. So I turned off my computer and hit the streets.

At ground level, I could observe certain neighborhood conditions that aren't visible in quantitative data. Statistics do not convey the differences between poor, minority neighborhoods that are cursed with empty lots, broken sidewalks, abandoned homes, and shuttered storefronts, and those that are densely peopled, busy with foot traffic, enlivened by commercial activity and well-maintained parks, and supported by strong community organizations. As I got to know the rhythms of life in various Chicago neighborhoods, I learned how much these local conditions mattered, both every day and during the disaster.

Consider Englewood and Auburn Gresham, two adjacent neighborhoods on the hypersegregated South Side of Chicago. In 1995, they were both 99 percent African American, with similar proportions of elderly residents. Both had high rates of poverty, unemployment, and violent crime. Englewood was one of the most perilous places during the disaster, with 33 deaths per 100,000 residents. But Auburn Gresham's death rate was 3 deaths per 100,000 residents, making it one of the most resilient places in the city—safer, even, than tony Lincoln Park and the Near North Side.

By the end of my research, I'd discovered that the key difference between neighborhoods like Auburn Gresham and others that are demographically similar turned out to be what I call *social infrastructure*: the physical places and organizations that shape the way people interact.

Social infrastructure is not "social capital"—a concept commonly used to measure people's relationships and interpersonal networks—but the physical conditions that determine whether social capital develops. When social infrastructure is robust, it fosters contact, mutual support, and collaboration among friends and neighbors; when degraded, it inhibits social activity, leaving families and individuals to fend for themselves. Social infrastructure is crucially important, because local, face-to-face interactions—at the school, the playground, and the corner diner—are the building blocks of all public life. People forge bonds in places that have healthy social infrastructures—not because they set out to build community, but because when people engage in sustained, recurrent interaction, particularly while doing things they enjoy, relationships inevitably grow.

During the heat wave, the people of Englewood were vulnerable not just because they were black and poor but also because their neighborhood had been abandoned. The residential blocks looked and felt "bombed out," and the social infrastructure that had once supported collective life had deteriorated. Between 1960 and 1990, Englewood lost 50 percent of its residents and most of its commercial outlets, as well as its social cohesion. "We used to be much closer, more tight-knit," says Hal Baskin, who has lived in Englewood for fifty-two years and currently leads a campaign against neighborhood violence. "Now we don't know who lives across the street or around the corner. And old folks are apprehensive about leaving their homes."

Epidemiologists have firmly established the relationship between social connections, health, and longevity. In the past few decades, leading health journals have published dozens of articles documenting the physical and mental benefits of social ties. But there's a prior question that scientists have not explored as thoroughly: What conditions in the places we inhabit make it more likely that people will develop strong or supportive relationships, and what conditions make it more likely that people will grow isolated and alone?

After the heat wave, prominent Chicago officials publicly declared that the socially isolated people who died had effectively chosen their own fate, and that the communities they lived in had sealed that fate. The mayor, Richard M. Daley, criticized people for not looking after their neighbors, and the human services commissioner, Daniel Alvarez, complained to the press about "people that die because they neglect themselves." But when I spent time in Chicago's most vulnerable neighborhoods, I observed something different. Those who lived there expressed the same values endorsed by residents of more resilient places, and they made genuine efforts to help one another, in both ordinary and difficult times. The difference was not cultural. It was not about how much people cared about one another or their community. It was that in places like Englewood, the shoddy social infrastructure discouraged interaction and impeded mutual support, whereas in places like Auburn Gresham the social infrastructure encouraged those things.

During the decades that residents fled neighborhoods like Englewood, Chicago's most resilient places experienced little or no population loss. In 1995, residents of Auburn Gresham walked to diners, parks, barbershops, and grocery stores. They participated in block clubs and church groups. They knew their neighbors—not because they made special efforts to meet them, but because they lived in a place where casual interaction was a feature of everyday life. During the heat wave, these ordinary routines made it easy for people to check in on one another and knock on the doors of elderly, vulnerable neighbors. "It's what we always do when it's very hot or very cold here," says Betty Swanson, who has lived in Auburn Gresham for nearly fifty years. It's what they always do, pe-riod, no matter the weather. And with heat waves becoming more frequent and more severe, living in a neighborhood with a social infrastructure like Auburn Gresham's is the rough equivalent of having a working air conditioner in every home.

I first reported my findings about the significance of the social infrastructure during the Chicago disaster in my dissertation, and then in a book called *Heat Wave*. When I finished, I began think-ing beyond that particular catastrophic event and investigating the ways that local resources such as libraries, barbershops, and community organizations affect people during ordinary times too. I took a closer look at the neighborhoods that proved so resilient during the heat wave, and I noticed something extraordinary: they were *always* significantly safer and healthier than other places that are demographically similar, and by margins that were star-tlingly large. A half decade before the disaster, for instance, life expectancy in Auburn Gresham was more than five years higher than it was in Englewood. The disparity was even greater—ten years—in another matched pair of adjacent neighborhoods that I'd compared extensively: longevity in South Lawndale (also known as Little Village) was significantly higher than in North Lawn-dale.

These differences were so dramatic, and so pervasive, that they made me wonder whether social infrastructure was even more im-portant than I'd realized. I needed to explore the hidden networks and taken-for-granted systems that support—or, in some cases, undermine—all variety of collective life.

This time, I really did leave Chicago. After all, my hometown's de-pleted neighborhoods are not the only places that suffer from social disconnection, and the problems affected by social infrastructure transcend heat and health. I moved to New York City, where I began teaching at New York University, and I spent two years at Stanford University. I conducted research in many American cities as well as Argentina, England, France, the Netherlands, Japan, and Singapore. While each of the places I've studied has distinctive ecological challenges, political systems, and cultural orientations, their residents share similar concerns. Today, societies around the world are becoming more fragmented, divided, and conflicted. The social glue has come undone.

According to Canada's Global News, "We all live in a bubble." The BBC warns that "class segregation" is "on the rise," in England. *Today Online* reports that "India is regressing in the happiness rankings primarily due to abysmal social capital and a lack of interpersonal trust." Distrust and fear stemming from extreme inequality have fueled a spike in gated communities and armed private security across Latin America. The Associated Press reports that "private guards outnumber public officers" by four to one in Brazil, five to one in Guatemala, and nearly seven to one in Honduras. *Foreign Policy* notes that in China, "stratification has emerged in a society that had hitherto tried to eradicate the very concept. . . . Social class has become increasingly entrenched, opportunities for upward mobility increasingly limited." Even the Internet, which was supposed to deliver unprecedented cultural diversity and democratic communication, has become an echo chamber where people see and hear what they already believe.

In the United States, the presidential election of 2016 was an especially disturbing example of political polarization, and the long campaign exposed social chasms far deeper than even the most worried experts had recognized. The language of red and blue states seems too weak to describe America's splintered cultural and political geography.

The oppositions are not merely ideological, and the divisions run deeper than Trump vs. Clinton, Black Lives Matter vs. Blue Lives Matter, Save the Planet vs. Drill, Baby, Drill. Across America, people complain that their communities feel weaker, that they spend more time on their devices and less time with one another, that schools and sports teams and workplaces have become unbearably competitive, that insecurity is rampant, that the future is uncertain and in some places bleak. Worrying about the decline of communities is a hallmark of modern societies and a trope among public intellectuals. Although I've written extensively about social isolation, I've long been a skeptic of claims that we're lonelier and more disconnected than we were in some mythical golden age. But even I am forced to acknowledge that, in the United States, as in other parts of the world, the social order now feels precarious. Authoritarian leaders threaten to undo entrenched democratic systems. Nations break away from political alliances. Cable news tells its viewers only what they want to hear.

These fissures are expanding at an inopportune moment. The United States, like most developed nations, faces profound challenges—including climate change, an aging population, runaway inequality, and explosive ethnic divisions—that we can address only if we establish stronger bonds with one another and develop some shared interests too. After all, in a deeply divided society each group fends for itself above all others: The rich may make philanthropic contributions, but their own interests are paramount. The young neglect the old. Industries pollute without regard for those downwind or downstream.

Few seem happy about these divisions—oddly, not even the winners. For much of the twentieth century, business leaders and wealthy families believed that they too would benefit from a social pact with blue-collar workers and middle-class professionals; after the Depression, they even supported housing and unemployment insurance for the poor. The system that the United States created was hardly perfect, and entire social programs (for housing, health, and education, among others) said to benefit "the public" actually excluded African Americans and Latinos, who were forcibly relegated into separate social worlds. But by sharing the wealth, investing in vital infrastructure, and promoting an ever-expanding vision of the common good, the nation achieved unprecedented levels of not only social stability but social security too.

Today, this collective project is in shambles. In recent decades, the 1 percent has taken home an outsize share of the nation's economic gains, while the bottom 80 percent of workers have seen their wages stagnate or decline. When millions lost their homes in the foreclosure crisis, the most affluent Americans locked up their spoils, buying "safe deposit boxes in the sky" in soaring urban condominium towers. Those who could afford it went one step further, building survivalist retreats in New Zealand or the wooded Pacific Northwest, secluded places where they can prepare for civilization's end. Meanwhile, the quality of public services deteriorated badly, as did the nation's critical infrastructure. A small number of extraordinarily wealthy people built parallel private systems for air travel, personal security, even electricity; the merely well-off got fast-tracked (in airports, on special toll roads, and even in amusement park lines). The result is apparent everywhere: the great majority endures systems that are crumbling from overuse and underinvestment. Public transit lines are shoddy and overcrowded. Parks and playgrounds are poorly maintained. Public schools are underperforming. Branch libraries have reduced their hours, and in some cases closed for good. Heat, rain, fire, and wind wreak havoc on places that could once withstand them. Vulnerability is in the air.

None of this is sustainable.

American voters said as much in 2016, electing (albeit through the Electoral College rather than by a majority at the polls) a president who promised to blow up the system. But America's divisions have only deepened since President Trump took office. Today, the specter of social unrest haunts cities, communities, and college campuses across the country. We fear one another, and everyone wants protection from the other side.

As a sociologist, I have grave concerns about the powerful trembling of these social fault lines. As a citizen, I can't help asking how we can rebuild the foundations of civil society in the kinds of diverse, democratic nations we find throughout the world today. As a student of history, I wonder how we can move beyond violent opposition to a perceived nemesis and develop a sense of shared purpose based on commitments to justice and decency. As a parent of young children, I wonder whether we can repair things so that they will have a chance to flourish and not spend their lives cleaning up our mess.

But how will we do this? Economic development is certainly one solution, though increasing national prosperity helps a society become more cohesive only if everyone—not just the most successful—shares in the gains. Besides economic growth, two ideas about how to rebuild society have dominated the conversation: One is technocratic, and involves engineering physical systems that enhance security and facilitate the circulation of people and goods. The other is civic, and involves promoting voluntary associations—the Masons, the National Association for the Advancement of Colored People, block clubs, gardening groups, and bowling leagues—that bind people into communities. Both ideas are important, but they're only partial solutions. Social infrastructure is the missing piece of the puzzle, and building places where all kinds of people can gather is the best way to repair the fractured societies we live in today.

It's long been understood that social cohesion develops through repeated human interaction and joint participation in shared projects, not merely from a principled commitment to abstract values and beliefs. Alexis de Tocqueville admired the laws that formally established America's democratic order, but he argued that voluntary organizations were the real source of the nation's robust civic life. John Dewey claimed that social connection is predicated on "the vitality and depth of close and direct intercourse and attachment." "Democracy must begin at home," he famously wrote, "and its home is the neighborly community."

Contemporary students of civil society have made similar observations. In *Bowling Alone*, the Harvard political scientist Robert Putnam attributes declines in health, happiness, education, economic productivity, and trust to the collapse of community and diminished participation in civic organizations. In *Coming Apart*, the conservative pundit Charles Murray argues that the "American project" has always been based on human beings "coming together voluntarily to solve their joint problems." This "civic culture" was once "so widely shared among Americans that it amounted to a civil religion," Murray writes, echoing Tocqueville. But recently—and here is the source of his title—the "new upper class" has effectively abandoned the collective project, forming a separate society based on "spatial, economic, educational, cultural, and, to some degree, political isolation." Unless the nation renews its sense of solidarity across class lines, Murray warns, "Everything that makes America exceptional will have disappeared."

Both Putnam and Murray advocate changing our cultural attitudes toward civic life and community building, and recommitting to the common good. For nearly two decades, Putnam's magisterial account of declining social capital and his clarion call for more public engagement have influenced political officials, religious leaders, activists, journalists, and scholars alike. Yet the problems that made Putnam anxious when he published *Bowling Alone* are just as prevalent today, and in some ways more extreme.

In the late 1990s, when the book was written, one of Putnam's principal concerns was that families had retreated from public life—the world of sports leagues and community groups—in favor of the private living room, where parents and children gathered together to watch TV. Today, of course, an evening when an entire family watches the same program in a common room is something like a utopian fantasy. Maybe on a special occasion: the Super Bowl, the Oscars, a presidential election, or a session of collective video gaming. But on typical nights it's everyone on their own device.

Drawing on the best available data on American social behavior, the Harvard sociologist Peter Marsden shows that, surprisingly, trends in social activity have been fairly steady since the 1970s. Americans spend a bit more time with friends and a bit less time with neighbors than they used to, and, to no one's surprise, they're more likely to socialize on the Internet than in a restaurant or bar. Membership in traditional voluntary organizations hasn't changed much either. But Americans are also more likely than they used to be to say that they cannot trust "most people." The most recent numbers from the Bureau of Labor Statistics show a modest but steady decline in rates of volunteering, with participation going down "across persons of all levels of educational attainment." Immersion in their private worlds, writes the Berkeley sociologist Claude Fischer, probably goes hand in hand with alienation from public life.

Moral suasion has failed to increase our level of engagement in local institutions, where democracy takes root. But cultural values, and exhortations to change them, are not the only influences on our everyday social routines. As proponents of the New Urbanism movement have demonstrated, people with the same interest in social connection, community building, and civic participation have varying opportunities to achieve those things depending on the conditions in the places where they spend time. The social and physical environment shapes our behavior in ways we've failed to recognize; it helps make us who we are and determines how we live.

This book argues that social infrastructure plays a critical but underappreciated role in modern societies. It influences seemingly mundane but actually consequential patterns, from the way we move about our cities and suburbs to the opportunities we have to casually interact with strangers, friends, and neighbors. It is especially important for children, the elderly, and other people whose limited mobility or lack of autonomy binds them to the places where they live. But social infrastructure affects everyone. And while social infrastructure alone isn't sufficient to unite polarized societies, protect vulnerable communities, or connect alienated individuals, we can't address these challenges without it. In this book, I'll explain how and why.

Infrastructure is a relatively new and entirely modern concept. It is "a collective term for the subordinate parts of an undertaking, substructure, foundation," says the *Oxford English Dictionary*, and the higher-order projects it supports could be economic, military, or social. "It is by definition invisible, part of the background for other kinds of work," writes Susan Leigh Star, the late scholar of science and technology, in a classic article, "The Ethnography of Infrastructure." It is embedded, "sunk into and inside of other structures, social arrangements, and technologies," she adds. It is "transparent to use, in the sense that it does not have to be reinvented each time or assembled for each task, but invisibly supports those tasks." Its scope, in time and in space, is large. It is "fixed in modular increments, not all at once or globally." It is taken for granted by members of the group that use it most often. And, crucially, it becomes most visible when it breaks down.

The Vanderbilt University anthropologist Ashley Carse writes that the word "infrastructure" first came to the English language in the late nineteenth century, from France, where it was used to refer to the engineering work required for new railways, such as building embankments, bridges, and tunnels. After World War II, infrastructure became a buzzword in military and economic development circles. "Infrastructure was more than a word," Carse claims. "It was world-making," because it justified "specific visions and theories of political and socioeconomic organization" that Cold War planners advocated. The infrastructure concept catapulted from policy jargon into popular American discourse in the 1980s, when, perhaps surprisingly, President Ronald Reagan said his foreign policy objective was to help developing countries foster "the infrastructure of democracy, the system of a free press, unions, political parties, universities, which allows a people to choose their own way."

Today, the word "infrastructure" usually makes us think of what engineers and policy makers refer to as hard or physical infrastructure: large-scale systems for transit, electricity, gas, oil, food, finance, sewage, water, heat, communications, and storm protection. Sometimes experts call these systems the "critical infrastructure," because policy makers perceive them to be essential for functioning societies.

When the levees break, cities and coastal areas flood, sometimes catastrophically. When the power goes out, most businesses, health care providers, and schools cannot operate, and many transit and communications networks stop running too. Breakdowns in the fuel supply can be even more consequential, since oil generates most of our heat and gas powers the trucks that deliver nearly all the food and medications consumed in large cities and suburbs as well as the automobiles that most people depend on to travel. No one needs a lengthy description of the problems that occur when the sewage system stops working. But the real problems come when several or all of these systems collapse simultaneously, as they do during extreme weather events or terrorist attacks. Unfortunately, history shows that such things are impossible to prevent, no matter how sophisticated our technology or design. And, as most policy makers and engineers see it, when hard infrastructure fails, as it did in the great Chicago heat wave, it's the softer, social infrastructure that determines our fate.

"Infrastructure" is not a term conventionally used to describe the underpinnings of social life. But this is a consequential over-sight, because the built environment—and not just cultural pref-erences or the existence of voluntary organizations—influences the breadth and depth of our associations. If states and societies do not recognize social infrastructure and how it works, they will fail to see a powerful way to promote civic engagement and social interaction, both within communities and across group lines.

What counts as social infrastructure? I define it capaciously. Public institutions, such as libraries, schools, playgrounds, parks, athletic fields, and swimming pools, are vital parts of the social infrastructure. So too are sidewalks, courtyards, community gar-dens, and other green spaces that invite people into the public realm. Community organizations, including churches and civic associations, act as social infrastructures when they have an estab-lished physical space where people can assemble, as do regularly scheduled markets for food, furniture, clothing, art, and other con-sumer goods. Commercial establishments can also be important parts of the social infrastructure, particularly when they operate as what the sociologist Ray Oldenburg called "third spaces," places (like cafés, diners, barbershops, and bookstores) where people are welcome to congregate and linger regardless of what they've pur-chased. Entrepreneurs typically start these kinds of businesses be-cause they want to generate income. But in the process, as close observers of the city such as Jane Jacobs and the Yale ethnographer Elijah Anderson have discovered, they help produce the material foundations for social life.

What doesn't qualify as social infrastructure? Transit networks determine where we live, work, and play, and how long it takes to move between places. But whether they're social infrastruc-ture depends on how they're organized, since a system designed for private vehicles will likely keep people separate as they travel (and consume enormous amounts of energy), whereas public sys-tems that use buses and trains can enhance civic life. Although they have obvious social impacts, waterworks, waste treatment facilities, sewage systems, fuel supply lines, and electric grids are usually not social infrastructures. (We don't congregate in these places.) But conventional hard infrastructure can be engineered to double as social infrastructure.

Take the case of levees. A simple levee is an artificial embankment that people build to prevent water from going into places they don't want it to be. "A levee," write Marshall Brain and Robert Lamb, on the popular HowStuffWorks website, "is typically little more than a mound of less permeable soil, like clay, wider at the base and narrower at the top. These mounds run in a long strip, sometimes for many miles, along a river, lake or ocean." This kind of levee is physical infrastructure that protects social life on the dry side, not a robust social infrastructure. But levees can be designed differently. In the late 1930s, for instance, engineers needed to protect Washington, DC's Federal Triangle neighborhood after a spell of heavy rains led to massive urban flooding. They could have put up a narrow mound of soil, but instead they built the Potomac Park Levee, a sloped walking path capped by a curved stone wall. In subsequent years the dual-purpose levee and parkland became one of the most popular public spaces in the city, a place where thousands of people go daily without even knowing that they're on top of a critical infrastructure. Today, a growing number of architects and engineers are designing hard infrastructure, such as seawalls and bridges, so that it also functions as social infrastructure by incorporating parks, walking trails, and community centers. These projects, which already exist in places like Istanbul, Singapore, Rotterdam, and New Orleans, provide multiple benefits, from protecting against storm surges to promoting participation in public life.

Different kinds of social infrastructure play different roles in the local environment, and support different kinds of social ties. Some places, such as libraries, YMCAs, and schools, provide space for recurring interaction, often programmed, and tend to encourage more durable relationships. Others, such as playgrounds and street markets, tend to support looser connections—but of course these ties can, and sometimes do, grow more substantial if the interactions become more frequent or the parties establish a deeper bond. Countless close friendships between mothers, and then entire families, begin because two toddlers visit the same swing set. Basketball players who participate in regular pickup games often befriend people with different political preferences, or with a different ethnic, religious, or class status, and wind up exposed to ideas they wouldn't likely encounter off the court.

Social infrastructures that promote efficiency tend to discourage interaction and the formation of strong ties. One recent study, for instance, shows that a day care center that encourages caregivers and parents to walk in and wait for their children, often inside the classroom and generally at the same time, fosters more social connections and supportive relationships than one where managers allow parents to come in on their own schedules and hurry through drop-off and pickup so they can quickly return to their private lives. Because much of our hard infrastructure—highways, airports, food supply chains, and the like—is designed to promote efficient circulation of people or vital resources, it can accelerate the trend of social atomization. Think, for example, about the contrast between a village where everyone gets their water from the same well and a city where everyone gets their water from faucets in their private homes.

Not all hard infrastructure leads to isolation. A recent ethnographic study of the New York City subway system, for instance, shows that people forge "transient communities" as they ride through the metropolis. The daily experience of spending time on crowded train cars rarely leads to long-term relationships, but it helps passengers learn to deal with difference, density, diversity, and other people's needs. It fosters cooperation and trust. It exposes people to unexpected behavior and challenges stereotypes about group identity. The subway is not only New York City's main social artery but also its largest and most heterogeneous public space.

While the subway is a form of social infrastructure that, like public athletic fields and childcare centers, promotes interaction across group lines, some social infrastructures encourage bonds among people who already have a great deal in common. In elite American communities, private country clubs, some of which forbid female members and informally exclude certain ethnic or racial minorities, help build strong social ties and business networks that ultimately deepen the nation's divisions and inequities. Border walls, including the one that currently separates parts of Israel and Palestine as well as the one that President Trump promises to build on the border of Mexico and the United States, are quintessentially antisocial infrastructures. Paradoxically, zones around border walls, including checkpoints and access gates, often attract a diverse set of people, including members of the very groups that the structure is meant to separate, and occasionally they become sites for political engagement and protest. But their net impact is unmistakable: on good days, they segregate, discriminate, and entrench inequalities; on bad days, they incite violence.

Given the world's cultural diversity, it's no surprise that there is great variety in the kinds of social infrastructure that people find essential. In rural areas, for instance, hunting clubs, town halls, and fairgrounds are key sites for gathering, and community suppers are a staple of local life. Watering holes are hubs of social activity in societies across the planet, and some are especially important. "Of all the social institutions that mold men's lives between home and work in an industrial town," writes the MassObservation collective, in a classic ethnographic study of British industrial culture, the pub is more prevalent, "holds more people, takes more of their time and money, than church, cinema, dance-hall, and political organizations put together." In other public places, ordinary people are "the audiences, watchers of political, religious, dramatic, cinematic, instructional or athletic spectacles," but in the pub, things are different. "Once a man has bought or been bought his glass of beer, he has entered an environment in which he [is] participator rather than spectator." Drinking grounds serve as sites of civic activity in other societies, of course. The Germans have their beer gardens, the French their cafés, the Japanese their *izakayas* and karaoke bars. They are vivid examples of those "third places," the small, warm, intimate settings where people in public can feel like they're at home.

I've observed all kinds of collective life made possible by strong social infrastructures in foreign settings. For several years my family and I spent part of the winter living and working in Buenos Aires, and some of our most rewarding encounters with local residents happened around a soccer field (which in fact was a playground that children informally converted for their purposes every afternoon) where my son became a regular. In Doha and Jerusalem, as in so many Middle Eastern and African cities, I was continually pulled into the magnetic cultural activity at the souk. I never joined the early morning Tai Chi or group dance sessions in the parks near the places I stayed in Shanghai or Beijing, but undoubtedly millions of older Chinese people participate in them regularly for the social as well as physical benefits. In Iceland, geothermal swimming pools called "hot pots" are vital civic spaces, where people regularly cross class and generational lines. The Mexican *zócalo*, the Spanish *plaza* (or *plaça*, in Barcelona), and the Italian *piazza* serve the same function. I've never been to Rio de Janeiro, the Seychelles, Kingston, Jamaica, or Cape Town, but I've spent enough time in other coastal areas and lakefronts to know that nearly everyone appreciates the social opportunities created by a well-maintained beach.

Few modern social infrastructures are natural, however, and in densely populated areas even beaches and forests require careful engineering and management to meet human needs. This means that all social infrastructure requires investment, whether for development or upkeep, and when we fail to build and maintain it, the material foundations of our social and civic life erode.

The components of social infrastructure rarely crash as completely or as visibly as a fallen bridge or a downed electrical line, and their breakdowns don't result in immediate systemic failures. But when the social infrastructure gets degraded, the consequences are unmistakable. People reduce the time they spend in public settings and hunker down in their safe houses. Social networks weaken. Crime rises. Older and sick people grow isolated. Younger people get addicted to drugs and become more vulnerable to lethal overdoses. Distrust rises and civic participation wanes.

Robust social infrastructure doesn't just protect our democracy; it contributes to economic growth. One of the most influential trends in urban and regional planning involves converting old hard infrastructure, like discontinued rail lines and shipping docks, into vibrant social infrastructures for pedestrian activities. The High Line, which has driven billions of dollars of real estate and commercial development in Lower Manhattan, generated explosive social activity—and, alas, fueled runaway gentrification and displacement—is the most prominent model of this emerging urban form. But many other recent or current projects are reviving dead infrastructure with social infrastructure networks that attract residents, tourists, and businesses. The BeltLine in Atlanta is developing slowly, but will ultimately repurpose a twenty-two-mile rail corridor circling the city into thirty-three miles of trails, as well as a string of parks, public artworks, and affordable housing projects, that help connect some forty-five neighborhoods. In New Orleans, the Lafitte Greenway is a bicycle and pedestrian trail that's designed to connect people and neighborhoods that might otherwise remain divided. The 606 Trail in Chicago, the Philadelphia Viaduct Rail Park, the Los Angeles River Revitalization, and the Petite Ceinture in Paris are being designed to do similar work. After burying the highway, Boston built a greenway on top of the Big Dig. Today, the Toronto City Council is trying to develop an urban park in the underpass of the Gardiner Expressway. A coalition in Sydney, Australia, is pushing to convert the Anzac Bridge into a massive pedestrian green space. The garden and walking path that Rotterdam developed on an abandoned elevated train track has environmental as well as social benefits. The designer, Doepel Strijkers, engineered a system that uses industrial waste to heat buildings along rails, dramatically reducing their carbon emissions and making the air that pedestrians breathe a little cleaner.

Across the planet, projects like these evince the value of social infrastructure, and the rising demand for it as well. Not long ago, Jane Jacobs and other prominent advocates for improving urban life argued that entrepreneurs, not governments, should build the spaces that support our social interactions. But places like the High Line have not emerged from the free market. They required thoughtful design, careful planning, and, crucially, enlightened leadership from the public sector. Often they advanced through partnerships, with nonprofit organizations and civic coalitions supporting initiatives that cities and states couldn't undertake on their own.

Today, the United States, like most other nations, is primed to make a historic investment in infrastructure, the kind we haven't made in generations. Despite their many disagreements, American voters are undivided in their support for such public works projects. The need for significant infrastructure spending, if not necessarily the way to pay for it, was one of the few things that both Trump and Clinton agreed on in the 2016 presidential campaign. In coming decades, perhaps even in the next few years, we will invest hundreds of billions of dollars in critical infrastructure across the country, trillions around the world. Given the extraordinary stresses that are coming from our growing population, rising consumption, and global warming, and the sorry state of the systems that Americans rely on for electricity, transit, food, water, communications, and climate protection, we have no choice.

What we must decide, however, is whether rebuilding our social infrastructure will be part of this project. Most current debates about infrastructure investment in the United States focus exclusively on conventional hardline systems, as if the material underpinning of our social and civic life were an unrelated concern. To be fair, one reason for that omission, in this country at least, is that social infrastructure is not yet a familiar concept. Other nations treat infrastructure more expansively, though, and we should too, lest we squander a historic opportunity to strengthen the places where we live and work.

To that end, this book will identify the elementary forms of social infrastructure and show how they shape conditions in different kinds of places, urban and suburban, rich and poor, in the United States and around the world. When possible, I'll use the same comparative method I used to study the fate of Chicago neighborhoods, since looking closely at positive and negative cases is a powerful way to illustrate what works and what doesn't, and sometimes even why. Most of the evidence I'll marshal to support my claims comes from my own research and experiences. But I will also draw heavily on pioneering studies by colleagues across the social sciences and design fields that show how places shape human interaction and determine our fate. Although they rarely use the term, the body of research they've produced helped me understand the value of social infrastructure and its potential role in rebuilding civic life.

In the chapters ahead, I'll show how social infrastructure can alleviate—or, when neglected, exacerbate—contemporary problems that we spend a great deal of time, money, and energy trying to solve: social isolation, crime, education, health, polarization, and climate change.

As we explore these global challenges, we'll see that in every case the social infrastructure is just as important as the critical networks we've always prioritized, and that each depends on the other in ways we've yet to fully appreciate. My argument is neither that social infrastructure matters more than conventional hard infrastructure, nor that investing in social infrastructure is sufficient to solve the underlying problems of economic inequality and environmental degradation that make this moment so dangerous. It's that building new social infrastructure is just as urgent as repairing our levees, airports, and bridges. Often, as we will see, we can strengthen both simultaneously, building lifeline systems that are also, to borrow the phrase that Andrew Carnegie used to describe the twenty-eight hundred or so grand libraries that he built across the world, "palaces for the people." But first we need to recognize the opportunity.

CHAPTER ONE

A Place to Gather

It's a balmy Thursday morning in the New Lots neighborhood of East New York, Brooklyn, 70 degrees and sunny on the last day of March. The sidewalks have awakened. Small groups of middle-aged men banter outside bodegas and on stoops of the small, semi-detached brick houses that are common in the area. Mothers and grandmothers push strollers and watch over preschool children who hop and skip and revel in the unseasonable warmth. It seems early for recess, but the schoolyards are buzzing. Traffic is light on the narrow residential streets, but occasionally someone honks, a motorcycle engine fires, a truck roars past.

Street life in East New York is busy, but not always congenial. The district is one of the poorest in New York City, with about half the residents living below the poverty line. It's also one of the most segregated. Nearly 95 percent of residents are black or Latino, and only 1 percent are white. Social scientists sometimes call East New York socially isolated, because its peripheral location and limited public transit options restrict access to opportunities in other parts of the city, while people who don't live there have little reason to visit and strong incentives to stay away.

The area is among the most violent neighborhoods in New York City, with especially high levels of homicide, felony assault, and sexual assault. Conditions like these are bad for everyone, but research shows that they're particularly treacherous for older, sick, and frail people, who are prone to hunkering down in their apartments and growing dangerously isolated when they live in inhospitable physical environments. That's not only what I observed in the Chicago heat wave; it's what social scientists who conduct large-scale studies of isolation have found as well.

Living in a place like East New York requires developing coping strategies, and for many residents, the more vulnerable older and younger ones in particular, the key is to find safe havens. As on every other Thursday morning this spring, today nine middle-aged and elderly residents who might otherwise stay home alone will gather in the basement of the neighborhood's most heavily used public amenity, the New Lots branch library.

At first glance, it's an uninviting facility. The run-down, two-story brown brick building is set back behind a wide sidewalk and bus stop, with a beige stone facade at the entry, a broken chain-link fence on one side and a small asphalt parking lot on the other. In recent years the city designated the library site "African Burial Ground Square," because it sits atop a cemetery used to inter slaves and soldiers during the Revolutionary War.

The library is small, and it's already crowded despite the early hour and the good weather. There are two banks of computer terminals with Internet access on the first floor, and patrons, sometimes more than one, at every machine. There's a small display case holding photographs and short biographies of Nobel Prize winners; tall wooden bookshelves with new releases, atlases, and encyclope- dias; an information desk with flyers promoting library events for toddlers, young readers, teens, parents, English-language students, and older patrons. One librarian asks if I need anything. Another stacks books.

I ask to see the second floor, and Edwin, a sweet and soft-spoken information supervisor, takes me upstairs. Here there are three separate universes. A designated children's space, which is worn but, Edwin says, about to get renovated; a set of tables for English- language courses, which are always oversubscribed; and, in the back, a classroom that serves as the library's Learning Center, a place where anyone over age seventeen who's reading below GED level can get special instruction, individually and in groups.

Everyone is welcome at the library, regardless of whether they're a citizen, a permanent resident, or even a convicted felon. And all of it, Edwin reminds me, is free.

I tell Edwin that I'm here for the event in the basement com- munity room, and it turns out he's heading there too. We walk downstairs together and he points out the building's deteriora- tion. The shelves, ceilings, stairwells, and wall panels are wearing out. Wires are exposed. There are rusted toilets and sinks in the bathroom. The doors don't close properly. In the community room there's an aging, cream-colored linoleum floor, glaring fluorescent lights, wood paneling, and a small stage strewn with plastic stack- ing chairs. I think about the burial ground that was here and I realize we can't be far from the bones.

The community room serves many purposes: theater, class- room, art studio, civic hall. But this morning two staff members, Terry and Christine, will transform it into something unusual: a virtual bowling alley. They've arrived early to set up a flat screen television, link an Xbox to the Internet, clear out a play space, and assemble two rows of portable chairs. It's opening day of the Library Lanes Bowling League, a new program that encourages older patrons in twelve libraries in Brooklyn to join local teams and compete against neighboring branches. Nine people at New Lots signed up to play, and after weeks of practice, they're about to take on Brownsville and Cypress Hills.

Branch libraries offer something for everyone, but the extra services and programming that they provide for older people are particularly important. As of 2016, more than twelve million Americans aged sixty-five and above live by themselves, and the ranks of those who are aging alone is growing steadily in much of the world. Although most people in this situation are socially active, the risk of isolation is formidable. A fall, an illness, or the inevitable advance toward frailty can render them homebound. If older friends and neighbors move away or die, their social networks can quickly unravel. If they get depressed, their interest in being out in the world can diminish. Street crime discourages everyone from going outdoors and socializing in public, but it's particularly intimidating for the old. In neighborhoods where crime is high or the social infrastructure is depleted, old people are more likely to stay home, alone, simply because they lack compelling places to go.

New Lots has its library, though, and today the doors open at 10 a.m. Soon after, ten patrons, eight women and two men (one who's here to watch) ranging in age from fifty to nearly ninety, walk downstairs. Among them are Miss Jonny, who sports wraparound sunglasses, tall red boots, a black-and-red polka-dot scarf, and a gray newsboy cap. There's Suhir, in a seafoam sweat suit and a white hijab. Santon, a soft-spoken man from Guyana, dons a blue baseball cap and loose-fitting green trousers. Una, Bern, Salima, Miba, Daisy, and Jesse round out the crew. They greet one another warmly. Some women hug. A few clasp hands. Daisy gives Una a gentle high five that turns into a longer touch and a smile.

Terry, an ebullient library information specialist with big eyes and a dazzlingly bright smile, hands each player a royal blue bowling shirt with a white public library logo on the front pocket and TEAM NEW LOTS in yellow on the sleeve. Terry is the team's coach and cheerleader, and she's trying to pump them up for the match. Christine, a veteran librarian who wears rectangular glasses and holds a pencil and a phone in her shirt pocket, is the main organizer, having recruited participants from the computer classes and book clubs she leads at the library. Terry and Christine walk around the room and help the participants get into their uniforms, buttoning and pulling them down so they won't snag when it's time to bowl.

When everyone is outfitted the players take their seats, making small talk and tapping their toes in anticipation. Christine tries to link the Xbox to the machine in the basement at the Brownsville Library, where their opponents, invisible to us but no doubt similarly composed, have put on their own uniforms and settled in for the match. It worked perfectly in practice, but this time there's something wrong with the connection. Christine calls Brownsville. Yes, they're there, just working on the Wi-Fi. In a few minutes, the machines are in sync and the game is on.

Brownsville goes first and the team watches the ball roll up the side of the alley, taking out a few pins but leaving most upright. There's some rumbling and a bit of nervous laughter coming from the seats. It grows louder when the next roll leaves the opponents' frame open. Everyone knows they can win.

Jesse bowls first for New Lots, and she's not fooling around. "Come on, Jesse!" Terry shouts. Her teammates clap enthusiastically. "Let's do this now!" Terry calls out again. Jesse approaches the screen and stops at the designated spot about fifteen feet in front of it. She seizes the hand control, raises her right arm to the sky until the Xbox registers her presence, and reaches out 90 degrees to take the ball. On screen, the ball rises to show that she's ready. Jesse reaches back and sweeps her arm forward, as if she were rolling a ball up the alley. It's a powerful roll, and at first it seems on target but it winds up too true to center and three pins stay standing. Some in the group applaud. Some sigh in exasperation. Jesse looks incredulous. "You got this!" Terry yells. "You good." Jesse approaches the ball again, looking determined. She lifts, rolls, nails the spare. The room erupts.

The New Lots bowlers kill it, extending their lead frame after frame. They are old, and some are enfeebled, probably too weak to hold an actual ball. Only one player had ever participated in an old-fashioned bowling league, the kind that requires gutters, slick shoes, and a shiny wood floor. Robert Putnam famously lamented the demise of these leagues during the late twentieth century. Their disappearance, he argued, signaled a worrisome decline in social bonds. But here a group of people who could easily be at home, cut off from friends and neighbors, is involved in something greater than deep play. They're participating, fully and viscerally, in collective life. The mood is electric. Turn by turn, the players stand, boosted by their teammates' applause and the librarians' exhortations, salute the screen, and demolish their digital targets. "I'm feelin' for Brownsville right now," Terry exclaims. *"But not too much!"*

The team's confidence is soaring when the second match gets going, but it doesn't take long to see that Cypress Hills is for real. The opponents go first and it's a strike. Jesse responds with a strike of her own. Then Cypress Hills rolls another, and Terry makes fish lips, popping her eyes in disbelief. Suhir makes a spare. New Lots is in it. But then Cypress gets a turkey, three strikes in a row, and Terry is incredulous. "There's some funny business going on here!" she insists. "That's Walter," the Cypress Hills librarian. "I *know* that's Walter. I'ma call him out."

She doesn't, though, and the Cypress Hills team gradually pulls away despite strong performances from most of the New Lots players. The game goes by quickly and the mood, naturally, is more subdued. When it ends there's a short pause and a little confusion about what will happen. "We should ask them for a rematch," Christine says. "I think we can beat 'em."

Christine jumps on the phone, a landline attached to the wall, and reaches Walter at the other library. She ribs him a little: "That wasn't you bowling, was it?" She smiles for a beat. "Uh-huh. Right. Well, hey, it's still early, you guys want to do another?" They did, and in a few moments they're back at it again.

This time New Lots takes nothing for granted. Terry, who's decided that if Walter is playing then she is also, jumps in and knocks down everything. Santon hits a spare. "It's all you, Miss Jonny!" Terry shouts, and Miss Jonny makes her first strike of the morning. Bern follows with another perfect roll, then Una does the same, and now New Lots has its own turkey and a sizable lead. Terry is ecstatic. She screams out encouragement and struts around the room in circles with each strike or spare. When Jesse seals the victory with a strike in the tenth frame, the entire group is joyous, like Yankee Stadium after a play-off win.

There are team photos, high fives, and hugs all around. Christine tells the players that there will be trophies for the top teams and a giant trophy for the library that wins everything. Miba, feeling bold and full of swagger, suggests that they just engrave New Lots on it now and bring the trophy over. Her teammates are in hysterics, their smiles as deep as a lifetime.

The celebration lasts just a few minutes. It's noon, the players are hungry, and there are hours of sunshine ahead. I congratulate the team and wish them good luck on the season. "Thanks," Terry says. "We gonna be *fine*."

I leave feeling uplifted by the cheering, the camaraderie, the joy of watching people who hardly know one another turn their neighborhood into a community. It was a rare moment of what the great French sociologist Émile Durkheim called "collective effervescence," and I hadn't expected it, not at the library.

Today, we may have every reason to feel atomized and alienated, distrustful and afraid—and the demographics are as challenging as the politics. There are more people living alone than at any point in history, including more than a quarter of Americans over the age of sixty-five, who are at particular risk of becoming isolated. That's worrisome, because, as a large body of scientific research now shows, social isolation and loneliness can be as dangerous as more publicized health hazards, including obesity and smoking. But some places have the power to bring us together, and the kind of social bonding I witnessed that morning in Brooklyn happens in thousands of libraries throughout the year.

Libraries are not the kinds of institutions that most social scientists, policy makers, and community leaders usually bring up when they discuss social capital and how to build it. Since Tocqueville, most leading thinkers about social and civic life have extolled the value of voluntary associations like bowling leagues and gardening clubs without looking closely at the physical and material conditions that make people more or less likely to associate. But social infrastructure provides the setting and context for social participation, and the library is among the most critical forms of social infrastructure that we have.

It's also one of the most undervalued. In recent years, modest declines in the circulation of bound books in some parts of the country have led some critics to argue that the library is no longer serving its historic function as a place for public education and social uplift. Elected officials with other spending priorities argue that twenty-first-century libraries no longer need the resources they once commanded, because on the Internet most content is free. Architects and designers eager to erect new temples of knowledge say that libraries should be repurposed for a world where books are digitized and so much public culture is online.

Many public libraries do need renovations, particularly the neighborhood branches. But the problem libraries face isn't that people no longer visit them or take out books. On the contrary: so many people are using them, for such a wide variety of purposes, that library systems and their employees are overwhelmed.

According to a 2016 survey conducted by the Pew Research Center, about half of all Americans aged sixteen and over used a public library in the past year, and two-thirds say that closing their local branch would have a "major impact on their community." In many neighborhoods the risk of such closures is palpable, because both local library buildings and the systems that sustain them are underfunded and overrun.

In New York City, where I live, library circulation is up, program attendance is up, program sessions are up, and the average number of hours that people spend in libraries is up too. But New York City doesn't have an exceptionally busy library culture, nor is it a national leader. The distinctions belong to other places: Seattle leads the nation in annual circulation per capita, followed by Columbus, Indianapolis, San Jose, San Francisco, Jacksonville, and Phoenix. Columbus has the highest level of program attendance: five of every ten thousand residents participate in library activities there each year. San Francisco and Philadelphia are close behind, as are Boston, Detroit, and Charlotte. New York City trails them all.

New York City also ranks low in per capita government spending for the system. The New York Public Library receives $32 for every resident, on par with Austin and Chicago but less than one-third of the San Francisco Public Library, which gets $101 per resident.

Urban library systems in the United States have long been public-private partnerships, and city governments have long relied on philanthropists to fund much of the library's work. Still, it's hard to understand why most cities give so little public support to their libraries. According to recent reports from the Pew Research Center, more than 90 percent of Americans see their library as "very" or "somewhat" important to their community, and in the past decade "every other major institution (government, churches, banks, corporations) has fallen in public esteem except libraries, the military, and first responders." Despite this support, in recent years cities and suburbs across the United States have cut funding for libraries, and in some cases closed them altogether, because political officials often view them as luxuries, not necessities. When hard times come, their budgets get trimmed first.

Doing research in New York City, I learned that libraries and the social infrastructure are essential not only for a neighborhood's vitality but also for buffering all kinds of personal problems—including isolation and loneliness. And while these problems may be particularly acute in struggling neighborhoods like East New York, they're hardly confined to them. Consider Denise, a fashion photographer in her late thirties whom I met in the Seward Park Library children's floor on a chilly April morning. She's wearing jeans, a long black coat, and large tortoiseshell glasses. As she sits, she scans the room and quickly decompresses. The children's floor might not be a second home anymore, not since her daughter started preschool, but during her first few years of being a mother Denise was here almost every day.

"I live close," she tells me. "We moved here six years ago. I didn't think about what it would mean to live by a library, not at all. But this place has become very dear to me. So many good things have happened because we come here." Denise stopped working when her daughter was born, but her husband, an attorney, didn't. On the contrary, the demands on his time increased, and he worked well into the evening, leaving her in a small Manhattan apartment with a baby she loved intensely but also with a feeling of loneliness beyond anything she'd experienced before. "I had a pretty bad case of postpartum depression," she tells me. "There were days when getting out of the apartment was just a huge struggle. I suddenly went from working in this job I loved to spending all my time at home trying to take care of things that really matter but that I didn't know how to do. I felt like I was in the trenches, you know? You can go crazy like that. I had to get out, but it was hard. And I didn't know where to go."

At first Denise tried taking the baby to coffee shops, hoping she'd nap or rest quietly while she went online or read. That didn't happen. "I'd go to Starbucks and there would be all these people there working or having meetings. It's a place for grown-ups, right? When the baby starts crying everyone turns around and stares at you. It's like: 'What are you doing here? Can't you take her away?' It's definitely not kid-friendly."

Denise had spent time in libraries as a child in California but hadn't used the system much since moving to Manhattan. On one especially stressful day, though, she put her daughter in the stroller and brought her into the Seward Park Library, just to see what was there. "An entire world opened up that day," she remembers. "There were the books, of course. You can't have a lot of them when you live in a small apartment, but here there are more than we could ever read. And then I discovered that there's a whole social scene going on between everyone who comes here. The parents, the nannies, the children, people in the neighborhood. The librarians! They are so kind here."

Immediately, Denise found herself surrounded by other first-time mothers who shared her struggles but could enjoy the fun parts of parenting too. She saw that her baby wasn't the only one crying when everything seemed fine, refusing to eat or nap. She realized that she wasn't alone. Denise also found more experienced mothers and babysitters who could answer most of her questions. "You just kind of start chatting," she explains, "and it's amazing but you wind up having these really personal, really intense conversations." I ask if something similar happens in parks and playgrounds, and Denise says that it does, to some extent, but that it's easier here in the library, especially on the children's floor. The room is warm and open, the children are protected, and there's an ethos that makes it easy for parents to connect with one another.

"It's like you become part of the mommy tribe here," Denise explains, "and that makes parenting a lot less lonely." The tribe endures, even when the kids go to school and mothers spend less time in the local branch. Some of the people Denise and her daughter met during those early years in the library remain close friends.

The accessible physical space of the library is not the only factor that makes it work well as social infrastructure. The institution's extensive programming, organized by a professional staff that upholds a principled commitment to openness and inclusivity, fosters social cohesion among clients who might otherwise keep to themselves. Friendships develop quickly in the library in part because the place sponsors so many shared activities for children and, by extension, for caretakers too. Denise and her daughter did lap-sit classes for early literacy, bilingual song and story hours, magic shows, and classes for music and art. "In those first years there's a lot of unstructured time that you're just looking to fill," Denise tells me. "You can pay to take classes in some places, but it's expensive, and sometimes you just can't get there, the schedule that day doesn't work out. The library is great because you can pop over and there's always something happening. You just check out the calendar and make it part of your week, or just show up and jump in."

Librarians, Denise discovered, play an important role helping parents and children feel comfortable in the library. Sometimes, she says, they provide even greater service. "At one point, you know, our cat was not doing very well. I was thinking, 'Oh my God, my daughter is so attached to this cat. What happens if it dies?' Our librarian had recommended a lot of children's books to me, so I asked her for a book that would help my kid understand death. And you know what? She actually had a few books about pets who die. She knew what I needed! She knew!" In the end Denise's cat recovered. "She really does have nine lives," she says, laughing. "But I learned about the kind of resource I have in the library. And I felt lucky to have that help."

The help at the library made a difference in the way Denise

felt about herself as a mother, and eventually she gained enough confidence to return to work. That meant hiring a nanny, and entrusting her daughter to a stranger wasn't easy. "That's such a big emotional hurdle," she says, "but there was this one nanny I saw at the library a lot, and I loved the way she was caring for this little girl. She was really involved and really sweet and really loving. I knew that's what I needed for my daughter too. I told the nanny I was going back to work and she referred me to the woman who became, like, not only my nanny, but my favorite person in the world." Denise now calls the library "a lifesaver," and though that may be an exaggeration, there's no question that the institution proved valuable in ways she'd never imagined.

Why have so many public officials and civic leaders failed to recognize the value of libraries and their role in our social infrastructure? Perhaps it's because the founding principle behind the library—that all people deserve free, open access to our shared culture and heritage, which they can use to any end they see fit—is out of sync with the market logic that dominates our time. (If, today, the library didn't already exist, it's hard to imagine our society's leaders inventing it.) But perhaps it's because so few influential people understand the role that libraries already play in modern communities, or the many roles they could play if they had more support.

In New York, as in cities across the United States and around the world, neighborhood libraries and librarians do all kinds of unexpected things for surprisingly large numbers of people. Their core mission is to help people elevate themselves and improve their situation. Libraries do this, principally, by providing free access to the widest possible variety of cultural materials to people of all ages, from all ethnicities and groups.

For older people, especially widows, widowers, and those who live alone, libraries are places for culture and companionship, through book clubs, movie nights, sewing circles, and classes in art, music, current events, and computing. When Library Lanes scales up to the city level, no old person in the five boroughs need bowl alone again. The elderly can also participate in some of these activities in senior centers, but there they can do them only with other old people, and often that makes them feel stigmatized, as if old is all they are. For many seniors, the library is the main place they interact with people from other generations. It's a place where they can volunteer and feel useful. It's where they can be part of a diverse and robust community, not a homogeneous one where everyone fears decline.

Libraries provide different benefits to young people. They expose infants and toddlers to books and stories that would otherwise be inaccessible. They help youths inch toward independence, giving them library cards and letting them choose how to use them. Libraries offer refuge and safe space to teenagers who'd rather study or socialize than hang out in the streets. Librarians help students with homework and offer after-school programs in art, science, music, language, and math. They recommend books, authors, even entire genres to young people who are searching for something different but can't yet name it. Libraries help children and teenagers feel responsible, to themselves and to their neighbors, by teaching them what it means to borrow and take care of something public, and to return it so others can have it too.

By doing all this, libraries also help families and caretakers. They provide a social space and shared activities for new parents, grandparents, and nannies who feel lonely, disconnected, or overwhelmed when watching an infant or a toddler by themselves. They help build friendships and support networks among neighbors who'd never met before taking a library class. They teach parenting skills to people who want or need them. They watch children, sometimes very young ones, whose parents work late or on weekends and who can't afford childcare. They give families confidence that their kids are in good hands.

Libraries may be the textbook example of social infrastructure in action, but other places and institutions do similarly vital work connecting people who need a hand. The Harvard sociologist Mario Small has looked at how the organization of different childcare centers shapes relationships among parents, particularly single mothers. In centers that encourage parental involvement, even if only at drop-off and pickup, mothers build friendships even when they're not looking for companions. These institutions, he writes, "are also spaces for interaction, buildings with halls, stairs, and lobbies where mothers certainly have an opportunity not only to make friends but also, when friends do not emerge, to see each other and each other's children repeatedly, becoming part of the daily marches from home to center to work to center to home that organize the habits of many working mothers." Through repeated encounters, mothers whose children attend these institutions develop high levels of trust in one another, and that quickly yields bonds of friendship and mutual support. The centers become critical sites of social activity, yielding play dates that give one mother a few extra hours to work or rest, information about schools and scholarships, tips about available jobs, and the kind of last-minute emergency help that every parent occasionally needs.

Not all childcare centers promote this level of support and solidarity. Donna, one of the mothers whom Small interviews, recounts her experience at a day care center in a downtown financial district, one that's set up to serve a busy corporate clientele. The center has a rolling drop-off and pickup schedule, designed to match the parents' long and erratic workdays, and as a consequence the parents didn't interact regularly or get to know one another's children well. The schedule is not the only issue. The space is compact and the environment is professional, in keeping with the neighborhood. There's not much room for parents to relax and hang out. For their part, the teachers make little effort to get parents to linger and play with the kids when they are in the building. The result, Donna says, is that there are "no parents sitting down and chatting or anything like that." The center offered reliable childcare when her son was in the building, but it didn't help her develop the relationships she needed in the rest of her life.

Most debates about education focus on the relationship between school quality and individual student achievement. That's sensible, since schools play such an important role in determining people's fate in modern societies, even in those where inherited privilege matters more for success than merit or hard work. But educational institutions do far more than teach individual students. From childcare centers to research universities, schools create social worlds that shape and sustain entire communities. They're our primary public institutions for establishing democratic ideals and instilling civic skills. Schools are our modern agoras, gathering places where we make and remake ourselves and develop a sense of where we belong.

Schools are organizations, but they're also social infrastructures. The way they're planned, designed, and programmed shapes the interactions that develop in and around them. For students, teachers, parents, and entire communities, schools can either foster or inhibit trust, solidarity, and a shared commitment to the common good. They can also set boundaries that define who is part of the community and who is excluded. They can integrate or segregate, create opportunities or keep people in their place.

Schools, of course, are particularly important social spaces for children. They're the physical places where students make the friendships that shape who they become. In fact, there's a considerable body of psychological research showing that peer groups and school social environments affect child development far more than parents do. Since the advent of social media, however, the Internet and the mobile phone have challenged the primacy of schools—and not just schools, but all other physical places where people meet for face-to-face interaction, from pubs to playgrounds, churches to community groups. Whether and how this affects social isolation and human connection are two of the most difficult questions of our time.

The Internet and social media have unquestionably made it easier to meet new people and maintain contact with friends and family. They allow us to share all kinds of information, from the most mundane to the most intimate, with huge numbers of people, in real time. (After all, there are more than two billion monthly Facebook users alone.) Today, as Aziz Ansari and I learned when we were doing research for *Modern Romance,* the Internet is where Americans are most likely to search for and find their spouse. It's where people go when they want to find out where to protest or rally. And, of course, it's where they go to post photographs of their children, their family vacation, their breakfast, themselves.

It's common, these days, to hear that the Internet, and particularly social media, is making us lonelier and more isolated than ever. These claims may well feel true to those who long for simpler, happier times—but there's no good evidence that they're accurate. Indeed, research by the Berkeley sociologist Claude Fischer suggests the opposite: drawing on forty years of social surveys, Fischer's work shows that the quality and quantity of Americans' relationships are about the same today as they were before the Internet existed. The most reliable behavioral data available show that using mobile phones, the Internet, and social media has a positive effect on both the size and the diversity of people's personal networks. For most of us, Facebook friends and Instagram followers are supplements to—not surrogates for—our social lives. As meaningful as the friendships we establish online can be, most of us are unsatisfied with virtual ties that never develop into face-to-face relationships. Building real connections requires a shared physical environment—a social infrastructure.

Sherry Turkle, an eminent psychologist and scholar of science and technology at MIT, is particularly interested in the way social media affect the quality of our interactions. According to her research, the incessant electronic messaging that's so common among young people is crowding out time for face-to-face conversation. That matters, she writes, because conversation is "the most human—and humanizing—thing we do. . . . It's where we develop the capacity for empathy. It's where we experience the joy of being heard, of being understood. And conversation advances self-reflection, the conversations with ourselves that are the cornerstone of early development and continue throughout life."

If in-person conversation is humanizing, online discourse can too often be the opposite. Apps like Tinder and OkCupid allow people to start electronic conversations with large numbers of strangers, but as Aziz and I found in our research for *Modern Romance*, these exchanges often devolve quickly, with people treating one another more rudely and crudely than they would in face-to-face interactions. In interviews, even well-meaning people confessed to feeling that the people they meet online sometimes seem more "like bubbles on a screen" than flesh-and-bone human beings. What's striking about this behavior is that it happens in forums where people are looking for love and intimacy. On other parts of the Internet, from Twitter to Reddit, the discourse can be even more venomous.

Making social life work well with the Internet isn't easy, and, as Turkle recognizes, people throughout the world are growing frustrated with the excesses of Internet culture. Turkle calls for us to turn away from our screens and "reclaim conversation," focusing on the people and places in front of us. Doing so requires searching for commonalities in those who are different and for humanity in those who disagree with us. It requires recognizing that communications technologies work best, and fulfill us most, when they direct us to physical places that everyone can access. Consider, for instance, the social group that's most often accused of shunning face-to-face interactions in favor of electronic communication: teenagers.

According to research by danah boyd, director of the research institute Data & Society, young people spend so much of their social time online because adults—from helicopter parents to hypervigilant school administrators and security guards—give them few other options. Despite higher crime rates, teens in previous generations had more freedom to roam around their neighborhoods and local public spaces than today's youths. They had more unstructured time after school and on weekends; they even had more free time during school, and far less surveillance. "Increasing regulation means that there aren't as many public spaces for teens to gather," boyd writes. "Facebook, Twitter, and MySpace are not only new public spaces: they are in many cases the only 'public' spaces in which teens can easily congregate with large groups of their peers. More significantly, teens can gather in them while still physically stuck at home."

The teens whom boyd interviewed insisted that they prefer hanging out in person to messaging on smartphones, but adults have restricted their mobility so thoroughly that they have few alternatives. The Internet has become young people's core social infrastructure because we've unfairly deprived them of access to other sites for meaningful connection. If we fail to build physical places where people can enjoy one another's company, regardless of age, class, race, or ethnicity, we will all be similarly confined.

Libraries are precisely these kinds of places, and in many neighborhoods, particularly those where young people aren't hyperscheduled in formal after-school programs, they're as popular among adolescents and teenagers who want to spend time with other kids their age as they are among older people and new parents. That's a claim that should be easy to verify: simply go into the branch library closest to you a few minutes before the school day is out, and watch as a steady stream of students pours in and settles down for the afternoon.

Why are libraries such popular places for young people? One reason is that, as public institutions, they're open, accessible, and free. Another is that the library staff welcomes them; in many branches, they even create special places where teenagers can be with one another. To appreciate why this matters, compare the social space of the library with the social space of popular commercial establishments, such as Starbucks or McDonald's. Commercial entities are valuable parts of the social infrastructure, and there's no doubt that classic "third places," including cafés, bars, and restaurants, have helped revitalize cities and suburbs. But not everyone can afford to frequent them, and not all paying customers are welcome to stay for long. Spending time in a market-driven social setting—even a relatively inexpensive fast-food restaurant or pastry shop—requires paying for the privilege. Inside almost every Starbucks, Dunkin' Donuts, or McDonald's, particularly those in neighborhoods where there are teenagers, poor people, or old people around, there's usually at least one sign that says No Loitering. And it's not just a suggestion.

Some New York City McDonald's franchises impose time limits of twenty or thirty minutes "while consuming food" that, depending on the client, management may or may not enforce. Race matters, but so too do class and age. Groups of teenagers are routinely asked to leave commercial establishments, even after they make their purchases. In 2014, a group of elderly Korean Americans in New York City publicly challenged a McDonald's franchise whose managers began to kick them out of the restaurant less than an hour after they'd ordered, charging them with colonizing the seats and quashing business.

Older and poor people will often avoid Starbucks altogether, because the fare is too expensive and they feel like they don't belong. The elderly library patrons I got to know in New York City told me that they feel even less welcome in the trendy new coffee shops, cocktail bars, and restaurants that are so common in gentrifying neighborhoods. Poor and homeless library patrons don't even consider entering these places. They know, from experience, that simply standing outside a high-end eatery or watering hole can prompt managers to call in the police.

You rarely see a police officer in a library, but libraries are places where people attend to one another, regardless of what else they are doing. In a world where we spend ever more of our time staring at screens, blocking out even our most intimate and proximate human contacts, public institutions with open-door policies compel us to pay close attention to the people nearby. After all, places like libraries are saturated with strangers, people whose bodies are different, whose styles are different, who make different sounds, speak different languages, give off different, sometimes noxious, smells. Spending time in public social infrastructures requires learning to deal with these differences in a civil manner.

This is not to say that public spaces are always peaceful and serene. During the time I spent in branch libraries, for instance, I witnessed a variety of conflicts: destitute men arguing over access to the bathroom; unattended children fistfighting during a special event; an unemployed man shouting that teenagers were playing video games on computers that should be for adults only; a mentally ill homeless person disrupting an entire section of patrons by muttering violent threats. According to a security guard at a branch I frequented, one day a heroin addict collapsed of an over-dose at a table and had to be rescued by paramedics, and another day someone defecated on the floor.

These problems are inevitable in a public institution that's dedicated to open access, especially when other institutions, from methadone clinics to homeless shelters and food banks, routinely turn away—and often refer to the library!—the very people who most need help. But what's remarkable is how rarely these disruptions happen, how civilly they are managed, and how quickly the library regains its rhythm afterward. Even in the roughest neighborhoods, branch libraries are not heavily guarded, nor are they staffed with social workers and counselors. Instead, they establish and informally enforce their own norms and codes of conduct, trusting patrons to honor them and getting compliance 99 percent of the time. "You have to try very, very hard to get kicked out of this library," one branch manager told me. "And we're going to do everything possible to find you a place."

Everyday life in libraries is a democratic experiment, and people cram into libraries to participate in it whenever the doors are open.

The openness and diversity that flourishes in neighborhood libraries was once a hallmark of urban culture; in fact, the most influential theories about what makes city life culturally distinctive emphasize the pleasures as well as the challenges of dealing with difference on a daily basis.

In some ways, American cities are growing more diverse. Immigration is booming, especially in New York City. Today, there are more than three million immigrants in New York, about one-third of whom have arrived since 2000. In cities across the country, you can hear languages, eat food, and find or partake in cultural activities that weren't much a part of America a few generations ago. The United States remains an open society that, as always, incorporates new people and reinvents itself.

In other ways, though, American cities remain divided and unequal, with some neighborhoods cutting themselves off from difference, particularly when it comes to race and social class. Some communities do this by building walls and gates, some by aggressively policing those who look like they don't belong. Others, including some enclaves of affluence in New York City, do it more subtly, perhaps without intent. The real estate gets so expensive that only the wealthy can afford to live there. Shops and restaurants go upscale, attracting a certain clientele. The neighborhood becomes homogeneous and insular, not open and diverse. The social environment grows less hospitable. The architecture becomes forbidding and severe.

The Seward Park Library, a stately red brick and limestone Italian Renaissance building at the edge of the nation's first municipal playground, Seward Park, might look elite and exclusive. It's a gorgeous structure, built from the opulence of a previous gilded age. But the library, which sits at the point of convergence for Chinatown, a mass of public housing projects, and a rapidly developing urban glamour zone for young professionals, has long been the heart of the Lower East Side community. Its doors are open to everyone, and everyone comes.

For the past 170 years, the Lower East Side has been a popular neighborhood for poor immigrants, in part because its location, on low-lying land near the river, made it unattractive for those who could afford a nicer setting, but mostly because—to this day—it has thousands of apartment buildings where enormous numbers of people squeeze into units that look a lot like the tenements that zoning codes no longer allow. In the mid-nineteenth century, Irish immigrants rushed into the area, pioneers whom the established New Yorkers blamed for turning a prosperous neighborhood into an ethnic slum. Then came the Germans, followed by Eastern

European Jews, who stayed in the neighborhood for much of the twentieth century. A few thousand older Jews as well as a handful of small synagogues remain there today. But today's Lower East Side is primarily Puerto Rican and Chinese and, with a 31 percent child poverty rate, is disproportionately poor.

In the past decade, the area around Seward Park has begun to gentrify. Next door, co-op apartments that were originally built for blue-collar union workers now sell for more than $1 million. Across the street, the former headquarters for *The Forward*, the leading newspaper for American Jews, was recently converted into a luxury condo building. Down the block there's Mission Chinese Food, the Manhattan outpost of a San Francisco culinary sensation whose chef won a Rising Star award from the James Beard Foundation, an upscale cocktail bar, and, of course, a juice bar. But for now the neighborhood remains an immigrant enclave, and the landmark library, one of the original sixty-five libraries in New York City funded by Andrew Carnegie's $5.2 million donation in 1901, serves its aspiring residents in more or less the same ways that it has since opening in 1909. It's also sustained its level of activity: Seward Park circulates more than five hundred thousand items annually (about fourteen hundred books and a handful of DVDs each day) and attracts more than twenty thousand people into its programs, making it one of the busiest branches in the system.

I first visited the Seward Park Library on a gray January morning. I took the F train from West Fourth Street to East Broadway, the last stop in Manhattan, walked past a small encampment where a homeless man was getting himself together, and went up the stairway to Rutgers Street. The first thing I noticed was the long string of high-rise red brick public housing projects clustered around the FDR Drive, near the East River. A few years before, I'd toured those buildings with the Rebuild by Design competitors to observe flood damage from Sandy. They'd been inundated with seawater. The first floors were uninhabitable; the elevators were malfunctioning; the power, phone, and cable lines in the basement were a tangled, corroded mess. The common areas outside were ugly and neglected, with cracked asphalt, uncomfortable benches, small patches of unkempt grass. At the time I hadn't thought much about where the thousands of people who lived in these buildings could go to escape the dreary environment. Visiting the library, it became clear.

When I entered the gates to Seward Park I immediately saw a group of twenty old people, mainly women, all Chinese, dancing for exercise despite the winter weather. A few preschool children were swinging. Small groups of old men walked circles around the path. A homeless man was asleep near the public restrooms, which were locked down and closed until spring.

The library itself, a regal, four-story structure with high arched windows and an imposing, rusticated limestone base, is at the northeast corner of the park, and there's a large public space with long stone benches in front of the entrance. I arrived there a few minutes before 10 a.m., when the library opens, and found four-teen people scattered around the area, some hovering by the door or on the short stone staircase leading up to it, others standing on the asphalt below. There was a young professional couple: he held a paper coffee cup from the gourmet café across the street; she held two DVDs. There was an old Jewish woman, hair wrapped in a kerchief, carrying a small book bag and talking to a gray-haired man in jeans and a parka about Donald Trump. Two heavy-set Latinas in their thirties or forties rested against the rail on the stairway, arms folded, occasionally reaching for a phone. An old Chinese man in a gray hat and a tan overcoat sat on the cold bench. A few college-age students with heavy backpacks stood alone, and four ragged-looking men, homeless or maybe coming from a shel-ter, clustered by the entrance. One kept checking the time.

At ten o'clock sharp a librarian in an oversize suit jacket

unlocked the front door and held it open. "Good morning," he said, with a warm smile and a nod of recognition for each familiar face, and a kind, welcoming one for mine.

The disheveled men rushed inside. One beelined for the first-floor bathroom, the only one that's officially open to all patrons, even though there are two more in the basement and another for children only on the second floor. One raced up the stairs, and the others dropped their bags on the tables by the big front windows and began to browse through the new books. Most patrons gave the men some leeway, trying to avoid the smell, and then everyone went to their spot. The couple returned their DVDs, grabbed another from reserve, and left. The old woman in the kerchief went right to the desktop computers and started checking her e-mail. The Chinese man took the stairs to the third floor, where, I soon learned, he and two friends spend every morning reading Mandarin newspapers. The Latina women walked around the circulation desk to the lounge area, which is open until it becomes part of the designated teen space at 2 p.m., and immediately pulled out their phones.

Once the first wave of patrons settled in I walked over to the library worker who'd greeted us at the entrance and introduced myself. "I'm Andrew," he replied, extending a bony hand that emerged from the long sleeves on his vintage black jacket, and clasped mine in a gentle grip. "How can I help?"

For branch librarians, helping people find more than they're looking for is the essence of the job. "There are few jobs that exist today where you're really just doing good things as a public servant," Andrew told me one day. "You're not screwing anyone over. You're not taking advantage of anybody. You're just offering a free service."

Andrew grew up in Los Angeles. He has a twin brother, and

often on weekends their mother, a British immigrant who didn't drive, would take them on long bus rides to either the main branch of the Los Angeles Public Library or the Beverly Hills Public Library. "They were nowhere near where we lived," he recounted. "But the buildings were so beautiful, and she wanted to expose us to that inspiring architecture. To this very day I think about how different it was to visit a library as opposed to everywhere else. Being in them just felt different. That's stuck with me to this very day.

"My father wasn't around much, and the library was a place where my mother could just relax while my brother and I would look through books. The one book that I associate with our trips there most of all is *No Fighting, No Biting!* I think it's by Else Holmelund Minarik, and it's illustrated by Maurice Sendak. We must have checked that book out more than, oh God, I don't know, more than any other. There were two siblings involved in it. And my mother would just sort of drolly look at the two of us as she was reading about these bickering siblings. That will be with me forever."

Andrew moved to New York City, where his brother lived, and applied for an entry-level job as an "information specialist" in the library system. It didn't pay well: the starting salary for librarians in the New York Public Library system is around $48,500, and pay for information specialists, who generally lack a graduate degree in library sciences, is considerably lower. But it was better than Starbucks, where he worked for a while, and it would put him on a career path that felt meaningful, and full of purpose. When he started working, he quickly knew he'd made the right choice.

"Here's something I realized once I got here," Andrew explained "At Starbucks, and at most businesses, really, the assumption is that you, the customer, are better for having this thing that you purchase. Right? At the library, the assumption is you *are* better. You have it in you already. You just sort of need to be exposed to these things and provide yourself an education. The library assumes the best out of people. The services it provides are founded upon the assumption that if given the chance, people will improve themselves." And, as I observed during my time in libraries, social interactions—with librarians and with other patrons—are one of the crucial ways that this self-improvement happens.

Both children and adults benefit from the relationships they build in branch libraries. "Children," Andrew said, "are still growing and they're still absorbing things. Hopefully adults are doing that too. But a lot of adults who use the library aren't just people who are trying to improve themselves in terms of, say, intellectual capacity. They're trying to improve themselves because they need an environment that's not like every other environment they've ever known, that judges them, that takes advantage of them, that doesn't want anything to do with them, doesn't understand their role in society. They want to be in a place where they can feel this generous assumption of human nature, and they should always get that here." The library is where they feel cared for and connected. It sustains them, especially during lonely times.

The library staff has more autonomy to develop new programming than I'd expected from an established public institution. Managers, it seems, assume the best of their librarians, and their information specialists too. The first thing Andrew introduced at Seward Park was Tea Time, which he held in the corner of the third-floor reference and reading room. "I noticed a lot of people come in early in the morning and never go to programs," he told me. "They're just using the library as a resting place. And I thought, maybe because my parents are British, 'What's more relaxing than a good cup of tea and a newspaper or book?'"

Tea Time quickly became one of the library's more popular programs, attracting a regular group of older patrons and a steady stream of newcomers who were happy to get a free hot drink and biscuits in the morning. It also became a reliable source of social activity: as they sat together, sipping tea, participants also shared newspapers, and then stories, until over time a small and unlikely community of Chinese, Turkish, Latino, Jewish, and African American patrons had formed. "I like the way the program brings people together," Andrew explained. "But that's not all. The other reason I like it is because Tea Time is one of the best ways that the library can express faith in people. There's a term you don't hear these days, one you used to hear all the time when the Carnegie branches opened: *Palaces for the People*. The library really is a palace. It bestows nobility on people who can't otherwise afford a shred of it. People need to have nobility and dignity in their lives. And, you know, they need other people to recognize it in them too. Serving tea doesn't seem like that big a deal, but the truth is it's one of the most important things I do."

CHAPTER TWO

Safe Spaces

The Pruitt-Igoe housing project, a complex of thirty-three eleven-story buildings that opened in North St. Louis between 1954 and 1956, is perhaps the most famous failure in the history of American public housing. The initial design, by the highly regarded architect Minoru Yamasaki (who went on to design the World Trade Center), called for a mixed-rise set of towers connected by walking paths and "a river of trees," but the Public Housing Administration forced a revision to bring down costs. The housing agency standardized the plan and substituted cheaper construction materials than those Yamasaki wanted. Ultimately, each of the thirty-three identical buildings featured an open first floor for community activity; a corridor with common rooms, laundry facilities, and a garbage room on several "anchor floors"; and elevators and stairwells shared by all of the roughly one hundred families residing in the tower. Families rushed into the new apartments, which were in great demand. In 1957, more than 90 percent of all units were occupied.

A few architecture critics initially praised the high modernist project for its spatial efficiency and abundance of green space. But major problems soon emerged. In the 1960s, Oscar Newman, a young professor of architecture and urban planning from Washington University in St. Louis, initiated a study to determine what was wrong. Newman had read about the conditions at Pruitt-Igoe, but that hadn't prepared him for what he saw in person. Vandals had destroyed the laundry and garbage facilities. Graffiti covered the common areas wherever he went. There was garbage all over the public areas, both inside and outside the buildings, and the sidewalks were coated with broken glass. Residents complained about the spike in prostitution, drug dealing, burglary, and violent crime. Families with children had grown fearful and began hunkering down in their private residences. "The corridors, lobbies, elevators, and stairs were dangerous places to walk," Newman writes. "Women had to get together in groups to take their children to school and to go shopping." People began moving out, and soon there was an exodus. By 1971, about half the units in the complex had been shuttered and the occupancy rate was 35 percent.

Newman acknowledges that his first reaction was to blame the residents for ruining what could have been a beautiful, modern housing development. "Walking through Pruitt-Igoe in its heyday of pervasive crime and vandalism, one could only ask: What kind of people live here?" he says. That's not surprising, since prevailing theories about the causes of crime have long focused on the characteristics of people who break the law. When criminologists examine the factors that lead to high levels of lawlessness, they typically consider "background" factors like a person's race, gender, income, family situation, and education level, or, in some cases, their moral values and capacity for self-regulation. Initially, Newman did the same, and he observed what most government officials did: a community with a high concentration of poor, black, single mothers and their children. It appeared as if no one was able to exert control.

But as Newman spent more time at Pruitt-Igoe, he realized that the situation was more complex. Most residents, for instance, kept their own apartments "neat and well maintained—modestly furnished perhaps, but with great pride." Moreover, Newman visited the small balconies shared by two families, and found them to be "pockets that were clean, safe, and well-tended." He wanted to know what accounted for the differences between the project's private and public spaces, and he began searching for answers.

The well-kept apartments and semiprivate landings offered Newman one clue; but what he observed in the housing project adjacent to Pruitt-Igoe taught him even more. "Across the street from Pruitt-Igoe was an older, smaller, row-house complex, Carr Square Village, occupied by an identical population," he writes. "It had remained fully occupied and trouble-free throughout the construction, occupancy, and decline of Pruitt-Igoe." People made good use of their semiprivate gardens and public areas, which meant that there were plenty of what Jane Jacobs, whose ideas greatly influenced Newman, called informal surveillance through "eyes on street." Families felt safe and relatively comfortable, and with good reason: the crime level was three times lower than it was in Pruitt-Igoe. Newman was fascinated. "With social variables constant in the two developments," he explains, the underlying reasons "that enabled one to survive while the other was destroyed" had to involve "physical differences," not the characteristics of the residents.

Newman compared the physical features of the two projects, and the differences were stark. In Carr Square Village, each row house contained just a few families, all of whom could identify one another as neighbors, if not friends. They shared a compact entry-way and a semiprivate outdoor area, and it was relatively easy to establish standards for using and maintaining the space since only a few neighbors would be sharing it. In Pruitt-Igoe, however, the design and management of the buildings made it impossible for residents to regulate behavior in and around them. So many people shared the same public areas that no one person could manage or maintain them, and, unlike high-rise buildings in middle-class areas, there were no doormen or resident superintendents who were paid to do that job. What's more, the population of the thirty-three-building complex was so large that it was "impossible to tell resident from intruder." For Newman, the lesson was straightforward. The dire situation at Pruitt-Igoe was not due to the characteristics of the people who lived there, but to the project's physical infrastructure. Building and landscape design "play an important role in reducing crime and in assisting residents in controlling behavior in their housing environments," he concludes. "Residents maintained and controlled those areas that were clearly defined as their own," but the larger, shared public spaces "evoked no feelings of identity or control [and] . . . made it impossible for even neighboring residents to develop an accord about acceptable behavior."

Newman included an account of the physical factors that made Pruitt-Igoe so much more dangerous than Carr Square Village in his 1972 report, *Defensible Space*. That same year, the government began to demolish the Pruitt-Igoe complex, a process that would go on until 1976, when the last doomed building came down. Newman's theory of defensible space gained considerable influence among urban planners and criminologists and helped shape the design of new housing projects throughout the world. (Newman even became a character in the 2015 HBO miniseries *Show Me a Hero*.) Subsequent research has questioned whether all of Newman's findings are generalizable. In some cities, we know, poor neighborhoods with high-rise public housing are safer than poor neighborhoods without it, and Newman failed to identify which conditions make some projects more successful than others. He was wrong to conclude that, in the case of crime and housing, "the apartment tower itself . . . is the real and final villain." But Newman's main point, that the built environment helps determine local crime levels, is widely accepted. In fact, the evidence for it is now stronger than ever.

Some of that evidence comes from a school of crime prevention that emerged around the same time as Newman's defensible space theory. Crime Prevention Through Environmental Design (CPTED) begins with the insight that a person who is likely to commit a crime in a certain environment would never consider doing so in another. As C. Ray Jeffery, the criminologist who conceived CPTED, puts it, "There are no criminals, only environmental circumstances which result in criminal behavior. Given the proper environmental structure, anyone will be a criminal or a noncriminal." It follows, then, that crime control measures are unlikely to work if they are designed to target individual offenders. Instead, crime is best managed "through the manipulation of the environment where crimes occur."

To this day, however, most policies that aim to reduce crime focus on punishing people rather than improving places. The president has called for a national "stop and frisk" police program; the attorney general wants more severe sentencing; advocates of "law and order" are resurgent. We invest little in housing and far less in safe sidewalks and neighborhood amenities like libraries, senior centers, and community gardens, which draw people into the public realm and put more eyes on the street. We spend even less to address criminal "hot spots": specific places, such as empty lots, abandoned buildings, and liquor stores, that are known to foster illegal activities. Funds for improving community and street-level conditions in the places most likely to suffer from crime and violence are in short supply.

Government officials may have political reasons to crack down on potentially dangerous people rather than on demonstrably dangerous places, but the scientific grounds are shaky.

We have other more effective and less expensive ways to reduce crime today. And a growing body of scientific research shows that some of the best options involve investing in social infrastructure.

In the nineteenth century, British researchers began studying the variation in crime rates between and within cities. While some of this work offered relatively simple accounts in which concentrated poverty led to higher crime, others pushed to another level, asking why there was so much variation in crime rates among poor neighborhoods. "Most of this work was descriptive and offered theories," writes the University of Pennsylvania criminologist John Mac-Donald, "but did not attempt to provide guidance on how to curb crime." He compares this tradition, unfavorably, with the work of British health scholars, most notably John Snow, whose research on cholera "noted the importance of the spatial environment in shaping human health and suggested the separation of sewers and drinking water wells to prevent water-borne diseases." Reducing crime is more difficult than preventing cholera, but MacDonald, who's done pioneering experimental research on how places influence crime rates, is one of many contemporary environmental criminologists with something new and significant to offer.

Social scientists have long played a major role in shaping crime policies. Consider the "broken windows" theory, which the Harvard political scientist James Q. Wilson and the Rutgers criminologist George Kelling introduced in the *Atlantic* in 1982. According to Wilson and Kelling, criminals perceive broken windows and other forms of neighborhood disorder as signals of weak social control and, in turn, as evidence that crimes committed there are unlikely to be checked. "Though it is not inevitable," they argue, "it is more likely that here, rather than in places where people are confident they can regulate public behavior by informal controls, drugs will change hands, prostitutes will solicit, and cars will be stripped. That the drunks will be robbed by boys who do it as a lark, and the prostitutes' customers will be robbed by men who do it purposefully and perhaps violently. That muggings will occur."

"Broken Windows" is not only one of the most cited articles in the history of criminology, it's also one of the most influential works of public policy research, sometimes referred to as "the bible of policing" and "the blueprint for community policing." Since the 1980s, cities throughout the world have used Wilson and Kelling's ideas as motivation for "zero tolerance" policing, wherein officers carefully monitor petty crimes such as graffiti, loitering, public intoxication, even panhandling, and courts severely punish those convicted of committing them. "If you take care of the little things, then you can prevent a lot of the big things," said the former Los Angeles and New York City police chief William J. Bratton, who used broken windows theory not only as a guide in both places but also in his global consulting work. In practice, this meant stopping, frisking, and arresting more people, particularly those who live in high-crime areas. It also meant a spike in reports that police were unfairly targeting minorities, particularly black men.

Despite some relatively recent experimental evidence supporting elements of the theory, broken windows always worked better as an idea than as a work of empirical science. As the Columbia University law professor Bernard Harcourt writes, "the famous broken windows theory has never been verified," and "the existing social-scientific data suggest that the theory is probably not right." The problems, which include the fact that perceptions of disorder generally have more to do with the racial composition of a neighborhood than with the amount of broken windows or graffiti, are numerous and well documented. A veritable A-list of renowned scholars, including the Harvard sociologist Robert Sampson, the University of Chicago sociologist Stephen Raudenbush, and the Berkeley criminologist Franklin Zimring, have identified flaws at all levels of the broken windows argument, and with the policies it inspired.

For present purposes, though, I'm less interested in the validity of the broken windows theory than in the way it was framed and interpreted. The authors, Wilson and Kelling, encouraged policy makers to crack down on the petty crimes that lead to things like broken windows, which meant more aggressive street-level policing. Had they been more interested in the influence of social infrastructure, however, they might have taken another tack.

Consider the famous scenario in which the authors propose how spirals of disorder and decay get started. "A piece of property is abandoned, weeds grow up, a window is smashed," they write. "Adults stop scolding rowdy children; the children, emboldened, become more rowdy. Families move out, unattached adults move in. Teenagers gather in front of the corner store. The merchant asks them to move; they refuse. Fights occur. Litter accumulates. People start drinking in front of the grocery; in time, an inebriate slumps to the sidewalk and is allowed to sleep it off. Pedestrians are approached by panhandlers." From there it gets worse.

What's curious, I think, is that the first two steps of this vicious cycle—"A piece of property is abandoned, weeds grow up"—have disappeared in the public debate about why some neighborhoods have such high crime rates. The third step—"a window is smashed"—inspired the article's catchy title and took center stage. In academic circles, scholars had long been concerned about the security risks posed by abandoned properties and empty lots. But the popular and policy debates about Wilson and Kelling's theory ignored the two problems at the root of their story and jumped straight to the criminal behavior. We get "Broken Windows," not "Abandoned Property," and a very different policy response ensues.

Imagine what might have happened if Wilson and Kelling had pushed their readers—many of whom were mayors and police chiefs—to think more carefully about the social infrastructure. What if vacant buildings and empty lots had gotten the attention that was showered on petty criminals instead? What if neighborhood crime prevention efforts focused on inspecting and remediating dangerous properties rather than stopping and frisking suspected people?

This is not a rhetorical question; it's a puzzle that drove John MacDonald, the Penn criminologist, and his collaborator, the epidemiologist Charles Branas, to start one of the most exciting research experiments in contemporary social science.

Branas, who's now the chair of epidemiology at Columbia University, is a leading scholar of gun violence, a topic he got to know viscerally while working as a paramedic. Branas often found himself responding to calls for victims of gunshot wounds. On a typical day, more than ninety Americans die from gun violence, and two hundred more are injured. And although gun violence has decreased dramatically in recent decades, it remains far higher in the United States than in other affluent nations—the US gun homicide rate is about twenty-five times greater than the average among other high-income societies. It is stubbornly high in particular cities, some midsize (New Orleans, St. Louis, Buffalo) and some large (Detroit, Philadelphia, Chicago); and, within these cities, it's especially high in very specific places—not just neighborhoods, but blocks. Branas and MacDonald wanted to understand why certain places were so dangerous.

It's unusual for epidemiologists and criminologists to collaborate, but Branas and MacDonald met in the 2000s when they were working at the University of Pennsylvania, first in a seminar on gun violence at the medical school's Trauma Center, and then, once the conversation got started, on the campus grounds. Both were frustrated by the science that linked crime to neighborhood disorder. "A lot of it, from 'Broken Windows' on, was just descriptive," Branas told me. "You didn't know exactly what counted as disorder. And it wasn't actionable. Outside of policing, which was obviously complicated, there wasn't much you could do about it." One day, Branas read an article in *Science* based on experimental research done by Kees Keizer in the Netherlands. "These researchers somehow got permission to *create* disorder in certain neighborhoods. They actually added graffiti and litter to some places and not others, and they could measure the effects." The paper showed a strong relationship between disorder and incivility— some, though by no means full, validation for the broken windows theory. But Branas was less interested in the findings than in the method. They knew that no institutional review board or community organization would ever let them add graffiti and litter to an American neighborhood, but perhaps they could design another experiment to test place-based crime reduction techniques.

While they were brainstorming, Branas was invited to discuss his research on guns and alcohol at a conference sponsored by the Federal Reserve Bank in Philadelphia. During his presentation, he briefly mentioned his interest in running an experiment on the physical factors related to gun violence. "When I finished, someone from the Pennsylvania Horticultural Society [PHS] approached me," Branas recalled. They were convinced that vacant properties were driving up violent crime in poor neighborhoods. Philadelphia had passed an ordinance that required owners of abandoned buildings to install working doors and windows, but there were thousands of buildings out of compliance, and tens of thousands of empty lots that were violating the anti-blight ordinance too. The horticultural society had incredible data, and they offered to help.

Branas and MacDonald were excited about the idea. There is, after all, an established literature showing a relationship between abandoned properties and crime. In 1993, the criminologist William Spelman published a paper showing that, in Austin, Texas, "crime rates on blocks with open abandoned buildings were twice as high as rates on matched blocks without open buildings." And, in 2005, the sociologist Lance Hannon showed that the number of abandoned houses in a given census tract was correlated with homicide levels in New York City's high-poverty and extreme-poverty areas. Branas, who had taken the lead on the project, invited more scientists to join them: a health economist, a professor from the Department of Emergency Medicine, and a medical anthropologist. There was an enormous amount of data to collect and analyze.

The team's first major research project involved assessing the impact of two natural experiments in Philadelphia. In one, the Penn group examined violent crime around 2,356 abandoned buildings that had been in violation of Philadelphia's anti-blight ordinance. A set of 676 buildings had been remediated by the owners, which meant they had been "treated" with replacement doors and windows; the rest had not. Every month, for a three-year period between 2010 and 2013, the researchers compared violent crime levels around the treated buildings with violent crime levels around a randomly selected, geographically matched group of buildings that remained in disrepair.

The team did something similar in the second project, which compared violent crime around vacant lots. There were 49,690 "abandoned parcels of open land with no buildings on them" in Philadelphia, the researchers report. PHS had remediated 4,436 of them, which meant they had cleared trash and debris, graded the land, planted grass and trees to create a parklike setting, and installed low wooden post and rail fences with walk-in openings to facilitate recreational use and deter illegal dumping. Again, Branas and his colleagues compared the treated sites with a set of randomly selected, geographically matched properties. In this study, they measured crime annually, over a full decade, from 1999 to 2008.

On a warm and windy day in September, I visited Philadelphia to observe the sites in their experiments, including empty lots and abandoned houses that PHS had remediated and the untreated properties that they used as controls. Keith Green, a bald, large-set African American man with a salt-and-pepper beard, picked me up in his blue Ford pickup truck, and told me that we'd begin by driving to West Philadelphia, where PHS maintains 2.3 million square feet of vacant land. Green, who grew up in a part of Philadelphia that's so gray they called it "the concrete city," started working at PHS twenty-one years ago, first as an intern and then on community garden projects. "I never thought I'd be doing this for so long," he told me, "but I found my niche when we started fixing up abandoned property. I remember one of the first jobs: The city asked us to clean up a two-block area in North Philadelphia where there was a flea infestation. We got there and it was like the entire area had turned into a jungle. Weeds, tall grass, messed-up trees. People were using it as a dumping ground. There were junk piles. Old cars. Broken bottles. Mattresses. Just a mess. We wound up treating 125 empty lots on four city blocks. I'm not kidding: 125! It was a horrible job, but when we finished you could tell that the neighborhood was going to be different. And people were so happy. I'd have kids running up to my truck yelling, 'Mr. Keith! Mr. Keith! Can you come back tomorrow?' They treated me like I was Mister Softee!" He laughed at the memory. "I kept thinking, 'You know, this is something we have to do all over Philadelphia.' And that's basically what we did."

Green drove slowly up Fortieth Street in West Philly. "You're gonna want to keep your eyes open," he instructed. "You won't believe what you're gonna see." In fact, the area looked a lot like the depleted neighborhoods I'd studied in Chicago, like Englewood and North Lawndale, places where row houses and apartment buildings, some empty, some well kept, sat adjacent to large open lots that were thick with weeds, debris, and six-foot-high grass. "See that?" He pulled over at a corner lot with a low-lying wooden fence, two benches, trimmed trees, and a neatly cut lawn. "That's one of our treated sites. You can tell because it's so well maintained." We got out, walked through the pocket park and over to a vacant house and large lot a few steps away. There, the grass had grown both high and wide, so that it now came through the sidewalk and out to the curb. "Now this, this is a disaster," Green said. "It's probably got an owner who wouldn't let us work here, or someone we couldn't track down. If you live here, you've got to deal with all the problems this attracts into the neighborhood: Pests. Insects. Garbage. Crime. And you know it's gonna make it hard for new development to work here. People see that and they want to run."

We crossed the narrow street to look at another property, and when we got there Loretta, an African American woman in her late twenties who was out for some exercise, was walking briskly in our direction. I paused and asked her if she lived here. "No," she replied. "But I walk around this neighborhood all the time."

"Have you noticed all the little parks with small fences?" I inquired.

"Not really." She looked around, took them in. "They're nice, though."

"What about the abandoned lots with all the weeds and garbage?"

"Um, yeah," Loretta answered, cracking a little smile. "Why do you think I'm walking on the other side of the street!" She paused for a beat, then looked over at the lot and started explaining. "Those places are scary. You don't know what's going on in that mess, who's around. There's a lot of places like that around here, and I just try to keep away."

Loretta returned to her exercise and Green and I headed up the road again before turning onto Westminster Street. He pointed to a large remediated lot that residents had converted into a community park, with picnic tables and a small garden. "A guy who owns a store a few blocks away helped fix up this block," Green explained. "He just wanted the neighborhood to look nice, to get more people out on the sidewalks and gardens. We see a lot of that. If we maintain things, residents go a little further, and put in what they like."

We crossed over to a set of three row houses that had pocket parks, one large, one small, on either side. Micky, who had gray hair, sunglasses, a wooden cane, and a few missing teeth, was sitting on a picnic table and talking on a flip phone. He stood up and nodded when he saw me approach. I asked if he came to the park often. "I sure do," he responded. "It's a popular place. The Muslims had an event this past weekend. There was a health fair not long ago too. I'm seventy-three years old and I walk around here every day. This is a nice spot to stop."

Green asked if the park made the neighborhood better. "Oh, you know it does," Micky replied. He pointed to the front porch of the row house next door, where Joyce, in sandals and a white T-shirt, was relaxing on a rocking chair. "Ask her, she knows."

Joyce was nodding. "I've been staying here ten, twelve years now. Those lots were bad when I first got here. Drugs and all that. Kids up to no good. People would let their dogs run all around them too, and oh, did it smell!" She grimaced and shivered a little from the memory. "But they fixed it up pretty soon after I got here. Put them tables in, big umbrellas too. Kids started coming around. We got the garden going. Before, everybody would avoid this block. It was ugly, and dangerous, 'cause you didn't know who was gonna jump out of those bushes. Now it's a lot better. We've got the park, we've got shade. It's a pretty good place to be."

Green and his colleagues at the horticultural society suspected that fixing up the empty lots and buildings was improving Philadelphia's poor neighborhoods, but they weren't certain. Branas and MacDonald had a more specific hypothesis: they thought that remediation would reduce gun-related crime around them. "It's not simply that they are signs of disorder," Branas told me. "It's that the places themselves create opportunities for gun violence; they take what might just be a poor neighborhood and make it poor and dangerous." The reasons are straightforward. Abandoned houses are good places for people involved in criminal activities to hide when they are on the run. They're also good places to store firearms. Untended empty lots are notoriously good places for drug dealing—in part because most law-abiding residents avoid them, and in part because dealers can hide their products in the weeds and tall grass if the police drive by. For communities, and for the police, they are hard places to monitor and control.

But compelling theories, as critics of broken windows know all too well, are often betrayed by evidence that discredits them. That's why Branas was so surprised by the dramatic findings from their first experimental study on blighted environments and violence: There was a 39 percent reduction in gun violence in and around abandoned buildings that had been remediated. There was a smaller but still meaningful 5 percent reduction in gun violence in and around vacant lots that had been remediated as well. These are extraordinary numbers, at a level of impact one rarely sees in a social science experiment. But they weren't the only ones that impressed Branas and his team. Equally powerful, he said, is that there was no evidence that the violence had simply shifted to nearby places: the declines were real. Moreover, these reductions lasted from one to nearly four years, making the benefit far more sustainable than those in other crime reduction programs. "Honestly," he confessed, "it was a bigger effect than we'd expected to find."

According to Branas, "the main goal of the two projects was to find a way of making inexpensive, place-based changes that can be scaled to entire cities and that are relatively straightforward to sustain." He'd failed to do this earlier in his career, he acknowledged, when he was doing more conventional antiviolence research and advocacy, the kind that focused on the people who are most likely to commit crimes. "When I started at Penn, we had been working hard to reduce gun crime in Philadelphia. We had the interrupters, the social workers, the community leaders. Some of them were amazing, and we had some successes. But they were always short-lived. They lasted only as long as we could keep the people there in the hood. We spent a considerable amount of money on that project, and in the end it wound up helping only, I don't know, about fifty kids, just the ones who were there at the time. We wanted to have a bigger impact, one that would continue even after we left."

The Philadelphia studies suggest that place-based interventions are far more likely to succeed than people-based projects. "Tens of millions of vacant and abandoned properties exist in the United States," write Branas and his team. Remediation programs "make structural improvements to the very context within which city residents are exposed on a daily basis." They are simple, cheap, and easily reproducible, so they can be implemented on a large scale. What's more, they impose few demands on local residents, and the programs appear to pay for themselves. "Simple treatments of abandoned buildings and vacant lots returned conservative estimates of between $5.00 and $26.00 in net benefits to taxpayers and between $79.00 and $333.00 to society at large, for every dollar invested," their paper in the *American Journal of Public Health* reports. It's not only more dangerous to leave the properties untended; it's also more expensive.

That's why, once Branas began publishing and presenting his findings on the impact of fixing up abandoned properties, cities and universities throughout the United States were eager to enroll in the experiment. "In the last few years we've had people here from so many cities," Keith Green told me. "Detroit, Chicago, Trenton, and Seoul. When the guy from Chicago was here, he kept saying, 'This is incredible! This is incredible! We need this in Chicago. I don't know why we don't do this there!'"

By 2016, the team had raised millions of dollars in federal grants and launched blight remediation projects in New Orleans, Louisiana; Newark and Camden, New Jersey; Flint, Michigan; and Youngstown, Ohio. Each experiment included local academic partners and, at Branas's insistence, the frontline researchers were community residents who were trained and paid for their contributions. "We're proud that we've been able to employ people in these neighborhoods," Branas said. "But the bigger, more sustainable effect will come from fixing places."

Policing will always be a key component of crime reduction, and there's no question that some policing strategies are better and more humane than others. But in recent years, small-scale, place-based policies in some of the world's most dangerous cities—including Rio de Janeiro, São Paulo, and Johannesburg—have yielded substantial declines in violent crime. In some cases, they've improved the quality of everyday life too.

In São Paulo, for instance, the local government has supplemented policing programs with policies that reduce opportunities for crime in specific "hot spots," while incentivizing young people to spend more time in safe places, particularly schools. Social scientists have long observed that the presence of bars and liquor stores tends to increase local levels of violence, especially in high-crime areas. History shows that prohibition is not a wise response to this problem, not only because it generates more crime but also because it fails to reduce overall consumption and often shifts consumption to more dangerous substances. But there's good evidence that reducing the hours when bars and liquor stores operate helps. Between 2001 and 2004, for instance, sixteen of the thirty-nine São Paulo municipalities implemented a "dry law," which forced bars and liquor stores to close between 11 p.m. and 6 a.m. When the Brazilian economist Ciro Biderman examined the impact on violent behavior, he discovered that the dry laws caused "a 10% reduction in homicides" and had similar effects "on battery and deaths by car accidents." Although the restrictions were suspended after the crime rate began to drop, they showed that subtly tweaking the social environment can dramatically increase safety.

While one of São Paulo's crime-fighting techniques involved reducing access to dangerous places, another aimed to increase access to a cherished safe spot that generates multiple benefits for children and communities: schools. The government had good reason to focus on the one place where young people have regular interactions with responsible adults. According to a World Bank report on crime prevention in Brazil: "In São Paulo, among those crimes for which the age of the suspected offender is known, between 20 and 25 percent of robberies, thefts and motor vehicle crimes are committed by individuals under the age of 18." In 2003, São Paulo initiated the Family School policy, which opened 5,306 public schools on the weekends and provided extensive programming for children. Drawing on models from Mexico and Colombia, the government also started CCT Bolsa Família, a policy that offered modest but meaningful cash transfers to poor families, on the condition that their children complete secondary schools. Both programs, the World Bank claims, made important contributions to São Paulo's great crime drop.

Not all environmental designs to reduce crime produce widespread benefits. Consider the gated community, an architectural form that has emerged throughout the world to assuage anxieties about crime and violence, and which some critics see as an extreme expression of CPTED's underlying principles. After all, gated communities facilitate local control of shared territory and establish clear lines between public and private space. They sponsor and, through signage, call attention to active surveillance by security guards and cameras. They often encourage the kind of informal social interaction among residents that allows for eyes on the street. They maintain all public areas, which sends a clear signal that residents monitor and care about the physical environment. Wherever possible, they reduce opportunities for crime.

In *City of Walls,* the Berkeley anthropologist and urban planning scholar Teresa Caldeira documents the fortification of urban space in São Paulo during the 1980s and 1990s. "In the last two decades, in cities as distinct as São Paulo, Los Angeles, Johannesburg, Buenos Aires, Budapest, Mexico City, and Miami, different social groups, especially from the upper classes, have used the fear of violence and crime to justify new techniques of exclusion and their withdrawal from traditional quarters of the cities," she writes. Caldeira attributes the rise of gated communities and private security in Brazil not only to high crime but also to anxieties about the end of military governance and emerging democratic politics in an unequal society. She calls attention to the pervasive "talk of crime," which "simplistically divides the world into good and evil and criminalizes certain social categories," while also legitimating the use of gates and private security "to ensure isolation, enclosure, and distancing from those considered dangerous." Caldeira grants that these systems protect those who can afford them, but worries, quite rightly, that they weaken democracy, deepen social divisions, and endanger as well as infuriate the people whom they exclude.

Urban critics raised similar objections to the rise of gated communities in postapartheid South Africa. Some, including the architect Karina Landman, blamed advocates of CPTED for not recognizing how their ideas could be used to justify new forms of social exclusion. In the late 1990s and early 2000s, Landman observed two distinct kinds of gated communities in South Africa: "Enclosed Neighborhoods," where white residents of formerly open residential communities put up gates, fences, and booms to reduce and control access points, and "Security Villages," which were larger places with mixed-use facilities, including office parks, retail outlets, and luxurious residential developments.

Landman reports that both types of gated community successfully maintained low crime levels inside their protected environments. But the segregated social infrastructures they supported created countless other problems and directly undermined the urgent project of rebuilding democratic order in postapartheid South Africa. "Many people object to a restriction of access to public roads. It is also prohibited by the South African Constitution," she observes. Moreover, "the question of access often leads to resentment," particularly among city dwellers who had previously been able to visit or travel through the enclosed neighborhoods without scrutiny. Landman does not explicitly condemn gated communities, but there's no question about the message written between the lines. She's essentially saying that in South Africa, fear of crime is doing the work that fear of blacks did during apartheid: justifying the creation of an unequal society sustained by segregated social infrastructure, in which one group can take extralegal measures to protect itself and the others can only fume.

Intriguingly, there is at least one well-documented case of an impoverished, crime-ridden community taking control of their own territory and using unauthorized security devices to monitor violence perpetrated against them by police. But their low status and lack of political power made the project short-lived. In 2001, while the University of Texas anthropologist João Costa Vargas was conducting fieldwork in Rio de Janeiro, a neighborhood association in the city's second largest favela, Jacarezinho, installed large gates and cameras at several access points. On a popular political website, leaders of the association demanded "their right" to "more and better social programs focusing on health, education, and job training, and public transportation. In short, they demanded full citizenship," Vargas writes. Gating themselves into a protected community was a political tactic that local leaders used to publicize both their social problems and their struggles with violently abusive police.

The Brazilian media was fascinated by the story. But, as Vargas reports, the stigma around Jacarezinho and the low status of its poor, dark-skinned community made journalists skeptical of the neighborhood association's claims that police, not residents, were the main perpetrators of violence. The news media consistently denied the legitimacy of the residents' demands and, in turn, of the gates. Officials insisted that drug dealers were using gates and cameras to create a zone of lawlessness where police couldn't operate. Whereas the white neighborhoods in South Africa had managed to defend their neighborhood enclaves, the poor, mostly black slum dwellers of Rio did not have that privilege. Their gates came down quickly, and the militarized police force reasserted control.

Battles to control the social infrastructure are usually not so dramatic. In the United States and Europe, disputes over safety and the social infrastructure are more likely to unfold slowly and quietly, and they're often centered in gentrifying neighborhoods where new commercial and residential developments change street-level conditions in ways that can either protect or—if they lead to displacement or heightened racial discrimination—imperil local residents. Gentrification is one of the most controversial issues in affluent urban areas, so it's no surprise that there's a burgeoning literature on how it affects crime rates. Unfortunately, there is not yet a clear answer. Some studies show an increase, likely because new commercial development creates new targets and opportunities for crime, while others show a decrease, often attributed to more eyes on the street. The variation suggests that gentrification plays out differently depending on the local context, and also that groups are likely to be affected by gentrification in divergent ways.

In all neighborhoods, though, commercial establishments are important parts of the social infrastructure. As Jane Jacobs and Ray Oldenburg famously argued, grocery stores, diners, cafés, bookstores, and barbershops draw people out of their homes and into the streets and sidewalks, where they create cultural vitality and contribute to the passive surveillance of shared public space. When I did research in Chicago, I discovered that poor neighborhoods with active retail corridors were surprisingly resilient during the devastating heat wave, because people who lived in them could easily go out and get air-conditioning or support from neighbors. Remarkably, the social activity generated by street-level commerce protected both the majority and the minority populations in Chicago neighborhoods: it wasn't the products that made residents safer, it was the people who came out to shop and socialize. Yet Chicagoans who lived in depopulated and commercially depleted neighborhoods didn't have the same opportunities for casual interaction, and as a result they were more likely to remain in their broiling homes.

But, as the story of São Paulo's successful dry laws illustrates, some commercial outlets are more likely to foster crime than to inhibit it. Bars and liquor stores are obvious examples; banks, currency exchanges, and automatic teller machines can have similarly deleterious effects on vulnerable neighborhoods, for the simple reason that they create new targets for robbery and assault. In the 1960s, the urban planning scholar Shlomo Angel examined patterns of illicit behavior in Oakland, which, like many cities at the time, was experiencing a worrisome spike in street crime. Angel found that retail corridors were hot spots, particularly after hours, when most consumers were at home and informal surveillance was weak. Although he shared Jane Jacobs's enthusiasm for the protective value of eyes on the street, Angel warned that commercial outlets were the wrong way to attract them, and urged cities to restrict their development.

Recently, though, social scientists have taken a closer look at these patterns, and they've discovered that most retail outlets and commercial corridors are more protective than Angel realized. This is especially true in gentrifying neighborhoods, where new retail businesses, such as coffee shops and restaurants, symbolize an "invasion" of white, affluent residents and often spark public debates about displacement. In one intriguing paper, "More Coffee, Less Crime?," a team of sociologists led by the Yale professor Andrew Papachristos examined the relationship between gentrification and crime rates, using the annual number of neighborhood coffee shops that opened as a proxy measure for new local retail development. The article is agnostic on the general question of whether gentrification is good or bad for residents and cities more broadly. But it makes a compelling case that retail outlets like coffee shops help keep a neighborhood safe.

After analyzing data from the Chicago Police Department, the US Census, and the Chicago business directories, Papachristos and his team make some striking observations. First, even after controlling for other factors, an increase in the number of neighborhood coffee shops is associated with a decrease in the number of murders. They report that this pattern holds regardless of whether the neighborhood is primarily white, black, or Latino. Second, and not surprisingly, not every group benefits equally. Street robberies, for instance, tend to go down when new coffee shops open in gentrifying neighborhoods that are primarily white or Latino. But they tend to go up in gentrifying neighborhoods that are primarily black, quite likely for the reasons that Angel proposed: they have fewer commercial outlets to attract a steady stream of consumers, and consequently they lack enough informal surveillance to deter crime.

Third, and importantly, business owners are less likely to open coffee shops in gentrifying black neighborhoods than in those that are white or Latino. When they do, it's often a sign that developers are planning a large-scale transformation of the area, one that will likely result in significant displacement of established African American residents. In 2017, this threat helped fuel a small-scale uprising in Denver's Five Points neighborhood, one of countless gentrifying urban areas around the United States. The flame came from Keith Herbert, the proprietor of a local Denver coffee chain, ink!, who allowed his staff to post signs saying "Nothing says gentrification like being able to order a cortado" and "Happily gentrifying the neighborhood since 2014" outside the company's new shop in Five Points. Herbert thought the signs would be funny, but residents and community organizations concerned about their fate found them offensive. Some responded by vandalizing the establishment; others organized protests against both ink! and the gentrification process it represented. "I am embarrassed to say that I did not fully appreciate the very real and troubling issue of gentrification, and I want to sincerely apologize to those who understand firsthand the hardship and cultural consequences that gentrification has caused," said Herbert in a Facebook post after the protests began. But this hardly satisfied his critics, who have continued pressing for their neighborhood to preserve places where everyone, not only affluent young professionals, feels at home.

Residents of the Cabrini-Green housing projects in Chicago organized a similar protest movement in the late 1990s, when the city announced that it would soon demolish, privatize, and revitalize the public housing stock, and civic groups accused officials of pushing poor African Americans off what had become valuable urban real estate. As protesters marched in front of City Hall, developers built a shopping center with a Starbucks across the street from Cabrini. The coffee shop, Papachristos and his team write, became a driver and a symbol of neighborhood transition, one that would "ensure this area will soon experience rapid gentrification." The housing project did experience a decline in homicide, but it remained far more dangerous than the areas around it. "Here, we might see a 'positive' effect of gentrification in the form of long-term neighborhood crime reduction," Papachristos and his coauthors write, "but at the severe expense of the displacement of Cabrini residents." For this reason, they are adamant that although local retail outlets may well make neighborhoods safer, gentrification imposes formidable social costs to impoverished and vulnerable people, and is by no means the ideal way to reduce crime.

As it happens, research conducted in another public housing complex in Chicago points to a more desirable way to reduce crime with social infrastructure. In a fascinating series of natural experiments, the landscape architect William Sullivan and the environmental scientist Frances Kuo, both professors at the University of Illinois, discovered the extraordinary power of vegetation to reduce crime in a high-poverty residential development.

Neither Sullivan nor Kuo knew what they would find when they began their two-year study of crime patterns across ninety-eight apartment buildings in the Ida B. Wells project on Chicago's South Side. They were advocates of greening urban neighborhoods. But it was the 1990s, and at the time urban planners who had studied places like Pruitt-Igoe were convinced that trees and grass in poor neighborhoods created opportunities for criminal behavior, because the green canopy made spaces beneath hard to monitor and control. Some older research supported this view, but Kuo and Sullivan noted that several recent studies reported lower levels of fear, less aggressive and violent behavior, and more civility in green areas. Their project, the first to use police crime data to measure the impact of green ecologies on public housing, would help establish a better answer.

Fortunately, the Ida B. Wells project was an ideal place to conduct a natural experiment. The residents of the buildings were demographically similar: nearly all were African American and poor enough to qualify for public housing, and the buildings contained a mix of family types. Kuo and Sullivan measured the amount of tree and grass cover outside the ninety-eight buildings, sorted them into categories, and analyzed which areas had higher or lower levels of crime. The findings were unambiguous: the greener the immediate surroundings of a building, the lower the rate of total crime. This pattern held for both violent crimes and property crimes, and it remained even after controlling for the number of apartments per building, building height, and vacancy rates.

In Ida B. Wells and another massive housing project on the South Side, the Robert Taylor Homes, Kuo and Sullivan probed to learn more about how green space helped reduce crime and violence. Part of the answer was predictable: when the green spaces were well maintained, residents used them often, and this meant more passive surveillance from eyes on the street as well as greater feelings of ownership and control. But they also discovered surprises. Through interviews and observations by public housing residents whom they trained to do research on their team, they found that people whose buildings were surrounded by vegetation felt less aggression and mental fatigue than those who lived amid concrete. Although the levels of aggression public housing residents reported were significantly higher than those in the general US population, people who lived in a green environment said they were involved in less aggression and violence against their partner and less aggression against their child than those whose environment was primarily gray.

The research by Sullivan and Kuo made a major impact on the way designers thought about public housing. Unfortunately, by the 1990s there was little funding available to build new public housing projects, and in some American metropolitan areas political leaders condemned those that existed as failures. Soon after Sullivan and Kuo released their research findings, Chicago and the federal government announced the "Plan for Transformation," which would demolish seventeen thousand public housing apartments throughout the city, including every building in the Ida B. Wells and Robert Taylor developments. There was a severe shortage of affordable housing in Chicago, and tens of thousands of families were stuck on multiyear waiting lists for public units. No matter. As in St. Louis during the 1960s and 1970s, local and national political officials believed that Chicago's hulking public housing projects were beyond repair.

The shortage of affordable housing is a national crisis today, and violent crime is once again on the rise in some cities. Public investment in these matters is inevitable, because the problems they generate are too difficult for citizens to endure and too serious for political officials to ignore. For decades, building prisons for the poor has been our main crime reduction policy, and the social costs have been as great as the economic expense. If we want a better, more equitable, and sustainable solution for the challenges facing our cities and suburbs, we'd be better off building social infrastructure instead.

CHAPTER THREE

Learning Together

I have young children, and for years taking them to school has been one of my greatest daily pleasures. We live about a mile from my children's school, and the walk, a straight shot down one of the big avenues in Manhattan, is occasion for conversations about everything from homework to homelessness, fashion (it's below Fourteenth Street, after all), family, and friends. It's neither bucolic nor relaxing. There's lots of street traffic and constant construction in downtown Manhattan. We occasionally encounter an aggressive panhandler or a trail of spilled garbage. But we all enjoy participating in the parade of humanity that animates the city's sidewalks each morning. We're together, with all kinds of stimulation around us, in a place that's full of strangers but still feels like home.

The small, progressive school they attend in Greenwich Village is the kind of place that strives to create community. There's lots of cultural programming and special events in the crowded, tenement-style building that, for lack of available outdoor space, serves as the school campus. But the real work of community development happens informally, if also by design. Parents of students in kindergarten and the early grades are encouraged to join their children in the classrooms for fifteen or twenty minutes each morning throughout the year. The official rationale for this practice is that it helps ease the students' transition into the school day. But within a few weeks most new parents figure out that it does something more important. It gives them time and space to get to know one another, so that they can build relationships that will help everyone, adult and child, get through a rewarding but challenging time of life.

The hallways, stairwells, and common areas of the school are comically cramped and busy, so there's no place in the building for parents to continue the conversations they begin in classrooms. By chance, though, there's an unusually large patch of open public space just outside the front door, a place with benches, small trees, and enough room for people to break into small groups and linger. That's exactly what parents do there, every morning, sometimes for just a few minutes but sometimes for much longer, because the workday starts late in New York City or because the banter is too good to end. Since it's Manhattan, it's no surprise that there's a coffee shop across the street from the school. When children get old enough to go to their classrooms alone, parents drop them at the front door, find their friends in the public area, and head to the café patio. Countless relationships evolve in the social space around the school building. Parents schedule play dates (for themselves as well as their children), learn about school issues, talk about their marriages and friendships, commiserate about work. For many parents, the morning drop-off is the most social time of the day.

Recently, my family and I spent a sabbatical year at Stanford University, and we moved into an idyllic suburb near the campus. We enrolled our children in the local elementary school, an excellent public institution with the kind of campus that could never exist in Manhattan. It has large, open fields for soccer and baseball, several play structures and swing sets, outdoor basketball courts, a shaded courtyard for lunches and snacks, and a large organic garden maintained by teachers and students. It also has an active parent-teacher association, which champions diversity (there's a growing Latino and Asian presence in the school, and many children with disabilities) and organizes social and cultural events for the community. The school could not be a more welcoming place.

But when the academic year began we quickly noticed some major flaws in the otherwise excellent social infrastructure. The campus, while beautiful, is mostly off-limits to parents, who are expected to drop off their children at the entrance and are allowed into classrooms on special occasions only. There's some space for casual interaction on the sidewalk in front of the school, but it's not designed for socializing, especially not at the beginning or end of the school day. The reason will likely be familiar to everyone who's spent time in large suburban schools: the entryway is dominated by a long, roundabout driveway, and every day hundreds of parents drive through it to drop off their children and quickly pull away. It's a remarkably efficient system—so efficient, in fact, that parents have little opportunity to get to know one another on or around the school grounds.

The infrastructure that makes this affluent suburban school less cohesive than it otherwise might be is probably not cause for serious concern, since families in the community have access to other well-run public institutions and marketplaces—swimming pools, libraries, athletic fields, farmers' markets, and pleasant commercial corridors—that foster community ties. But in the many towns and neighborhoods that don't have all these resources, educational institutions are essential parts of the social infrastructure. When they're set up to promote social connections, they can strengthen the support networks and dramatically improve the lives of parents and children. When they're not, each family is more likely to be on its own.

Of course, the design and programming of schools also shapes their core mission: educating children. The physical layout and organizational structure of a school affects how learning happens—in classrooms, on campus, and in the neighborhood where it's situated. This is just as true for elementary schools as it is for elite universities. Consider, for instance, the difference between the traditional Oxbridge college model, organized around small rooms where individual students study with tutors, and the latest design trends in contemporary universities, which feature large, open, multipurpose spaces that encourage serendipitous encounters and promote collaboration with people from different fields.

Campus landscapes, teaching halls, research centers, and dormitories are the most visible elements of a school's social infrastructure. But the edges and borders matter too, because they shape whether and how students learn to engage in public culture and interact with people who are not like them. Some schools—private as well as public—have open, accessible grounds with amenities for everyone in the area. Others put gates and security guards on the perimeter to ensure that only a select group comes in. In recent years, some high schools and universities have discarded the idea of a physical campus altogether, using the Internet as the main infrastructure for delivering education and eliminating most of the school's social life. But the most notable improvements in academic achievement are concentrated in schools that have doubled down on the places where face-to-face interaction between teachers and students happens regularly. Small, intimate settings where people get to know one another well are not only ideal places for young people to develop skills for civic engagement and community building but also ideal places to learn.

In the 1980s, when American political leaders had grown anxious about a new "urban underclass" and local governments throughout the country deployed armed security guards to monitor high school campuses, public schools—particularly those in poor areas—had ceased to be ideal places for anything. With metal detectors at the gates and pass cards restricting the circulation of students, educational institutions had come to resemble prisons. And that's where a growing number of students were heading, after failing out of schools that were set up to fail them.

Deborah Meier, a teacher, a principal, and an advocate with nearly three decades of experience in tough urban districts, belonged to a long tradition of education reformers who believed that schools worked best when they modeled the best practices of civic and intellectual life, with small classrooms serving as settings for safe but searching and honest debates. That's how the most prestigious urban private schools operated; why shouldn't urban public schools do that too? As Meier saw it, the move to militarize large school campuses represented a dangerous turn in American education, one that threatened to depersonalize the school experience and bring out the worst in the nation's most vulnerable children. Instead of cracking down on schools, she called for administrators to carve them up into institutions with about one hundred students per grade and no more than five hundred total. The goal was to create smaller learning communities—again, roughly the size of private institutions—where students and teachers could grow closer, staff could nimbly respond to emerging issues and needs, and parents could develop deeper local knowledge and a greater sense of ownership over their child's school. "Young people cannot learn democratic values in a setting that does not value individual achievement, that cannot notice triumphs and defeats, has no time to celebrate or mourn, or respond with indignation or recognition as the situation requires," she wrote in an influential *New York Times* essay. "Small schools offer opportunities to solve every one of these critical issues."

Meier acknowledged that small schools would not solve all the problems in American education. Drugs, violence, and vandalism would not go away simply because students had been moved to a new environment, or because a giant campus that once held two thousand students had been transformed into a set of five campuses, each with four hundred students. But "hugeness," she believed, "works against lively intellectual intercourse" and prevents both administrators and parents from improving conditions at ground level. "In small schools," on the other hand, "parents hear about the same teachers, students and families year after year in a variety of formal and informal ways. Trust builds and issues that arise get settled handily. Accountability to parents, as well as to the community, is a less knotty problem. In a small school, strangers and strange behaviors stick out and can be addressed with dispatch. Trouble-making strangers can be identified and peer pressure has an inhibiting effect on violence or other anti-social behavior."

It was a compelling argument—so compelling, in fact, that in the 1990s and 2000s several large urban school districts began small school initiatives, and major philanthropies, including the Carnegie Corporation of New York, the Annenberg Foundation, and the Bill & Melinda Gates Foundation, poured resources into small school projects. The Gates Foundation alone invested $650 million, hoping it would yield immediate results.

The experiments were indeed ambitious. In New York City, for instance, the Department of Education opened dozens of small high schools, including specialty schools—for arts, computers and technology, health, languages, and science, among others—that occupied portions of formerly large school buildings. Graduation rates at the new small schools quickly rose high above the city average, and in some failing schools, they spiked. In Flatbush, a predominantly poor, African American neighborhood in Brooklyn, the city transformed Erasmus Hall High School into the Erasmus Hall Educational Complex, with five separate schools. Before the change, graduation rates at Erasmus were around 40 percent. Within a few years they topped 90 percent. The change at the Evander Childs High School building in the Bronx was even more dramatic. In the 1990s and early 2000s, Evander Childs exemplified the problems of large urban school buildings, with high rates of violence, truancy, and, as of 2002, a four-year graduation rate of 31 percent. Some students, afraid of conflict, viewed skipping classes as a survival strategy, if not the best way to get ahead. Parents had no good options: they could either send their children into the fire or let their futures burn away slowly without a high school degree. Reducing the school size resulted in an astoundingly rapid transformation. Parents and administrators regained control of the campus. Attendance stabilized. By 2007, the combined graduation rate reached 80 percent.

On a warm spring day in 2016, I joined a librarian from the Seward Park Library on an outreach visit to the Seward Park Campus, a six-floor, "vertical campus" in a hulking gray industrial building where five small schools occupied the space of one old high school. We were there to bring library programming—that day would be an arts class focused on *manga* drawing—into a school system whose budget could hardly cover basic needs. Fifteen years before, as the Seward Park High School, the institution was overwhelmed by the challenge of educating students from the Lower East Side's poor, largely immigrant community. In 2001, its graduation rate was 32 percent. The small school experiment began there in 2006, and by 2012 the cumulative graduation rate from its five small schools—the High School for Dual Language and Asian Studies, the New Design High School, the Essex Street Academy (formerly the High School for History and Communication), the Lower Manhattan Arts Academy, and the Urban Assembly Academy of Government and Law—was above 80 percent.

I wasn't around to observe daily life in the old school, but fortunately the great journalist Samuel Freedman spent a year there in the late 1980s, reporting his book *Small Victories*. Freedman portrays the students, 90 percent of whom were children of immigrants who did not speak English, as bright and ambitious; at least, the ones who attended were, since more than 40 percent of entering freshmen dropped out before graduating, which placed Seward Park High on a list of the ten worst schools in New York State. The physical campus and organizational structure, however, created all kinds of obstacles, so many that one boy ran for student government on the slogan "Are you ashamed to go to Seward?"

Classrooms were impossibly crowded. There was a gaping hole in the roof and the ceiling of the faculty lounge was crumbling. Some two hundred windows were broken. The metal fence surrounding the school's annex was in disrepair. Basic materials—books, pens, paper, chalk—were in short supply. Teachers were overloaded and exhausted. Jessica Siegel, the book's protagonist, threw herself into teaching and helped the students accomplish more than seems possible. But she was an anomaly, and, regardless, the work was so taxing that she quit at year's end. The principal, diligent, dedicated, and entirely admirable, was outmatched by the school's problems. Most students were too.

The five schools I observed on my visit to the Seward Park Campus were neat and well organized, and students seemed to have a warm and familiar relationship with teachers and staff. External reviewers from the New School's Center for New York City Affairs found something similar when they assessed the institution in 2011: "The tone throughout the building is calm. Hallways don't get too congested during change of classes; students were relaxed and well-behaved during the lunchtimes we observed in the cafeteria. 'Like any high school, we have our incidents, but the kids are good. It's a safe place,' a security guard said." Each institution controls its own floor, and although their layout is identical, the schools distinguish themselves through their posters, announcements, fashion, and culture. They share some common facilities, including a gym and a small library on the sixth floor. But generally, they operate as separate institutions, and each is a good place to learn.

Reducing a school's physical size does not solve all of its problems, but it has proven to make a tremendous impact on student attention, achievement, and college matriculation as well as teacher satisfaction and positive feelings about the school climate. A recent study of twenty-one thousand New York City students by the independent, nonpartisan research firm MDRC found that, compared with students in ordinary high schools, students who attended small schools were 9.4 percentage points more likely to graduate, 8.4 percentage points more likely to enroll in college, and even more likely to attend selective universities. These numbers may not sound high, but—as countless school administrators and academic researchers know from experience—producing meaningful improvements in educational outcomes is notoriously difficult; there's a heated, long-standing debate, for instance, over whether spending more money on schools has any impact on performance at all. In this context, gains near 10 percent are extraordinary. There's no magic bullet for improving school performance in difficult environments, but designing campuses that students, teachers, and administrators can collectively control is among the most effective techniques we've found.

Designing campuses that promote learning and community building may be a relatively new priority in public education circles, where resources are scarce, but it has always been a central concern of universities, which play an outsize role in modern societies. The late Richard Dober, a renowned scholar at Harvard and MIT who designed college campuses throughout the world, estimated that, as of 1992, about 40 percent of the American population had spent at least one year as a full-time student on one of the nation's 3,500 or so college campuses. "Campus design is a civic art that resonates with meaning and significance for our culture," he wrote. "The Greeks had their agora, the Romans their Forum, the Middle Ages their cathedral and town square, the Renaissance their palaces and enclaves for the privileged, and the 19th century their centers of commerce, transportation and government. The campus is uniquely our generation's contribution to communal placemaking and placemarking." When designed well, it should "promote community, allegiance, and civility, while at the same time encouraging diversity in discourse and vision."

The time we spend on college campuses shapes our ideas about what we want to pursue and who we want to become. It changes our social networks and work opportunities. It breaks down ethnic and religious divisions, leading to what we once called "mixed marriages" between people who'd otherwise never form families together. And even as a growing number of people on both sides of the political spectrum express concern that colleges—and particularly partisan student groups—have become inhospitable to civil debate about controversial topics, there's no better institution to prepare us for civic life in democratic societies, giving us the tools we need to understand difference, evaluate evidence, and engage in reasoned dialogue with people who don't share our perspectives or values.

This hasn't always been the case. Many of the earliest European universities were designed to solidify social boundaries, not open them. In *Campus: An American Planning Tradition,* the Stanford professor Paul Turner recounts that the first universities, in Bologna and Paris, were part of the city, and students typically lodged with their families or with townspeople. As universities developed, local entrepreneurs built halls and hostels for the students. But many school administrators disliked this arrangement, as did the aristocratic parents of university students, and universities began to erect gates and walls to separate their sacred grounds from the profane communities in which they had been embedded. New College, at Oxford, built the first enclosed quadrangle that housed all university functions in 1379. Many schools followed, giving rise to the model of the college as a segregated residential community as well as an educational institution where students studied, largely in private rooms, under the direct tutelage of a learned instructor.

Turner identifies several reasons for the use of the enclosed quadrangle in British colleges, from efficient land use in crowded towns to the influential tradition of the cloistered monastery. "Simply from an architectural point of view," he writes, "the monastic and collegiate 'programs' were nearly identical: the housing of a community of unmarried men and boys, with space for sleeping, eating, instruction, and religious services." The walls that divided the college campus from the town served defensive purposes, protecting students and faculty not only from occasional wars and local conflicts but also from townspeople. "The early histories of Oxford and Cambridge abound in incidents of town-gown antagonism leading to fighting, warfare, and murder on both sides," Turner reports. "The ability to close off a college at a few gate-points also gave college authorities the advantage of greater control over the students, a concern that was a major factor in the growth of the collegiate system." By 1410, Oxford required all students to live in colleges rather than in the town, and that policy remains intact, albeit only for freshmen, today.

Oxford and Cambridge opened up in other ways, however. In the sixteenth century, when a graduate of Cambridge named Dr. John Caius raised concerns about the health risks of confining students to stagnant, foul air, the university built its first three-sided courtyard. (Some attribute the form to rising fashions in France's new chateaux.) Whatever its origin, Turner writes, the new, open campus spaces "suggested a more sympathetic and less defensive attitude toward the world outside the college." So too did the schools' push to reform admissions policies. During the seventeenth century, the great British universities made their first efforts to incorporate local, nonaristocratic children, and a larger proportion of the general population entered higher education than at any time except the twentieth century. These trends influenced the first American colleges, which were more accessible and expansive than anything in the Old World.

Since 1963, when Richard Hofstadter published *Anti-intellectualism in American Life*, but especially today, it's hard not to worry about America's weak commitment to intellectual culture. But early American colonists were interested in the pursuit of ideas, and soon after they settled here they began building colleges to support higher education. "By the time of the Revolution there were nine degree-granting colleges in the colonies," Turner writes. Harvard College was founded in 1636; the College of William and Mary in 1693; Yale College in 1701; the College of New Jersey (now Princeton University) in 1746; the College of Rhode Island (now Brown University) in 1764; Queen's College (now Rutgers University) in 1766; and Dartmouth College in 1769. These schools built grand buildings, the largest in their regions. They tended to be located in rural, frontier areas rather than distrusted, irreligious cities, and they encouraged students to spend time in pure, natural environments, "removed from the distractions of civilizations."

The *campus* is an American concept, probably coined around 1770, to describe the open grounds around the College of New Jersey. Turner reprints the first recorded use of the term to refer to the area around a college, from a letter written by a student in 1774: "Last week to show our patriotism, we gathered all the steward's winter store of tea, and having made a fire in the Campus, we there burnt near a dozen pounds, tolled the bell and made many spirited resolves." After 1776, the word gained popularity at colleges throughout the new United States, and by the mid-nineteenth century it had become the most common term to describe the grounds around American universities. Eventually it would take on new meaning for the grounds around corporate offices as well.

There has never been a dominant architectural style for American college landscapes or buildings. Brown University doesn't even have a dominant style on its own campus. But most American schools adopted the British residential college model and built dormitories to promote a robust campus culture. Old College, the first building at Harvard, had a spacious hall on the first floor that served as the hub of most activities. It was, at various times in the day, a lecture hall, a dining room, and a general living space. A library and a set of dormitories lined the second floor. Students shared bedrooms, and even beds, which was not unusual at the time. But, following the English model, they were each given a private space for studying, because most educators believed that learning happened when an individual was alone, memorizing facts and silently contemplating the day's lessons.

Yet from the beginning, the architects of America's universities rejected the monastic model that influenced European institutions, and designed them to be deeply social places. The primary motivation was intellectual. American campus architects wanted to build universities where knowledge from different fields would circulate freely, across academic domains and into the world as well. The intellectual life they promoted was never meant to be contained or disciplined. They aimed for cross-pollination, and the campus—its classrooms, libraries, dormitories, and dining halls—was an instrument of convergence.

American campus designers were also intent on building new communities, and they had novel ideas for fostering social ties. Harvard was but one of many American schools to organize student life around colleges, each with its own spaces for dining, studying, and fraternizing. Princeton developed dining societies, which later became eating clubs, as the foundation for college social activities. Students played a role in creating campus culture too. In 1776, five men at the College of William and Mary started a new student society, Phi Beta Kappa, which eventually added chapters at universities across the country, becoming the first intercollegiate fraternity.

Fraternities whose agenda was more social than academic are, of course, another hallmark of American universities. The first, the Kappa Alpha Society, was started in 1825 by a group of male students at Union College in New York who wanted to form an exclusive collegiate organization that would mirror the social clubs for affluent white men that were prominent at the time. In 1846, a chapter of Chi Psi at the University of Michigan opened the first fraternity house in a wooded area off-campus, where they could operate without official supervision. At the time, most college fraternities were secret societies, and administrators—at Union, Princeton, and Brown, among other schools—tried to prohibit them. But fraternities slowly gained acceptance as legitimate social institutions, in part because they were so popular among elite students, and in part because they offered universities a free solution to an emerging problem: housing the growing ranks of enrolled students.

By the late 1890s, fraternities and the women's equivalent, sororities, began to open chapter houses on or around university grounds. Eventually they'd become a staple of the US undergraduate system. Today, there are more than six thousand fraternity chapters across roughly eight hundred college campuses; about 10 percent of all male, degree-seeking college students join a fraternity each fall, and millions of young adults frequent their parties and social events. The Greek system, as it has become known, is beloved by students and alumni for whom it defines the collegiate social experience. Its advocates claim that those who participate in fraternities and sororities have higher graduation rates than those who shun them. But this achievement comes at the expense of campus health and safety, and the system has increasingly come under fire from university administrators concerned about its effects on campus life.

Fraternities, both as organizations and also as physical places, are an exemplary form of exclusive social infrastructure. The residential houses often contain dining facilities, indoor and outdoor recreational areas, bars, common rooms for entertainment, and ample party space, all of which encourage members to anchor their lives around them. Since most fraternities select people with similar backgrounds and interests—ethnicity, race, religion, class, or often sports (and occasionally academics)—joining one is an effective way to avoid the diversity and difference a university offers. Members gain brothers and sisters, but too often lose the chance to be part of something greater.

Fraternity houses are typically embedded in "rows," the vibrant social spaces that sustain a campus's Greek life, particularly on party nights. They are also dangerous spaces—sites of rampant discrimination, violent hazing, excessive drinking, and, too often, sexual assault. The National Study of Student Hazing, which includes 11,482 surveys with students from fifty-three American colleges and universities, reports that half of all students involved in Greek organizations experience hazing, most commonly involving forced alcohol consumption, humiliation, isolation, sleep deprivation, and sex acts. In 2013, Bloomberg News reported that more than sixty students had died in fraternity-related activities across US campuses during the previous eight years, at schools including Penn State, Baruch, Northern Illinois University, and Fresno State. Studies consistently find that men who are associated with fraternities are several times more likely to perpetrate sexual assault than those who are not. And health scholars have shown that fraternity membership is a significant cause of binge drinking, even after controlling for background factors. In other words, the high incidence of trouble at fraternities is not merely due to the people who join them—it's also about the places themselves.

In recent years, concerned faculty, students, and the victims of violence on fraternity rows have called for universities to reform the Greek system. After completing a massive study of sex on college campuses, however, the sociologist Lisa Wade concluded that nothing short of abolition would stem the damage. "Reform is not possible because the old-line, historically white social fraternities have been synonymous with risk-taking and defiance from their very inception," she writes. "They are a brotherhood born in mutiny and forged in the fire of rebellion. These fraternities have drink, danger and debauchery in their blood—right alongside secrecy and self-protection." It's difficult to abolish a social institution that has so many loyal and influential champions, and equally difficult to unbuild a social infrastructure that shapes so much of university life. But fraternities have earned an expulsion.

Fraternities are not the only divisive social infrastructures on college campuses. American universities rarely built the kind of high walls that protected colleges at Oxford and Cambridge from the communities around them, but many schools, particularly those in cities, have buttressed their exclusive admissions standards with elaborate physical and organizational systems that separate students and faculty from neighboring people and places perceived as dangerous. Today, large campus security operations reinforce these perceptions at universities throughout the country, and make the distinction between insiders and outsiders especially sharp.

Conventionally, college administrators and city planners think of "town/gown" divisions as especially bad for residents, not students, because they're the ones excluded from campus amenities and stuck dealing with a raucous population of young people who haven't learned to be good neighbors. But universities that cut themselves off from surrounding communities also hurt students, giving them a false sense of superiority and depriving them of opportunities to learn from their neighbors and develop the civic skills that they—and all of us—urgently need.

In recent years, several schools have begun experimenting with new models of civic engagement. In 2017, for instance, Colby College announced that it would lead a collaborative urban revitalization project that includes business owners, philanthropic organizations, and civic groups in its struggling hometown of Waterville, Maine. Colby announced that it would invest $10 million to purchase five properties in the downtown area, which it would convert into a hotel, a tech hub, and a 100,000-square-foot, five-story, mixed-use dormitory that would bring about two hundred students off-campus and into the community. When completed, the complex will include retail outlets as well as a public meeting space on the ground level, facilities designed to bridge the historic gap between town and gown. To bolster the effort, Colby faculty and administrators are developing a new "civic engagement curriculum," which will involve partnerships with the Waterville Public Library and a local homeless shelter, for all students who live in the downtown dormitory.

Partnering with the local community is more complicated at the University of Chicago, an affluent and prestigious school with a long history of excluding its African American neighbors. Despite a rhetorical commitment to liberalism and tolerance, during the 1950s the university's leaders established a fund they could use for "area protection" against what the former director of community interest called "negro invasion." The university president incentivized the board of trustees to support this initiative by taking members on a bus tour of "typical colored neighborhoods," which was designed to provoke anxieties about what would happen in Hyde Park if the university didn't acquire more real estate in the area surrounding the school. The scheme worked, as the trustees donated $4.5 million to a fund that would, as the chancellor, Lawrence Kimpton, put it, "buy, control, and rebuild our neighborhood."

Substantial as it was, the fund proved woefully inadequate to secure the area around campus from the crime that pervaded Chicago's postindustrial ghettos in the 1970s and 1980s. By the 1990s, university leaders had largely given up their efforts to control adjacent real estate. They invested in policing instead of property, a move made possible by the Illinois Private College Campus Police Act of 1992, which gave universities in high-crime areas all the legal powers of a police force but few of the public reporting obligations. Within a few years the university had built one of the nation's largest private security forces, and it made sure all prospective and entering students knew how well they would be protected once they arrived on campus.

But only if they stayed on campus: although the university's officers had jurisdiction to patrol off-campus, former students report that school officials advised them not to cross into the black neighborhoods around them, including Woodlawn, Washington Park, South Shore, Kenwood, and Oakland, because they'd be targets of crime. As compensation, the University of Chicago invested heavily in its own, internal social infrastructure: libraries, bookstores, cafés, art museums, theaters, and athletic facilities. It assured students that everything they needed was right on campus—or, if they felt adventurous, in the wealthy neighborhoods far to the north.

The university's student body has grown more diverse in recent decades, but today African Americans constitute less than 10 percent of the undergraduate population, compared with 85 percent in the adjacent neighborhood of Woodlawn, 68 percent in Kenwood, and 96 percent in Washington Park. In the twenty-first century, college leaders have made serious efforts to pierce the bubble of student culture and help the young people who study on its South Side campus engage their neighbors. In 2000, it released the Midway Plaisance Master Plan, which revitalized parks that are heavily used by local African American communities as well as students. In 2005, it launched the Urban Health Initiative, which improved access to public health programming and high-quality medical care in underserved areas around campus. It opened an Office of Civic Engagement, and declared that the school would now act "as an anchor institution on the mid–South Side." Leaders promised that they would "partner within our city and surrounding communities to share talent, information, and resources to have a positive impact on our city's well-being." They maintained the strong police presence in the area, but they stopped advising students to avoid neighboring communities.

More recently, they even began building social infrastructure that bridges the divide.

In the late 2000s, the celebrated local artist and University of Chicago faculty member Theaster Gates persuaded the university to purchase a string of abandoned buildings on Garfield Boulevard, a corridor in the Washington Park neighborhood just west of campus that was once a hub of commercial activity but had been hollowed out by decades of depopulation and economic decline. The plan, which the university hatched with the City of Chicago, Cook County, and several neighborhood organizations, was to transform the zone into an "Arts Block." The University of Chicago Arts Incubator, which would include galleries, studio space, classrooms, a community room, and a garden, would reside in the largest corner building. The two adjacent buildings would be leased to Gates for two for-profit, entrepreneurial projects: the Currency Exchange Café and BING Art Books. The university promised that the complex would stimulate economic growth and add cultural vitality to the struggling neighborhood. The Arts Incubator would offer extensive programming for local children and paid fellowships for local artists. The businesses would generate new jobs and attract more people into the community. And, as Gates and other University of Chicago leaders envisioned, they would bring students off the "safe space" on campus and into a place where they would interact with people whose race, class, and status were different from those they had grown up with at home.

When I first visit the Arts Block, in early 2017, I can't help but notice how much the streetscape resembles places like North Lawndale and Englewood, where the decrepit social infrastructure led to such high death tolls during the heat wave and degrades the quality of life every day. Garfield Boulevard is lined with empty lots, shuttered factories, and boarded-up businesses, and the residential blocks stemming from it are similarly depleted, with large grassy fields where grand homes and apartment buildings once stood. I park in front of a beat-up hardware store, one of the few open businesses near the Arts Block, and see two homeless men salvaging garbage from the lot next door. We nod at each other, I cross the street, and the men get back to work.

The Arts Incubator, which opened in 2013, is on the west corner of the complex. There's a bright, open gallery encased in large glass windows on the ground floor, but when I pull on the front door it's locked—a sign that the management remains on guard. Immediately, though, a young woman with long, wavy hair and a wide beige scarf pops out from a back room and motions that she's coming. She smiles warmly, opens the door, and introduces herself. Her name is Nadia, and she'd been working there for a year after leaving her job in a public school. There's a student art exhibit there, and Nadia tells me that it was entirely produced and curated by kids from neighborhood schools. "You should have come last week, for the opening," she says. "We had more than 150 people."

Nadia closes the door behind me, walks me around the exhibit, and offers a tour of the building. As we leave the gallery a group of middle-aged women carrying yoga mats comes downstairs. "We have classes two days a week now," Nadia explains. "They're free, so people just pop in from the neighborhood. I'm jealous!" We walk down a long hallway, past the private studios and into a backyard that local students and staff are turning into a rain garden. Next to it there's a large woodshop, where the staff runs a design apprenticeship program for teenagers, thirty of whom come each day. Theaster Gates is involved in the program, and the shelves are full of his objects and supplies. Nadia points to a set of ceramic teacups. "Theaster made these," she says. "And now every design class begins with a tea ceremony. It's just a way of marking the time as special, of getting everyone to truly be here."

The Arts Block, I can discern, is wholly dedicated to that project. Gates, renowned for recovering decaying objects from abandoned city buildings and transforming them into "urban interventions" with aesthetic and economic benefits, is the creative force behind the initiative. And while he oversees the university's community arts programming, on Garfield Boulevard he's focused on his two small businesses, the Currency Exchange Café and BING Art Books next door.

After my visit to the Arts Incubator, Nadia points me next door to the café, which Gates, in signature style, decorated with the original, hand-painted signage from the down-market neighborhood financial institution that once occupied the space. Megan Jeyifo, the café manager who joins me for a lunch of jambalaya and corn bread, explains that "it's no accident that the most visible, public-facing places that Theaster has developed used to be commercial establishments." The biggest aim of Gates's project is to provide stable employment to local residents while also proving that small businesses on Garfield Boulevard can be successful. "Theaster always says that this has to work because he has skin in the game!," Megan tells me. "It's not a community organization. It's not just an art project. We want it to be a model for entrepreneurs who believe in this neighborhood. And the first big challenge is getting people here."

It seems to be working. The café is bustling and there's a diverse clientele: students poring over books, freelancers on laptops, retirees sipping coffee. "The café was more of a formal restaurant when it started," Megan explains. "That appealed to some of the older clientele. But most people were coming in and hoping to stay awhile, and they didn't need to be bothered by waiters every few minutes. We switched to counter service and loosened things up." They also started to do more special programming, including a regular Jazz Monday series that has become a popular neighborhood social event and Story Time, a reading program for local kids.

Most of the customers are local residents, but Megan has worked hard to get the university community there as well. "They invited me to do a panel on community service at the first-year orientation," she tells me. "And the fact that they did is a sign of how things have changed. All the other panelists talked about volunteering, so I just said: 'The only thing I ask of you is to come and sit at our communal table. Just visit. Get something to eat or drink. That will make a difference. And I bet you'll come back after that.'

"The next week this kid, blond and baby-faced, came and sat at the communal table. He sat right next to one of our regulars, someone who's pretty active and entrepreneurial in the neighborhood too. Well, one of our servers saw the kid and got worried. He thought it was a twelve-year-old here without a parent and wanted to make sure he was okay. I went over to say hello, just see what was going on. And the kid said he'd seen me on the panel and wanted to take me up on the request! And, you know, now the students are coming. Sometimes too many come and they're working here at the wrong time—like on a Saturday, when we actually need the tables! But they show up. They're hanging out. And that's beginning to make a difference. It's a long, complicated history, the university and this neighborhood. We're not going to change it overnight, but we're going to make a start."

No one thinks that the deeply rooted town and gown conflicts in places like Chicago's South Side will be resolved quickly, but there is one set of higher-education institutions that's attempting an immediate, radical transformation of the way that colleges interact with the outside world: new online universities that rely solely on massive open online courses, or MOOCs. Rather than building traditional campuses, or any kind of physical structure embedded in a larger town or city, these schools use the Internet as the lecture hall and seminar room, and as the core social infrastructure too.

MOOCs first gained public attention in 2011, when a handful of prominent professors and administrators from elite universities suggested that they could help reduce costs and expand access to higher education. Initially, universities opened select courses, free of charge, to anyone with an Internet connection, and enormous numbers of people signed up. When the Stanford computer scientist Sebastian Thrun offered his artificial intelligence class as a MOOC, more than 160,000 people from 190 countries enrolled. Stanford, and several other universities, quickly set up nonprofit online ventures to supplement their offerings.

The extraordinary enrollment numbers also attracted the attention of entrepreneurs in the technology industry, who saw MOOCs as a natural way to "disrupt" the roughly $500 billion higher-education market. Silicon Valley venture capitalists partnered with the first stars of online education, including Thrun and his Stanford computer science colleagues Andrew Ng and Daphne Koller. Soon several commercial, for-profit ventures were competing for student dollars, including Thrun's start-up, Udacity, and Coursera, cofounded by Ng and Koller. On the other coast, Harvard and MIT partnered to start a nonprofit MOOC business, edX. Many of the world's leading scholars signed up to record online versions of their lecture courses, and millions of people around the world registered to take them.

As MOOCs gained press and popularity, college administrators worried that online education really would disrupt their operations, taking students—and their tuition dollars—out of the university and into the pockets of new technology firms. But their anxieties waned as the first waves of data on student performance went public. Although, according to a Pew Research Center survey, 16 percent of American adults reported that they'd taken at least part of an online course in the previous year, the great majority of them had already completed two- or four-year college programs. They were taking individual classes to develop new skills and knowledge on sites like KhanAcademy.org, a free online learning platform created by the entrepreneur Sal Khan, not enrolling in certificate or degree programs. Moreover, as several studies have concluded, only a small fraction of the students who enrolled in MOOCs actually completed the courses. A research team that includes Coursera cofounder Daphne Koller and the University of Pennsylvania professor Ezekiel Emanuel, for instance, reports that "just 4% of Coursera users who watch at least one course lecture go on to complete the course and receive a credential." The courses reach millions of people, many of them in the developing world, who otherwise would not have access to leading professors in the United States and Europe, but they have not succeeded in their threat to take down brick-and-mortar colleges, at least not yet.

One reason that online universities have failed to develop long-term, degree-granting programs is that they lack a strong social infrastructure. Students who enroll in Coursera or Udacity, which as of 2016 had twenty-three million and four million registered users, respectively, simply cannot build the personal relationships and career networks that make a university education so valuable, nor can they participate in the campus activities that make a college experience so rich. Online universities have tried to address this deficiency. Some offer online discussion forums, others have virtual laboratories, and a few—following the model established by the Open University, Britain's massively successful distance teaching project—organize regional meet-ups. None of them come close to reproducing the social experience of a residential college, nor even the thinner campus life at commuter schools where flesh-and-blood, part-time students study together for shorter terms.

In 2012, the tech entrepreneur Ben Nelson assembled a small

team of education experts, including the former Harvard president Lawrence Summers; Stephen Kosslyn, director of Stanford's Center for Advanced Study in the Behavioral Sciences; and Bob Kerrey, former US senator and president of the New School, to try a different approach. Billing itself "Higher Education for the 21st Century," Minerva promised to combine the best features of online education with a truly global university experience. Students would take all of their courses online, in small seminars conducted through an active learning interface that allows faculty—who work from locations all over the world rather than near the students—to give individual feedback in real time or after class. Each cohort, 120 at first and then larger as the program developed, would spend the first year in San Francisco, where Minerva leased dorm space in a renovated residential hotel. They would spend each of the following six semesters living in a different city—Berlin, Buenos Aires, Hyderabad, London, Seoul, and Taipei—where together, in leased dorms and hostels, they would share an immersive, collective, flesh-and-bones experience. And the entire four-year education would cost a fraction of what students pay for a traditional American college degree, because, as the Minerva website explains: "Instead of investing in maintaining the expensive buildings, campus facilities, and amenities found at other top universities, Minerva uses the vast resources of major world cities as its infrastructure."

I first visited Minerva's headquarters in downtown San Francisco in the spring of 2017, toward the end of its second academic year. Jonathan Katzman, the chief product officer, told me that his team designed the school's infrastructure to match contemporary lifestyles and learning styles. "We had two tenets," he explains. "First, if we house students in a city, we should take advantage of the city's features and amenities. Students should use the city library for studying, or else local cafés. We don't need to build a symphony hall, a theater, or an athletic complex, because the cities where our students go have all of these things, and we can make sure they know how to use them. We can do more too. Major cultural institutions here have staff that do outreach and education. Our students got to learn how to sing opera ... in the San Francisco Opera House! They performed plays ... on the stage of the A.C.T. Theater. They volunteer to work on homelessness, public health, all kinds of things. They interact with the real city, every day." Clearly someone is paying for the social infrastructure being used by Minerva, but it's not the students.

Though it's a new university, Minerva is trying to establish its own rituals and traditions, which it layers onto the social infrastructure. "There are a few big things already," says Capri LaRocca, the city experience manager. "We have legacy groups, which are kind of like the Sorting Hat groups in *Harry Potter.* They're named for things in San Francisco, like Ocean, Gate, and Tower. The students meet in special places, and they've been making videos and stories to pass on to the next cohorts. And the big common thing is the 10:01. Assignments are due every Sunday at ten p.m., and so we started a weekly ritual meal that everyone attends. The students are from all over the world, and each week a group from one of the countries or regions makes dinner and does some cultural programming. Usually it ends with their favorite party music, and everyone dancing until way too late."

Minerva is serious about the social side of university culture, but school leaders want the school to become prestigious because of its academic offerings, and they've built an infrastructure to support that. Katzman tells me that the second tenet of the school design is that the teaching technology, a portal that his team developed, must deliver an educational experience that's at least as good as what students get from an in-person seminar, possibly better. "We have excellent professors, faculty from all over the world who can teach for us because of our technology," he explains, "and we only do small seminars [live, highly interactive, and usually including only twelve to eighteen students], not lectures, because that's the best way for students to learn."

I've spent my career teaching in person, not on the screen, and naturally I express some skepticism. "Honestly," Katzman pushes back. "These are some of the most intense classes you will ever see, and the technology helps, because you see everyone's face on the screen, all at once, unless the instructor wants to do breakout groups or some other layout. Everyone is on the same level. There is no back row, no place where you can disappear. And there's this incredibly rich interaction between students, and between students and faculty. Also, every class is recorded, which means professors can literally review what happens when someone is struggling with the material. They can give the kind of feedback you just don't get in a traditional classroom."

Recently, Minerva released some data that backs this up. In 2016 and 2017, the school administered the Collegiate Learning Assessment, a standardized test that assesses how much students learn during a single academic year. In the fall, Minerva freshmen ranked in the 95th percentile compared with freshmen at other schools, and, because the program is highly selective and students are quite advanced when they enter, they ranked at the 78th percentile compared with college seniors as well. After eight months of intensive instruction at Minerva, the freshmen performed at the 99th percentile—not only among college freshmen but also when compared with seniors across the United States. "The average score of our students at the end of their freshman spring term was higher than the scores of senior graduating classes at every other university and college that administered the test," writes Stephen Kosslyn, the founding dean and chief academic officer. "Minerva's performance is unique in [the Collegiate Learning Assessment] history." The new school was already ranked number one in the measure it takes most seriously: helping students learn.

I asked Minerva if I could speak to some of the students, and they introduced me to three who are finishing up their first year. Each of them seems older and more mature than the first-year students I've taught in Manhattan, and perhaps that's not surprising. Although about twenty thousand people applied for one of the

160 spots in the class of 2022, those who get accepted, and then select the school over more conventional options, are clearly unlike the typical freshman.

In some ways, though, they are just like most university students. They're looking to discover things, to build relationships and have experiences that will shape them forever. "We're a close-knit community. Pretty much everyone knows everyone," says Zane, a precocious eighteen-year-old from Southern California. "But we're also incredibly diverse. I keep thinking that if I'd gone to UCLA, where a lot of my high school friends are, my life would have been totally predictable. I'd have studied computational mathematics. I'd have hung out with my old friends, stayed around California or LA. But this is an adventure. Everything is open and uncertain. I really believe that where you are shapes who you will be. And I am going to be all over the world, getting to know these different places and cultures. I already know that I'm going to be very different because I'm here. And I can't believe how much I'm learning."

When we finish our group conversation, Zane asks if he can walk me to the garage and get some advice. We leave the Minerva office, head up Market Street, and cross over toward the San Francisco Civic Center. We see another student, and he and Zane shout out to each other as they approach, slap hands, make plans for later. There's a man drumming on a plastic bucket, and Zane uses the moment to tell me he wants to spend the summer in New York City, doing an independent study on drumming circles. "I can bartend. Couch surf a bit. There are some Minerva students from there and I'm sure they can help me out when I get there," he explains. "Like I told you, we're all pretty tight." The advice he wants turns out not to concern academic research; he wants to know if I have friends or students who can give him a place to stay.

We stop at a traffic light and scan the plaza in front of us. There are government types in jackets and ties, European tourists, homeless people walking toward the library, cyclists whizzing past. Zane breathes out and his body relaxes, as if he feels at home.

Minerva students, like those at most universities, live close to a library, but theirs is run by the City of San Francisco rather than the school. It's a fitting arrangement, since in San Francisco, as in so many contemporary cities, the library may well be the single institution that's most responsible for inspiring people to learn. When I'd done fieldwork in the Seward Park branch of New York City's library system, Andrew, the library worker who called for more "palaces for the people," told me that helping children learn how much there is to learn in the world is the most rewarding thing about his job. "In three years here I've seen a lot of this neighborhood's children grow up," he explained. "I've seen kids learn to read. I've seen teenagers become regulars. I've seen some get in trouble, then turn things around. And it's great to witness growth in people, to watch kids become adults."

I observed this myself in various branch libraries. In Seward Park, most days began with groups of children from local day care centers and elementary schools parading through the building hand in hand, or with each small person holding on to a common line. They headed directly to the second-floor children's space, where a team of librarians and thousands of books awaited them. In Chinatown, where most parents are immigrants, often with limited knowledge of English and little money for buying books, the library is the key site for teaching literacy. The library staff offers classes for children, parents, and caregivers throughout the day. Among the programs I attended: story time, bilingual sing-along and reading, arts and crafts, basic computing, how to do research, homework help, college preparation. I watched teachers from elementary schools that, due to funding cuts in the public education system, no longer have their own libraries bring their entire class to Seward Park for special projects and to simply borrow books. I spent afternoons in the company of high school students who hung out, studied, and played computer games in the dedicated teen space because it was better than being out in the streets. I saw children's librarians organize special programs for families with an incarcerated parent, so that kids whose sense of shame and isolation made it hard to focus on schoolwork and build solid friendships could meet other kids in their situation. I met young people who said that outside the library they faced a world of constraints, whereas inside they saw only abundance, and permission to take whatever they wanted.

I interviewed dozens of people about their memories of growing up in libraries and learned about all kinds of ways that the experience mattered: Discovering an interest that they'd never have found without librarians, open stacks, or a video collection. Feeling liberated, responsible, intelligent. Forging a new relationship, deepening an old one. Sensing, in some cases for the first time, that they belong.

Sharon Marcus, for instance, grew up in a working-class family in Queens where money was tight and everyone was busy. "Home was not peaceful," she recalls. "And the park, where I spent a lot of time, was rambunctious. There was never really any spot that you could just sit and be by yourself. I was an introvert, and I needed some time when I wasn't gonna talk to anyone. I wanted to read for as long as I wanted, to be completely in charge of my time, my energy, how I was using my attention, where I was directing it, for how long. And the library was a place I could go and ignore people, but also know that I wasn't alone. We didn't go on vacations, we didn't travel. So the library was where I went to escape everything, and where I could glimpse a better reality."

Sharon has vivid memories of the books she read in her branch library. It started with stories about ordinary kids in New York City living lives very different from hers, and in time she grew interested in books about female actresses and film stars. "I remember finding a whole bunch of biographies of women who were queens and saints. Even now, I can physically see where this section was in the building. I was interested in queens because, well, why wouldn't I be? They were like men who had done something. I got interested in Queen Elizabeth the First because she was Henry VIII's daughter. I used the card catalog and found a book, and then next to it there was some other Elizabeth, some crazy Hungarian Christian saint who got leprosy deliberately or something, I remember reading that too. I don't know how they organized that section but it was basically about women who had achieved things. I devoured it."

The library became even more important to Sharon when she entered adolescence. "I was so excited when I realized you could read old newspapers on microfilm, and watch old movies at the library too. The librarians always let me, and they didn't ask a lot of questions. That was so important," Sharon tells me. "I never, ever encountered a librarian who said something like 'Why would you want to do that?' or 'I can't let you use that machine, you're too young.' I was shy, but they never made me feel weird. Nobody treated me like I was special or supersmart, either. They were just neutral. And that, I think, was a real gift. It made the library a space of permission, not encouragement that pushed you in a certain direction, where you feel like people are watching you and like giving their approval, but just freedom to pursue what you want."

No other place in Sharon's life worked that way: not home, where her parents monitored her choices; not synagogue, where she felt intense moral pressure but no sense of belonging; not school, where teachers and staff were quick to judge. The library, she learned, could accommodate nearly all of her interests, especially if she left her neighborhood and visited the main Queens Library or the stunning central library on Forty-Second Street and Fifth Avenue in Manhattan. "I remember going there to do a big research paper in high school," she explains. "It was before the Internet, and finding things took so much more effort. I remember feeling really good then. I was so far beyond the children's room, and even the collection at my little branch library. I realized that there were all these things I wanted to understand about how the world worked, and that here I could find the answers through books and reading." She remains a regular, to this day, though now that she's the Orlando Harriman Professor of English and Comparative Literature at Columbia University, finding time for public library visits isn't as easy as it was when she was a kid.

Jelani Cobb, who grew up in Hollis, Queens, during the 1970s, also believes that the most important part of his education happened in his neighborhood library. His father, who migrated from southern Georgia, was an electrician who started working at age nine and had only a third-grade education; his mother, from Alabama, had a high school degree. "This was a middle-class African American community with a lot of migration-generation folk who had southern accents," he says. "They'd found a foothold in the city and were beginning to make some progress for themselves. They hadn't been able to get formal education, but education was very important to them. They'd take a great deal of pride in reading the newspaper every single day, going to the library, taking out books and so on, supplementing what they didn't get as kids."

Jelani remembers getting his first library card. "I was about nine years old and going to a new school, and on the way back we stopped at the public library on 204th Street and Hollis Avenue. We went in and my mother told me to tell the woman what I wanted. I said that I wanted a library card and the woman couldn't quite hear me and so she leaned over to hear better and my mother said to her, 'No, sit back up.' And she told me to speak loudly so the woman could hear."

"And so I did. I said I wanted to get a library card. I think if you were old enough to sign your name you could get a card. And she gave me the thing! I signed my name and the card was mine!"

One of the first books he took out was about Thomas Edison, and it reported that as a child Edison read a one-foot stack of books each week. "I set out to do the same thing, and of course, I don't think I did it," Jelani recalls. "But that sparked a lifelong habit of spending many hours reading, which is amazing. And I remember being fascinated by the idea that as a young person, you could go to this place and read anything that you wanted. All these things were on the shelves! It was almost kind of like, 'Do people know about this?' It was like, 'Is the jig up?' I was worried they'd find out what happens here and shut it down!"

Jelani and his mother spent a lot of time together at the library. As he got older, she went back to school, getting a bachelor's degree and then a master's at New York University. One time, he remembers, "my mother took out a small book. It was maybe thirty pages and I couldn't believe that this was like a book for grown-ups. I thought that grown-ups read books that were really big and so I was interested in this book. I wanted to read it but she was like, 'No, this book is for grown-ups.'

"And I was like, well, 'I can read it! I can!' And so I read it, and it's about this man who has this bag of gold and he's going around with it and he wants to go swimming but he can't, and he wants to do something else but he can't. And all these times the bag of gold is getting in his way. And eventually he loses the bag, but then as he was looking for it, he winds up doing all these things that he couldn't do while he had it. I was like, 'Okay, this is a nice story.' And my mother was like, 'Do you get it?' And I was like, 'Yeah, the man lost his bag and then he did this and then he did that.' And then she said, 'No, this is what is called a metaphor.' And I specifically remember that. It was when I learned what a metaphor was and how it functioned in literature. She explained that the reason the story is so short and is still for grown-ups is that it's actually making a deeper point, that a book is often more than what the story is saying on the surface. That was quite a thing to learn!"

Jelani also spent a lot of time alone in the library, exploring politics, art, and literature, and sometimes delving into controversial topics that he'd grown curious about during conversations at home or in church. "I was raised Catholic, and when I was fifteen I somehow got interested in euthanasia and began to form an opinion about it. I had to do a report for school, and I started by interviewing my priest. He had baptized me, actually. And he explained that as Catholics, we were opposed to euthanasia, and I was kind of like, 'Okay, right.' But then I went to the library and started reading these things on my own. And I realized, you know, I think I disagree with this! People should have the right to choose when to die. And it wound up being an opinion that I hold to this day. And honestly, had I not kind of gotten into that topic on my own and actually just done that reading at the library, I probably would have just said, you know, this is what we believe as Catholics, and that's it." The library, he says, helped him become his own person, free to question authority and think for himself. Today, those are skills that he uses often. He's a staff writer for the *New Yorker* and a professor of journalism at Columbia.

Jelani's mother died in 2011, and he wanted to do something to honor her love for the library and his memory of the time they spent there together. "The year she passed away, I purchased a computer at our branch of the Queens Library, the one where she'd taken me to get my first library card. I put a little plaque on it that says 'For Mary Cobb.' I thought it would be a contribution to a place that my mother felt was valuable. And I felt like it was the right thing to do because it was so central for both of us. I mean, everything I do started from being able to read all those books when I was nine or ten."

Today, our communities are full of children whose future, like Jelani's, will be formed in the places where they go to learn about themselves and the world they'll inherit. They deserve palaces. Whether they get them is up to us.

CHAPTER FOUR

Healthy Bonds

Every four years, the American Society of Civil Engineers (ASCE) issues grades for the nation's infrastructure, and if the federal government were a high school student, it would tear up the report before bringing it home. In 2017, as in 2013, America's overall infrastructure score was a D+, but it could have been worse. The rail network, despite high-profile failures of the Amtrak line in the busy Northeast Corridor and the New York City subway system, got a B. Seven systems, including hazardous waste, levees, ports, schools, and wastewater, received modestly better grades than in the previous assessment. Parks, transit, and solid waste did worse, while others, such as aviation (D), roads (D), drinking water (D), and energy (D+), retained their miserably low scores.

It's not surprising that the ASCE does not grade social infrastructure, which is only now becoming a common concept. But it's strange that the ASCE refrains from scoring the nation's health and food infrastructures, which are as essential to our well-being as any other vital systems. As anyone who has been treated in an urban public hospital, visited a fallen industrial town or destitute rural community, or shopped for fresh produce in a low-income neighborhood knows, the places that make healthy living possible are also in disrepair. No one questions the urgent need for investments in the nation's outdated systems for transit, electricity, energy, and storm protection. But are the dire health problems that stem from shoddy social infrastructure any less pressing or dangerous?

Consider, for instance, the largest American public health crisis since the HIV/AIDS epidemic: opioid addiction. Since the late 1990s, the United States has experienced a dramatic increase in the sale, use, and abuse of prescription pain relievers, such as codeine and hydrocodone, as well as street drugs like heroin. The results have been devastating. Hundreds of thousands of people have died and countless communities, particularly in small towns and rural areas, have been ravaged. The addiction crisis has taken a financial toll as well. One 2016 study estimated that the opioid epidemic had already cost the US economy almost $80 billion.

The most serious consequence of the opioid crisis is an alarming rise in overdose deaths. In 2016, sixty-four thousand Americans were killed by overdoses—triple the number of 2000—with the vast majority of deaths linked to opioid abuse. To put this in perspective, it means more Americans died of overdoses in a single year than during the entirety of the Vietnam War. And the problem appears only to be getting worse. Health officials believe it likely that, absent a drastic intervention, five hundred thousand Americans will die from opioids in the next decade alone.

There is no single cause of the epidemic, but there's growing evidence that an important and often overlooked factor is the loss of social cohesion and social support. In 2015, the Princeton economists Anne Case and Angus Deaton identified a historically unprecedented increase in the number of white Americans dying in middle age. This was due largely to fatalities from drug and alcohol abuse as well as suicide, which Case and Deaton would later term "deaths of despair." The economists, who had been influenced by the French sociologist Émile Durkheim's classic account of suicide as a consequence of profound social disruption, argued that these fatalities were tied to large-scale economic and social changes. In addition to facing a decline in job opportunities, white people with little education were experiencing a loss of traditional rituals and social institutions that had long served as sources of support. Marriage rates are down. Divorce remains common. Families are fragmented. Local government agencies are strapped for resources. Libraries and childcare centers have fewer open hours. Churches are scrambling to meet new challenges and demands. "These changes left people with less structure when they came to choose their careers, their religion, and the nature of their family lives," they write. "When such choices succeed, they are liberating; when they fail, the individual can only hold himself or herself responsible. In the worst cases of failure, this is a Durkheim-like recipe for suicide."

How does a loss of community result in more people using painkillers? Intriguingly, there's a growing body of neurological research showing that opioids are, chemically speaking, a good analog for social connection. In one recent lab study, subjects were given naltrexone, a chemical that blocks the body's ability to produce its own, naturally occurring opioids. Without these chemicals, individuals felt more socially disconnected from other people. This reminds us that taking synthetic opioids, of the sort currently wreaking havoc on struggling American communities, can soothe physical pain, psychological anguish, and the agony of social disconnection as well.

Today, much of the evidence that social isolation and opioid addiction are linked is anecdotal, based largely on users who say that they turn to drugs after losing a job or a sense of belonging. One heroin addict in the Rust Belt city of McKeesport, Pennsylvania, told the sociologist Katherine McLean that the city's drug problems stemmed directly from a shredded social fabric. "There is no sense of community here," she said. "Not one, not one iota of community here. . . . So, left to your own devices, somebody that's drinking and drugging is gonna continue drinking and drugging. Nothing else, cause there ain't shit else to do."

But anecdotes are not our only evidence. There's new empirical work that establishes a clear connection between the strength of a community's social ties and its ability to withstand opioid abuse. In 2017, a study by the Harvard graduate student Michael Zoorob found that communities with strong social capital—as measured by things like the density of civic organizations and the rates at which citizens voted—were more likely to be insulated from the opioid crisis than comparatively fragile communities. This remained true even when Zoorob took into account factors such as income, education level, and the rate of painkiller prescriptions. Such a finding may indicate that people in stronger communities are less likely to become addicted to drugs or, possibly, that socially isolated people who use drugs are more likely to die from them. One of the most intriguing ideas in Zoorob's study is that overdose deaths—not unlike deaths from heat waves—may be higher among people with weaker social networks. Among the many reasons: if someone overdoses while they're alone, there's no one there to find them and call 911.

While restoring a broken social infrastructure is a critical long-term project, many cities and towns in the United States are asking what they can do right now to reduce the rate of overdose deaths. To answer this question, it's worth looking at another country that once faced a similar problem: Switzerland.

Beginning in the 1970s, Switzerland saw an alarming number of its citizens become addicted to heroin. Initially, the Swiss

responded to this in the same way the United States has tradition-
ally responded to drug use, with tougher law enforcement. Courts
issued stiffer sentences for drug users and dealers, while police dispersed people who took drugs in public places. But the problem
only got worse. In addition to seeing more young people take up
the needle, the country also witnessed a frightening increase in
property crime, HIV infection, and overdose deaths.

In 1987, increasingly desperate, authorities in Zurich tried the
opposite approach. Instead of facing harsh penalties, addicts would
now be allowed to use drugs openly, but only in a specific area
of the city, Platzspitz Park. Fans of the television series *The Wire*
will recognize this strategy as similar to the one deployed in Baltimore's fictional "Hamsterdam." As in Hamsterdam, this approach
did little to stem the problem of addiction and created intense
spillover effects, such as increased crime in areas around the park.
Meanwhile, legalization did little to stem the number of overdoses.

Switzerland is not an especially progressive country. Swiss
women, for example, only gained the right to vote in 1971. Yet, a
country of bankers is nothing if not pragmatic. Stymied, authorities struck on a plan that was both radical and full of common
sense. What was killing people, authorities realized, was not heroin use per se, but using heroin alone, under unsafe conditions. The
Swiss government ultimately decided that the best way to protect
users was to give them the drug. However, the heroin would be
administered only in clinics where the addicts could receive proper
supervision, and the drugs would be pharmaceutical-grade, free
of any unknown and potentially fatal additives. Doses were large
enough to allow users to function and not suffer withdrawal, but
modest enough to prevent them from getting high. The program
was run like any other medical facility and the users treated like
any other patients. People even had to purchase health insurance
to participate.

The Swiss found that once heroin users didn't have to worry
about how they'd get their drug, they were often able to take on the

larger problems that had led to their addiction in the first place. Social workers were able to build trust with users, helping them get jobs and counseling. By reducing the stigma of heroin, and creating physical places where drug users and counselors could meet together without the threat of punishment, the Swiss government was able to reintegrate its users back into society.

In all cases, recovering from substance abuse requires the support of a community, be it family, friends, therapists, or twelve-step groups. Addiction experts refer to these kinds of social connections as elements of "recovery capital." The heroin maintenance zones that the Swiss government established were not merely sites for drug injection. They were social infrastructures, places where addicts, counselors, and medical providers interacted regularly, under conditions that, though not exactly salubrious, were as healthy as possible.

Between 1991 and 2004, overdose deaths in Switzerland dropped by 50 percent. While many still overdosed at the supervised injection sites, not a single person died. Meanwhile, fewer people were choosing to start taking heroin. The number of new users dropped 80 percent between 1990 and 2002; in turn, HIV rates plummeted. The program also had positive effects for nonusers. Most notably, the country saw a 90 percent drop in heroin-related property crimes. In a national referendum held in 2008, Swiss citizens overwhelmingly voted to maintain their public health approach to opioid addiction. It's now part of national law.

It's also an international model of effective, if still controversial, social infrastructure, and one with a proven record of saving lives. Australia and the United Kingdom have run successful experiments with safe injection clinics. In 2014, Vancouver, Canada, an early leader in clean needle distribution programs, became the first North American city to open a fully legal heroin and methadone maintenance facility as well. The program made an immediate impact. Within two years of opening, the rate of fatal overdoses in the immediate vicinity of the clinic dropped by 35 percent; in the rest of the city, deaths dropped less than 10 percent. In Vancouver, as elsewhere, opponents of the legal injection sites predicted that they would encourage more people to try heroin, yet subsequent studies have shown that this hasn't happened. As in Switzerland, cordoning off a safe yet tame zone for users made the drug less appealing, and there are far fewer new users there than in comparable places.

US cities have been reluctant to adopt the Swiss model for opioid maintenance, but some places are inching toward the idea. Boston, which was one of the first American cities to experience a spike in lethal opioid overdoses and has been unable to reverse the problem, has allowed a sparsely populated corridor on the edges of the South End, Roxbury, and Newmarket neighborhoods to develop into the city's "Methadone Mile." It's not a legally protected drug safety zone, but the area, which overlooks Interstate 93 and has little commercial activity, now hosts an open-air drug market, homeless shelters, addiction clinics, and the Boston Medical Center, one of New England's largest safety-net hospitals and trauma centers. The thick concentration of services has attracted opioid addicts from all over New England, including some who are looking for treatment and others who just want a safer place to shoot up.

The city is struggling to keep up with the demand, but recently it opened what the journalist Susan Zalkind, in an article on the "infrastructure of the opioid epidemic," calls a "no questions asked 'engagement space'" that operates like a library, without requiring names or identification from its patrons. The clinic aims at getting addicts and drug abusers off the streets and into therapeutic programs, as does its neighbor, the Supportive Place for Observation and Treatment (SPOT), which monitors drug users to prevent overdoses and protect them, particularly women, from assault. Both programs achieved early successes. Within a few months of opening, Zalkind reports, SPOT staff had initiated 3,800 interactions with about five hundred users, 10 percent of whom went on to seek treatment, and prevented more than one hundred hospital trips. The addicts Zalkind interviewed told her that they'd made new friendships in the corridor. "You just know if something happens, you know that you have certain people that regardless are going to have your back," one man told her. There's a community, and a level of trust that's unusual among opioid users on the streets.

Not everyone is enthusiastic about the project, however. There's little question that Methadone Mile promotes the health and safety of opioid addicts, but social infrastructures designed for sick and vulnerable people, some of whom have criminal records, do not fit neatly into larger residential or commercial areas. Walk near the corridor, Zalkind writes, and you'll notice that "people tend to walk toward the area in a determined march and away in a foggy stupor. Men with backpacks may whisper 'brown' and 'that hard' in your ear as you pass, and you'll see a large number of people wearing lanyards with medical IDs hanging around their necks." It's easy to appreciate the benefits of building designated drug use and treatment zones if you live in another part of the city. Inevitably, though, people who live and work close to them complain.

Boston officials and leaders of the nonprofits and medical facilities that are working on Methadone Mile have been trying to do outreach with residents and small business owners who are worried about problems spilling over from the drug corridor. They are adding security and experimenting with designs that separate the therapeutic and medical facilities from the rest of the city. Fortunately, old industrial cities like Boston tend to have abandoned or undeveloped land where drug safety zones will not stretch into anyone's backyard. If it works, it's scalable: across the country, there are hundreds of places where a Methadone Mile could go. It's too early to assess the Boston project, but the evidence thus far suggests that it's reducing the risk of overdoses and helping people get into treatment. It's sparing the city the cost of managing overdoses in public hospitals. Most important, it's saving lives.

As devastating as the opioid crisis is, it's not the only—or the biggest—threat to public health in the United States. Indeed, in many poor and segregated African American neighborhoods, the most urgent problems stem from the absence of basic goods and services that other Americans take for granted, including the most fundamental form of market activity: selling healthy food.

Consider Englewood, the neighborhood on the South Side of Chicago where so many people died in the heat wave, and where life expectancy is far below the city average. Abandoned homes, boarded storefronts, and empty lots with tall grass and weeds the size of trees actively discourage people from walking around the area, and there are frighteningly high levels of violent crime on the broken-down, depleted city blocks. "We've lost so many people here that I had to stop counting," said Cordia Pugh, who has lived in the neighborhood for nearly five decades. "It was just too much."

Pugh worries about drugs, gangs, and guns in the neighborhood, and she still gets rattled by the sounds of conflict in the streets. But for decades, the most frustrating daily problem she and her neighbors faced was the lack of fresh meat and produce in the neighborhood's markets and corner stores. "I'm a fourth-generation farmer," Pugh explained. "My father's father's father was a farmer, from Mississippi, and we just kept on doing it. It's our heritage. With the Great Migration, which my family did in the 1930s, we took farming up North. We moved to Chicago when I was six, in 1959, from the place that's now Ford Heights. And I'll tell you, that was as rural as Mississippi. We had hog farms, cattle farms, all kinds of vegetables. You wouldn't have known you were out of the South." There were plenty of good food options in Englewood when Pugh's family first moved there. "Back then it was still a mixed neighborhood," Pugh recalled. "We had all kinds of shops and grocers, and there was a lot going on. I did Girl Scouts and the Boys & Girls Club in the neighborhood. I went to the YMCA after school. I did the Cadets [a music and marching program]. All right here. But in the 1970s things started falling apart here. All the white people left. There were riots after Martin Luther King was killed. The city disinvested, and all those programs for kids evaporated." The groceries disappeared too.

By the 1980s, Pugh told me, Englewood had become "the heart of Chicago's food desert"—the term that the US Department of Agriculture uses to describe urban areas where people have limited access to supermarkets, supercenters, or large grocery stores. The USDA reports that about 13 percent of low-income census tracts are food deserts, and in these areas, the absence of healthy food can be just as dangerous as the presence of gangs and guns. According to the US National Academy of Sciences, living in a food desert is associated with obesity and a host of chronic, diet-related diseases. It makes residents, including children, more likely to drink soda and consume processed foods that are high in salt, sugar, and chemical preservatives. It's linked to diabetes and cancer. And, for people like Pugh, it makes each ordinary meal an occasion for regret about the sorry offerings on the table instead of joy.

There are not many upsides to living in a place like Englewood, but one of them, Pugh told me, is that so many lots are empty—there's at least one open property on every block, and most have several—that the neighborhood is ripe for agriculture. "It took some time to see it," she explained, "but after a while we realized that Englewood could be farmed just like Mississippi." It's an ideal place not only for developing community gardens but for urban farming, potentially on a large scale.

She wasn't the only one to see the possibility. In 1992, Les Brown, who founded the Chicago Coalition for the Homeless, began advocating for an urban job-training program organized around farming. It was a bold idea, but a premature one, since the concept of urban farming was not yet established, and few shared his vision for transforming Chicago's empty lots into sites of agricultural production. He persisted, as did one of his colleagues, Harry Rhodes, and in 1998 their organization, Growing Home, acquired land for a farm in Marseilles, Illinois, seventy-five miles from Chicago, which they used to train production assistants. Brown died in 2005, but that year Rhodes worked with an Englewood community organization and persuaded the City of Chicago to let them use a vacant property for an agricultural site in the neighborhood. The lot turned out to be located at the crossroads of three distinct gang territories, and it was polluted with PCBs. But after four years of remediation, which involved bringing in truckloads of new soil, building good relationships with nearby residents, and persuading the city to amend a local zoning ordinance, Growing Home opened the Wood Street Urban Farm in Englewood. It was Chicago's first organic urban farm. Two years later, it opened the Honore Street Farm nearby. "Our goal," Rhodes told me, "is to turn Englewood from a food desert to a food destination."

Rhodes understands that it will be a long, difficult process, and he vividly recalls how bad things were when the farm project began. "Before we got to Englewood most people didn't have access to fresh produce," he explained. "They got their food from corner stores, Walgreens, or the gas stations in the area. People who really wanted fresh food would go to Whole Foods in the South Loop or the food co-op in Hyde Park, but most people didn't have the time or the money to do that. It wasn't hard to see why so many people had unhealthy diets. It was just hard to get good food."

"Englewood was obviously struggling in 2006," he said. "But a lot of families were doing okay. They had block clubs. The housing stock was filling. Things were starting to change." Then the Great Recession started, and the wave of foreclosures that swept through Chicago's African American neighborhoods hit Englewood especially hard. "It happened so fast," Rhodes recounted. "One foreclosure after another. Before we knew it, every block had at least three or four houses that got boarded up. Even today, a decade later, there are blocks where half of the houses are empty. There are more empty lots. And there's a lot more violence too."

Today, thanks to a decade of labor by civic organizations like Growing Home, there are already more than eight hundred identifiable community gardens and urban farms in Chicago, and they deliver tangible benefits to the people who are fortunate enough to live near them. According to the American Public Health Association (APHA), which recently issued a policy statement and review of the scientific literature on how access to nature affects health, community gardens do more than provide shade and reduce the temperature in overheated urban environments. They foster interactions within and across generations, resulting in less social isolation as well as more cohesion, civic participation, and neighborhood attachment. They reduce stress levels for people who visit or frequently walk by them. They help children develop positive feelings about nature and facilitate scientific learning. And they provide healthy food: more than five hundred gardens or farms in Chicago produce fruits or vegetables, many in places where fresh food is hard to find. The city, which has more than twenty thousand empty lots, most of them concentrated in poor and segregated areas, could use many more small-scale green spaces. But that won't happen without the resources that Chicago's political and philanthropic leaders have devoted to other vital infrastructure, including the impressive green roof on its own City Hall.

The 21,000-square-foot, $2.5 million City Hall roof garden is one of the grandest and most expensive green roofs in the world. First planted in 2000, it features about 20,000 plants of more than 150 species, each of which helps reduce heat and absorb rainwater in storms. Chicago reports that, on hot days, the roof temperature on City Hall is approximately 30 degrees lower than on comparable buildings with conventional roofs, and that this reduces energy costs by thousands of dollars per month. The massive roof is an impressive piece of green infrastructure, exactly the kind of project that cities will need to build out at scale as the world confronts climate change. It's aesthetically pleasing and ecologically responsible. It's inspiring not only to international visitors but also to local developers, dozens of whom have planted gardens on the roofs of other Chicago buildings. It is not, however, a work of social infrastructure. It does nothing to help people in Chicago neighborhoods connect with one another on a regular basis. It doesn't give people who are surrounded by asphalt better access to parkland or clean air. It doesn't make those who are vulnerable to extreme weather any safer, nor does it make the places they live healthier. To do all of that Chicago would have to invest in less glamorous but far more accessible green spaces: community gardens and urban farms.

Pugh, who had a long career in the private sector before moving into philanthropy, told me that one motivation for getting so involved in Englewood's farm and garden movement is establishing proof that the concept works. In addition to her own garden, she has developed two urban farms, the Hermitage Community Garden and the Englewood Veterans Gardens, in partnership with Growing Home. The new green spaces yielded much more than fresh produce. "The farms and gardens are giving people a peaceful place to go," Pugh explained. "Young people. Old people. We even get people coming from other neighborhoods, because they get so much pleasure from being outside, working the land with other good people. And we need that, because you can't have a community without a community space."

The farms and gardens are not just community spaces, Pugh added. "They're safe havens. Even the gangbangers respect what we are doing." They have parents and grandparents in the neighborhood, after all, and they appreciate fresh food too. "When there's a conflict they tell everyone to stay off our block now. They know we're doing something good here. And there's a good chance that their relatives will be out here too!"

"When we first got to Wood Street there was a turf war among gangs right there," Rhodes told me. "And we were building just as everything else was getting boarded up, so we had some kids vandalize our property, breaking windows and the like. But we were working closely with community groups and residents, and after a while people came to see us as a local resource. They saw that we had something to offer. And since then it has been pretty peaceful here. The gardens are just beautiful places. We're trying to build new ones too, because it's clear that the neighborhood needs more."

Englewood is still far from a food destination, but Growing Home is helping to end the food desert. Its two farms are producing a steady supply of fresh produce, and they now run a weekly farmers' market with cooking classes. Recently, two other community organizations built farms on empty lots nearby, and Kusanya, a locally owned nonprofit café, opened there too. The neighborhood, long stigmatized as a den of urban violence, is slowly gaining a reputation as a special place for urban agriculture. This change in its status has already affected local economic development. In September 2016, a shopping center with a Whole Foods, a Starbucks, and a Chipotle opened in Englewood, leading journalists to call it a "food desert no longer." This was perhaps premature, since not everyone can afford the fare at these establishments. But Englewood residents waited in long lines to shop in the Whole Foods on opening day, lured partly by the high-end grocer's pledge to offer reduced prices on staple items, including fresh produce, and partly by its commitment to hire scores of local residents.

Growing Home has also maintained its original commitment to job training and economic development. "When we spoke with people in the community, we learned that helping to break the cycle that led from poverty to prison and back was incredibly important here," Rhodes told me. "So we set up a program for people who'd just left prison, giving them fourteen-week jobs as production assistants and then helping them get full-time jobs when they finished." Once that was set, Growing Home formally added community development to its mission. "It makes a big difference to have a place that produces good food *and* helps to make all these social connections. We now see a lot of ways that we can help make Englewood a healthier place."

It took years, and an enormous amount of hard labor in the long-neglected urban soil, to persuade public officials that they could use infrastructure funds to support urban farms and community gardens. "When we first started the city kind of laughed at us," Rhodes recalled. " 'A farm in Englewood! Right.' Now they can see that this is a good idea. We're about to get a new site next to the farm on Honore, and for that one the city will actually do the environmental cleanup, cap it, fence it. That's a lot more support than we had a decade ago. It would be nice if the support was more systematic. But they see the difference we're making, and maybe we will get that someday."

They will if the American Public Health Association has influence in the emerging space where social infrastructure planning meets urban health. According to one of the main policy recommendations from the APHA report on nature: "Community gardens should be considered as a primary and permanent open space option as part of master planning efforts; gardens should be developed as part of land planning processes rather than as an afterthought in neighborhood redevelopment projects."

Policy makers have ignored this recommendation, but should know better. After all, modern infrastructure—for reliable power, clean water, fast transit, affordable food, and resilient structures—has done more to improve public health than any other modern intervention, including scientific medicine. "The early 20th century saw great changes in health and safety brought about through collaborations that today would be viewed as odd or unusual—[between] physicians and city planners, sanitarians and civil engineers," write Charles Branas and John MacDonald, who expanded their research on mediating urban blight to see if it does more for public health than reduce violent crime. "Episodically treating small numbers of people, while ignoring the obviously unhealthy social and environmental surroundings within which people live, has stunted our treatments and moved the health of the nation forward at too slow a pace." Today, as the world grows more urban and unequal, there's an urgent need to build healthier places, and social infrastructure is the key.

Fascinating research by Branas's team in Philadelphia shows not only *that* small green spaces in poor urban neighborhoods improve public health but also *how* they do. In a study led by Eugenia South, a professor of emergency medicine at Penn, the team found twelve people (eight men, four women, all African American, mostly older, and the majority with annual incomes under $15,000) who were willing to walk through an area within two blocks of their home with Garmin monitors measuring their heart rates continuously. They did two walks, separated by several months. On the first, the participants walked by untreated empty lots, the kind of urban blight that, as Branas's earlier research showed, tends to attract crime. On the second walk, they walked by empty lots that had been converted into small, accessible gardens with trees and other vegetation. Heart rate, the authors note, is a clear and dynamic marker of stress response; tracking its variations as the study subjects walked by the treated and untreated lots would show whether being within view of well-maintained green places affects a crucial element of human health.

The results were unmistakable: When residents walked by the untreated vacant lot, acute stress caused their average heart rates to increase by 9.5 beats per minute—this despite the fact that the sites had long been in the area and were familiar to the study participants. A spike of 9.5 heartbeats per minute may not sound too dangerous, but to Branas's team it was a worrisome number. It suggests that living near blighted urban spaces generates recurrent surges in stress and, with them, "inflammatory changes and dysregulation of cardiovascular, neurological, and endocrine systems over a lifetime for persons repeatedly exposed." Walking, which in most cases is precisely what people need to do to improve their health and fitness, can become instead a source of anxiety.

The effects were reversed when the subjects walked by lots that had been transformed into green spaces. "Our results indicate that in-view proximity to a greened vacant lot decreases heart rate, compared with in-view proximity to a nongreened vacant lot," South and her colleagues conclude. "The reduction in heart rate suggests a biological link between vacant lot greening and reduction in acute stress." More pragmatically, it indicates that "improvements to . . . physical conditions"—even inexpensive changes, like turning vacant lots into pocket parks—"may lead to widespread downstream health benefits." Like the APHA, they urge governments to consider structural improvements to neighborhoods as "first-line solutions to difficult urban problems." In Philadelphia, and around the world as well, the evidence that vibrant green places promote health by reducing stress, especially among the most vulnerable, is hard to ignore.

I've been concerned about the fate of one rapidly expanding group of vulnerable people, the elderly, since I began studying the Chicago heat wave. There are nearly six hundred million people aged sixty-five and above around the world today, and the United Nations estimates that "almost half of women living independently [i.e., not with family or in an institution] live alone." These numbers are expected to rise dramatically in coming decades, as the population ages. According to a joint report by the World Health

Organization and the US federal government, the total number of people aged sixty-five and over will reach 1.5 billion, or about 16 percent of the global population, by 2050.

In another research project, which became the book *Going Solo*, I argued that the rise of people living alone is one of the most significant but least examined demographic changes in modern history. Although the rise of living alone results from many positive changes (including the increase in longevity and the rising status of women), it has generated one extremely worrisome social problem: a spike in the number of old people at risk of becoming sedentary and isolated, particularly if their mental or physical health diminishes. Public policies that provide professional caregivers can help address this problem. But there is another, far more beneficial and considerably less expensive way to help the elderly maintain their health and vitality: invest in social infrastructure, and build places that promote active lifestyles and frequent interaction in the public realm.

In the United States, branch libraries, particularly those that offer programs like video bowling leagues, book clubs, and karaoke sessions, play a significant role in helping old people remain active. Designated senior centers also draw people out of their private homes and into the social world, albeit a somewhat stigmatized one where they only encounter people in their age group. Thanks to Social Security and Medicare, the American elderly receive basic support for managing the financial challenges of old age, yet the United States does little to promote physical and social activity among the elderly. Parks, for instance, may occasionally host programming for older people, but they are rarely designed to meet the needs of an aging population; the same is true of most libraries and public housing facilities. Other countries, however, have made larger and more thoughtful investments in social infrastructure that help the elderly flourish. These projects get little public attention, but as promoting good health in the world's aging population becomes a major social challenge, it's important to understand how they work.

I've spent years seeking out places that help old people maintain their physical health and social vitality, and one of the most remarkable examples is Singapore, where the life expectancy, 83.1, ranks third in the world. (Japan is first, at 83.7, and Switzerland is second, at 83.4. The United Kingdom ranks twentieth, at 81.2, and the United States is thirty-first, at 79.3.) About 80 percent of Singapore's citizens, and an even greater proportion of old people, live in publicly developed housing projects with privately owned flats, sold to residents with generous state subsidies. Most of these complexes offer residents easy access to vibrant common areas, including parks with exercise areas, generous meeting spaces, and affordable dining options at the outdoor "hawker centers" (or food courts) that typically occupy the ground level. "These places are busy all the time," says Wei Da Lim, my host during a research visit with Singapore's Centre for Liveable Cities, as we slurp *laksa* in a crowded hawker center on the ground floor of the Toa Payoh development. "Of course there are a lot of old people, because there are a lot of old people in Singapore"—today about one of eight people is over age sixty-five; by 2030, it will be one of five. "A lot of them live alone, and this is a place where they can always come and find people they know."

Toa Payoh is a typical Singapore housing estate: a series of high-rise towers, connected by stone walking paths and sidewalks, with small gardens scattered around the area and an expansive, open-air shopping center at the base. I visited five other housing complexes in different neighborhoods during my time in Singapore, and while their designs varied, each supported an extraordinary level of social programming, offered verdant green space for outdoor relaxation, and hosted commercial activity, from shopping to dining, that attracted people across generational lines. The common areas were heavily used, but the grounds were always clean and well maintained. People worried about crime, and a few complexes featured large signs where officials could report recent offenses. But the crime rates are low by almost any standard—at Toa Payoh, the "Crime Alert" sign was blank—and most criminal acts are petty. Old people looked to be at home in the public areas, whether they were walking, shopping, or, in a sight I saw often during long and humid afternoons, sleeping on a shaded bench.

The Singapore government engages in strict social planning, and it allocates units to achieve a mix of ethnicity and income level in each complex. But it is only beginning to grapple with the problem of what to do with such a rapidly aging population. I met with several city officials during my visit: the Centre for Liveable Cities is a research arm of the state, with tight connections to policy makers. Some worry that residents who age in place will grow isolated and estranged from their children and grandchildren, because the tight housing market makes it difficult for multiple generations to live in the same neighborhood. Others are concerned that large units designed for large families will be occupied by old couples and singles who won't use the space, further intensifying the housing crunch in one of the smallest and most densely populated places on earth. There are limits to the government's social planning, and it respects the rights of home owners to remain in their flats. But the housing agency is considering new developments that would help reintegrate elderly people with their children, whether in larger, multigenerational units or in new complexes that offer a mix of housing types for younger families and older singletons.

These ideas are not unique to Singapore. In Sweden, where a greater proportion of people live alone than in any other nation, I observed mixed-generation residential communities designed to bring people from different families together in active, socially supportive environments. At Färdknäppen, a cohousing project for people aged forty and above, everyone keeps their own private apartment but there are all variety of common spaces and programs, including a large kitchen and a nightly dinner that residents can cook and eat together whenever they choose. In the United States, some developers—and far more individual families acting alone to solve what feels like a private problem of caring for an elder—are experimenting with multigenerational housing types that allow younger and older members of a family to live in separate units on a common property. These projects, which come primarily from the private and philanthropic sectors, are hardly common. But they signal an emerging recognition that more and more people are looking for better places to live as they age.

Visiting Singapore was striking because government officials there are worrying about problems for the elderly that, thanks to the design and social order of their estate housing, they're already solving better than most other places. Singapore is an unusually affluent and educated society, with an authoritarian government and norms of social intervention that no democratic nation shares. Yet the current model of urban planning that Singapore uses to improve the health and welfare of its older citizens works by promoting the same things governments around the world are beginning to advocate: busy food corridors, commercial strips with local vendors, neighborhood parks, and vibrant public spaces. In most societies, creating healthier places for old people doesn't involve changing core values or systems of government. But it does require confronting two major social developments that few nations have been willing to confront honestly: there have never been so many old people, and there has never been such a dire shortage of housing that meets our current needs. Designs for the world's rapidly aging, increasingly urban societies will, inevitably, involve the kinds of large-scale housing and commercial complexes that Singapore is already developing. In the meantime, however, there are a number of small-scale improvements to the places where we live that can help keep old people healthy.

In *Placemaking for an Aging Population*, the urban planning scholar Anastasia Loukaitou-Sideris, along with a team of policy researchers at UCLA, highlights innovative social infrastructures designed for older people around the world. The most common projects are for parks and green spaces, which can easily be rebuilt to encourage more active use by older residents and more interaction across generations. In China, for instance, the elderly have long used public parks for collective exercise, including fast walking, dance, and Tai Chi. But in the late 1990s and 2000s, as China prepared to host the 2008 Olympic Games, the government began urging its rising older population to be even more active. It built thousands of new parks in urban areas, and many feature low-impact exercise equipment designed for the elderly.

Loukaitou-Sideris and her colleagues report that Spain has built more specialized recreational areas for old people—they call them "geriatric parks"—than any other European nation. The province of Málaga has thirty-two geriatric parks, mostly set within larger green areas. They typically include balance beams, pedals, stairs, ramps, and turntables, as well as space for group activities, and they're complemented by multigenerational exercise equipment in the adjacent areas. In 2009, London installed a similarly equipped "playground for seniors" in Hyde Park, and although middle-aged adults are welcome to share the area, children under fifteen are prohibited. Residents in Blackley, in Manchester, built their own senior park around the same time, but they opted for proximity to younger users, whose playground is on the nearest lot.

The most ambitious attempt to promote cross-generation interaction through outdoor play comes from Finland, where the playground manufacturing company Lappset has been working with local governments to create "three-generational play spaces." Lappset's parks feature equipment such as crawlers, climbing frames, and swings that are designed to be accessible regardless of age. They require some risk taking and cultural adaptation, since middle-aged and old people can feel awkward and uncomfortable on recreational facilities long associated with early childhood. According to market research, the French are least inclined to jump in and use the playgrounds, while the Germans and Scandinavians show the most enthusiasm for multigenerational play. No matter their nationality, once older people start using them, the benefits come quickly: A study by researchers at Rovaniemi Polytechnic, for example, found that three months of exercising on the playground equipment improved the balance, speed, and coordination of a group of forty senior citizens between the ages of sixty-five and eighty-one, reducing their vulnerability to falls. One sixty-three-year-old told the BBC that when she started using the playground's balancing equipment she felt like "an elephant walking on a narrow beam," but that after three months she'd cut her time from more than a minute to seventeen seconds. The real payoff, however, came outside the playground, on the streets and sidewalks where she could walk with the power and confidence she'd had when she was young.

Old people, of course, are not the only ones who need easy access to parks and other recreational facilities for their well-being; we all do. Children's need for open-air play spaces is particularly important: their physical health and social development depend on them. But in recent decades, as research by the renowned environmental psychologist Roger Hart and the scholars he has assembled at the City University of New York [CUNY] Children's Environments Research Group establishes, children throughout the developed world have been steadily losing their outdoor play spaces. Even playgrounds, Hart argues, have become excessively constraining for developing bodies and minds. The CUNY team identifies several reasons for the decline in accessible spaces for outdoor activities: public divestment from parks and recreational facilities; rising concerns about violence; new regimes of continuous adult supervision; parental pressure for academic achievement;

the emergence of professionally managed after-school programs; and, cutting across all classes and regions, the popularity of small-screen culture, with video games, apps, and social media as the dominant sources of youth entertainment. The effects of this loss include higher levels of child obesity and stress, and, Hart argues, diminished skills for participating in civic life.

This concern about the loss of civic skills may be surprising, since we rarely think of spending time on swings and slides or playing in sandboxes as preparation for democracy. But when Hart and his team go to the playground, they focus on behavior that most parents treat as secondary: How does a child decide when it's time to give up a swing so that another can have a turn? What happens when the wait feels too long? When do kids include strangers in their games and projects, and when do they set boundaries? How do they manage disagreement and conflict? Context matters. Hart and his colleagues are not only interested in what happens in the schoolyard or neighborhood playground where children make regular visits. They believe that social dynamics among children change when they explore new places and encounter different people and groups. Kids are especially likely to develop interpersonal skills that will help them in civic life when they wander into "foreign" places and have to navigate the new social situation on their own. But that's the kind of thing that happens less often now that parents monitor their children so closely, and they get little opportunity to roam.

One recent paper, by Hart's colleague Pamela Wridt, draws on oral histories, childhood autobiographies, and archival research to show how access to public space varied among three generations of New Yorkers: those born in the 1930s and 1940s, the 1970s, and the 2000s. For those born in the 1930s and 1940s, the neighborhood sidewalk was the main play area. Victoria, an Italian American who grew up in the East Harlem/Yorkville neighborhood in the 1940s, recounts that on her street "the whole block was full of kids. Almost all the activity was done outdoors. . . . You went outside and on the sidewalk you drew [with chalk] a potsie, those little squares where you used to play jacks, [and] bottle tops." Mothers allowed their children to play late into the evening, Wridt explains, "as they knew neighbors were keeping a watchful eye on their sons and daughters. Parents could also keep an eye on their children with great ease by peering out their tenement windows." There were risks involved in outdoor play, from benign conflicts with other kids or adults to, more seriously, getting involved in a gang or being hit by a car, and reform organizations lobbied for the city to develop contained play spaces, like playgrounds, to better protect kids. But bad things rarely happened to kids like Victoria. The sidewalks were their safe haven, the place where they grew up.

Most New Yorkers born in the 1970s had a different experience. By then, Wridt shows, rising crime made parents reluctant to let their children roam freely on the streets and sidewalks, and supervised areas, including playgrounds and athletic fields, had become more popular. But when the fiscal crisis hit, the city cut funds to parks and playgrounds. Professional supervisors disappeared. Conditions deteriorated. Gangs and drug dealers took charge of public spaces. Reggie, an African American who grew up in East Harlem/Yorkville around that time, tells Wridt that racial conflict was common, and black and Latino children often found themselves targeted in places that lacked an adult presence. As a teenager, he still wandered the area with friends, going to outdoor concerts ("open jams") in parks and playgrounds and building friendships through music and dance. But for younger children, these areas were gradually becoming off-limits, particularly after dark. A rising number of parents and caretakers were retreating from outdoor public spaces and forcing their children to hunker down indoors instead.

By the 2000s, children's access to outdoor public spaces was even more restricted. Noel, a thirteen-year-old Italian American who is growing up in the Isaacs Houses, the same complex where Reggie lived, tells Wridt that as a young child her parents let her play in the playground within the Isaacs, but forbid her from going to other local parks. "Noel's parents are extremely protective of her," Wridt writes, "and invest an enormous amount of energy monitoring her everyday life." Occasionally they let her join friends for movies or window-shopping on Eighty-Sixth Street, a more affluent commercial corridor near her neighborhood. And occasionally she goes to a professionally managed after-school or summer program in one of the commercial organizations that have become so common in middle-class and affluent communities today. But Noel says that her mobility is restricted, and as a result she spends most of her free time going where most people her age go. "I'm always on the Internet," she reports, "instant messaging . . . not as much email, but instant messaging. The television is always on, and the computer is always on too. I text message on my cell phone." It's social behavior, to be sure, but it seldom involves physical activity or spending time in green spaces outdoors. It may well protect Noel from violence, but it exposes her to risks of other health hazards, from obesity to stress to attention deficit disorders, that were far less prevalent in previous generations.

Noel's parents are choosing to keep her out of their neighborhood's degraded public play spaces, but by some measures they and their fellow New Yorkers are better off than other American families, because at least they have a local option. In the United States, the United Kingdom, and most other industrial countries, access to nature and outdoor play areas varies by social class, sometimes dramatically. In Los Angeles, for instance, where good weather should entice children outdoors in all seasons, nearly half of all low-income households lack immediate access to a park or playground. And, as Billi Gordon, a UCLA neuroscientist who studies the relationship between obesity and stress reports, many who do live near an outdoor play space are so close to a freeway that they stay indoors to avoid the dirty air.

Los Angeles didn't have to be this way. In 1930, with a commission from the chamber of commerce, the landscape architect

Frederick Law Olmsted Jr. published *Parks, Playgrounds and Beaches for the Los Angeles Region,* an elaborate proposal to build a network of parks, playgrounds, beaches, and forests for Los Angeles County. According to the City Project, a civic organization that advocates for equity in access to green space, the Olmsted Report "recognized that low-income people often live in less desirable areas, have fewer leisure opportunities, and should receive first consideration in parks and recreation." Its recommendations included "doubling public beach access," "greening the Los Angeles and San Gabriel Rivers," and "integrating forests and mountains within the regional park system." Although the plan was well received, Los Angeles power brokers killed each of Olmsted's key proposals. Worse, in subsequent decades the city's growth machine used racially restrictive covenants and constricting zoning laws to make Los Angeles even more divided and unequal than it was when Olmsted tried to fix things. Today, the city has some of the most lavish private estates, beaches, and country clubs in the United States, and residents of Los Angeles's affluent neighborhoods live amid some of the world's most beautiful natural sites. But in the impoverished neighborhoods, parks are in short supply.

They're also financially strapped. Los Angeles's refusal to invest in healthy, accessible green spaces did not end in the 1930s. Today, after decades of massive urbanization, Los Angeles County estimates that the parks it does support face roughly $12 billion in deferred maintenance costs, while the system needs some $21.5 billion for improvements. Los Angeles, like many American cities, is politically fragmented, and dozens of small municipalities have raised their own funds for parks, playgrounds, swimming pools, and senior centers because the public resources are insufficient. But that merely compounds the city's environmental injustices. After the Los Angeles city controller conducted a series of audits, it formally declared what everyone already knows: "that more high quality recreation programs are available in wealthy communities than in low-income communities, and the policies and formulas for

143

distributing public funding exacerbate rather than alleviate inequities." Local leaders have been aware of this problem for decades; yet, as the City Project concludes, "the City has failed and refused to implement the Controller's recommendations to improve parks in every neighborhood."

Recently, however, Los Angeles voters expressed their overwhelming frustration with the city's disinvestment from parks, beaches, and open spaces. In November 2016, they passed Measure A, a 1.5-cents-per-square-foot parcel tax to help build and maintain city parks, with nearly 75 percent of voter support. It's a modest measure, to be sure, with projected returns of less than $100 million per year. But it has no expiration date, so it promises to deliver a steady supply of new resources to the city's parks and public spaces. For now, though, whether the funds go to the people and places that need them most remains an open question, and the history of Los Angeles suggests that directing public investments in outdoor amenities to poor minority areas will always require a fight.

The research on environmental inequalities leaves little doubt that race and class shape who has access to nature. But poor people are not the only ones who suffer when they live far from green social infrastructure; middle-class and affluent people also need time in verdant settings, and those who cannot get it pay a high price. That, at least, is the conclusion of a fascinating paper by a team of British researchers headed by the geographer Jamie Pearce. Pearce and his colleagues wanted to know which environmental characteristics help drive health disparities in the United Kingdom. They developed a "Multiple Environmental Deprivation Index," which incorporates a wide set of ecological "disamenities," and measured census wards across the United Kingdom.

At the national level, the new index confirmed what Pearce's team expected: on average, impoverished neighborhoods had far fewer ecological amenities than wealthier ones. The effects are readily apparent. Mortality records at the census ward level show that environmental deprivation has a significant effect on health, even after controlling for a ward's age, sex, and socioeconomic status. The relationship is straightforward too: the more physical environmental deprivation, the worse the community's health. This finding was important to Pearce and his collaborators, because until recently some scholars, including Richard Mitchell, an epidemiologist who was part of Pearce's team, had wondered about "confounds," such as social class, that might better explain why environmentally deprived people fare worse than those in greener surroundings. Here, using reliable and comprehensive national data, the British researchers showed that environmental deprivation matters, period.

The real surprise from Pearce's study, though, concerns the effects of environmental deprivation on the health and longevity of people in more affluent districts. In previous studies, mainly conducted in the United States, epidemiologists had found that the impact of environmental deprivation on health was "disproportionately detrimental" in low-income neighborhoods. But in the United Kingdom, Pearce discovered, "the effect of multiple environmental deprivation was greatest among the least income-deprived populations." In London, for instance, affluent people who live in densely populated neighborhoods, such as Islington and Clerkenwell, that are coated with asphalt and far from open green spaces face greater health risks than their peers who live in places like Knightsbridge or Bayswater and enjoy easy access to all of Hyde Park. In the United Kingdom, at least, even wealth cannot protect people from the dangers of a poor environment. To stay healthy, everyone needs some green.

CHAPTER FIVE

Common Ground

In 1890, my great-grandfather, Edward Klinenberg, moved from a small village outside Prague to Chicago, and within a few years he settled down on the city's South Side. The University of Chicago was founded nearby that same year, but Edward didn't come to the United States to study—that would be a luxury for future generations. Chicago already had a string of small Jewish neighborhoods, with tightly knit communities organized around a synagogue, a school, a kosher market, and all the other establishments Jews had relied on in the European ghettos. Edward wanted none of that. He was intent on escaping military service to the Austro-Hungarian Empire and experiencing the kinds of opportunity America promised. His first challenge was to make ends meet, which he did by selling small batches of coal on street corners. Soon, Edward found work steering cattle from agricultural towns south of the city into the sprawling Chicago stockyards, making him one of the few Jewish cowboys in the great Midwest. As he rode through the borderlands of Illinois and Indiana, Edward couldn't help feeling awe at the massive industrial facilities for steel and manufacturing that were quickly transforming the landscape. Nor could he help noticing the streams of migrants—Germans, Irish, Scots, Serbians, Croatians, Poles, and Italians—who were flocking to the area to work in the mills or start their own small businesses. South Chicago, as the area would become known, was exactly the place he'd been hoping to find.

Edward spent most of his life on the far South Side of Chicago, raising eleven children in an ethnically diverse neighborhood that was unmistakably American. Although he refused to confine himself to a religious community, Edward's "primary group," the term that the pioneering University of Chicago sociologist Charles Cooley introduced to describe the core network of close friends and family with whom one maintains the deepest and most enduring bonds, consisted mainly of people with his background, Bohemians and Jews. Such "homophily" was, and still is, quite typical. Aristotle famously wrote that "people love those who are like themselves," and Plato believed that "similarity begets friendship." (Although elsewhere both also claimed that opposites attract!) Even in diverse societies, most people seek out confidants who are, in some important way or another, like them. Once they find each other, "birds of a feather" grow closer by engaging in recurrent, shared activities: eating, drinking, praying, playing, learning, and the like.

Had he stayed in his home village in Europe, Edward would likely have spent most of his life with members of his primary group. In Chicago, however, he developed a large "secondary group" of casual friends, colleagues, and associates, with whom he spent a considerable amount of time. Many of Edward's relationships developed through business. Industry dominated the area, and industrial life—rooted on the shop floor and the marketplace but extending out into the neighborhood's clubs, taverns, restaurants, and political organizations—set the terms for most local social interaction. Ethnic groups clustered together in certain churches and on particular residential blocks. People tended to marry their own kind. But South Chicago was not yet racially segregated, and in addition to bonding with members of their own ethnic communities, the area's residents built bridges that transcended group lines. Factory workers of different ethnicities helped one another out during long, grueling days in steel mills. They joined unions, picked leaders, and learned to bargain as a collective. They drank together, competed with one another in sports leagues, and took their wives dancing in neighborhood music halls. They got to know each other's families, and helped each other's sons get hired when they reached the right age. They got involved in local political clubs. Often, if not always, they fought on the same side.

In the 1960s, the sociologist William Kornblum moved into South Chicago's "blue collar community," taking a factory job so that he could understand how the neighborhood's social dynamics worked. By then, dark-skinned, non-European migrant groups— Mexicans and African Americans—had established themselves in the area, and they'd been subjected to the kinds of prejudice and discrimination for which Chicago had grown infamous. The white ethnic industrial workers were willing to accommodate Mexican Americans when they first came to South Chicago, but for blacks it was a different story. There were race riots when African Americans crossed the neighborhood's unofficial color lines. Whites strictly enforced the boundaries of racial segregation, and blacks had no choice but to build residential communities of their own. Kornblum came to South Chicago expecting to find that these divisions would extend into the factory and its social environment. Instead, he discovered that members of different groups shared a surprising level of trust and intimacy. "Men from interracial work groups routinely share wakes, funerals, retirement parties, weddings, and a host of family activities over the course of their lives in the mill," Kornblum observes. "And out of this interaction between peers of different races comes the possibility that black men may be treated not only as peers but as leaders in competition among peers."

Taverns, athletic fields, and political clubs were especially important sites of social bonding. Some tended to attract mainly people from one ethnic group, but many others were places where white ethnics, Mexicans, and African Americans came together regularly to converse, commune, and compete. Sometimes talk turned to things that happened on the factory floor. But more often coworkers and neighbors used their social time to take up other topics: family, sports, travel, politics, and all sorts of personal matters. Union newsletters and local newspapers helped the residents of South Chicago imagine their community; the neighborhood social infrastructure allowed them to build it.

Segregated neighborhoods and workplaces are breeding grounds for stereotypes and suspicion. But in the factories of industrial South Chicago, laborers developed intimate, face-to-face, sometimes heated but often jovial relationships with one another. "The white ethnic steelworker routinely works next to black men from the South Side ghetto; the Mexican worker from Millgate shares a locker room with Serbian steelworkers from Slag Valley," Kornblum writes. After work, "South Chicago families could attempt to segregate themselves within ethnic cultural worlds, or they might associate with diverse groups of neighborhood friends, but in every case ethnic segregation was limited by the more universalistic experiences of life on rolling mills, blast furnaces, coke ovens, ore docks, and the switchyards of the steel industry." Of course group divisions did not disappear altogether. Churches, social clubs, and, especially, intimate relationships were largely insular affairs. Ethnic tensions were always just beneath the surface, and occasionally they erupted into violent clashes. But in that social environment, prejudices didn't hold up well.

Unfortunately, the industrial communities that developed in places like Chicago, Detroit, Milwaukee, St. Louis, Pittsburgh, Buffalo, and Kansas City didn't hold up well, either. By the late 1960s and early 1970s, the social world that the steel mills had created was already breaking down. Massive deindustrialization hit American and European cities and continued through the last decades of the twentieth century. As factories shuttered, so too did the union halls, taverns, restaurants, and civic organizations that glued different groups together. Unmoored, unemployed, and unable to find new opportunities, people moved away. Between 1970 and 1990, nearly six hundred thousand people left Chicago, and most of them came from industrial areas like the one my great-grandfather settled in a century ago.

Sociologists have thoroughly documented how deindustrialization devastated neighborhoods, making cities and suburbs throughout the United States even more segregated by race and class. But we are only now coming to terms with how much damage deindustrialization and the decline of blue-collar communities did to the body politic, how fractured and distrustful we have become.

The presidential campaign and election of 2016 was hardly the first sign of America's social and political polarization, and deindustrialization is by no means its only cause. Until recently, though, leading public opinion scholars showed that pundits and policy elites were more polarized than voters. America, claimed the Stanford political scientist Morris Fiorina in 2005, was "closely divided," not "deeply divided." Citizens identified strongly with or against one of the two major parties, but—with exceptions for issues such as abortion, sexual morality, and capital punishment—they generally did not have firm or extreme views on most major policy matters.

That's changed in the last decades, however, as social inequality and class segregation have deepened, national news programs that transcended ideological lines have lost viewers, and the Internet has generated the rise of "filter bubbles," where everyone can find facts and opinions that confirm their beliefs. All of this feeds the kind of in-group connection that social scientists call "bonding social capital," but starves us of the "bridging social capital" we need to live together.

Since 2008, Americans have become deeply divided on a wide variety of issues, and on some, such as climate change, criminal justice, and immigration, leading political officials and popular media personalities champion "alternative facts" over mainstream scientific findings. Moreover, as the sociologist Mike Hout has found, today almost every attitude or identification has a political edge, and believing in one seemingly innocuous thing and not another puts people squarely among the reds or blues. In 2015, research by the political scientists Shanto Iyengar and Sean Westwood showed that "the polarization of the American electorate has dramatically increased," such that today "partisans discriminate against opposing partisans, doing so to a degree that exceeds discrimination based on race." The intensity of partisan disdain was visible during the 2016 election, when 55 percent of Democrats said that the Republican Party made them "afraid" and 49 percent of Republicans said the same about the Democratic Party, while more than 40 percent from both parties said their opponents' policy ideas "threaten the nation's well-being." Polarization is even more evident in collective gatherings. During the 2017 California Democratic Party Convention, for instance, the chairman stuck out his middle finger and got the crowd to chant "Fuck Donald Trump!" At the 2016 Republican National Convention, an entire arena chanted "Lock Her Up!"

Americans have always disagreed about politics and policy, but today our beliefs have hardened, as have our negative views of the people with whom we disagree. Sixty years ago, the nation was divided. But back then roughly one-quarter of employed Americans worked in factories, one-third of nonagricultural workers belonged to unions, and there were neighborhoods like South Chicago throughout the United States. Voluntary organizations were more diverse, write the sociologists Peter Bearman and Delia Baldassarri, "with respect to social class, race, ethnicity and religious orientation." So too were partners in marriage. While today, people in the United States and Europe are more likely to marry someone from a different ethnic background, they are also far more likely to marry someone from the same social class. The United States was segregated and unequal, but the social infrastructure supported shared experiences and forms of group mixing that are uncommon today.

"We are living in different political universes," writes the Harvard political scientist and legal scholar Cass Sunstein. "Of course mixed groups are no panacea.... But mixed groups have been shown to have two desirable effects. First, exposure to competing positions generally increases political tolerance.... Second, mixing increases the likelihood that people will be aware of competing rationales and see that their own arguments might be met with plausible counterarguments." Sunstein draws on classic studies and experimental research to show that, as in South Chicago during its industrial heyday, in-group attachments and prejudices against others diminish when people interact across the usual social boundaries. Democratic politics, Sunstein argues, works better when we are regularly exposed to different people and competing positions. Civil society does too.

Sunstein's book *#Republic* focuses on the Internet and social media, whose "architecture," he warns, insulates us in echo chambers and shores up group identity. I'm also concerned about the digital divide, but it's only one part of the problem. The architecture of division extends beyond our screens and onto the sidewalks, streets, and shared spaces where we make and unmake our communities every day. It's encroaching into the entire social infrastructure, polarizing us at a moment when we need to build common ground.

But if, in some places, the driving spirit behind new infrastructure projects is best captured by the refrain "Build a Wall," in others it remains "Only Connect!" The integrated blue-collar community may no longer be a viable model for large-scale development, but there are other exemplary forms of social infrastructure—some small scale, some large, some old, some relatively new—that suggest better ways to work and live together. It's urgent that we understand them.

Iceland is a small, homogeneous nation, without the fierce racial, religious, and regional divisions that make civic life so challenging in places like the United States and the United Kingdom. But it's not without its share of social problems and divisions, many of which deepened after the country's economic crisis in 2008. For much of the year Iceland is cold and dark, yet in recent decades the place that has best sustained warmth, intimacy, and spirited interaction across generational and class lines is the *sundlaug*, or public pool. The *sundlaug*, which often includes large swimming areas, "hot pots" for adults, and shallow children's pools, is a relatively recent invention: one guidebook reports that in 1900 less than 1 percent of Icelanders knew how to swim. But today, thanks to public investment in a geothermal heating system that runs throughout the country and social infrastructure projects that help residents commingle despite the frigid weather, there are more than 120 public pools in the nation of some 330,000 people, one for every 2,750 residents. Most Icelanders live near a pool, and they use them day and night, throughout the year, as a social space for gatherings of friends and family and as a forum for casual banter or more political debate among strangers. Access is basically universal, since most hot pots are free and the select swimming complexes that charge ask for only a modest entrance fee. "People from all walks of life go to the pool," says the folklorist Valdimar Hafstein. "So you have, mixing in the same hot tub, people living in the area, whether it's the professor or the student, construction worker or the businessman, the billionaire or car salesman—they all meet up."

The diversity of users, and the rule that everyone must strip naked and wash off in a public area before entering the tubs, make the pools an equalizing force in Icelandic society. So too does the substance of the conversations. When Dan Kois traveled to Iceland to do a story on its civic culture, he met immigrants in small towns who told him that the pools were ideal places to get to know neighbors and learn local customs, and new parents who recounted going to the hot tubs for tips and advice. Young women told him that seeing a variety of other female bodies at the pool helped them feel more comfortable and secure in their own skin. In Reykjavik, he learned, local council members routinely go to the pools to speak informally with their constituents, even if it means getting an earful of complaints. "The pools are more than a humble municipal investment, more than just a civic perquisite that emerged from an accident of Iceland's volcanic geology," writes Kois, who left the country convinced "that Icelanders' remarkable satisfaction is tied inextricably to the experience of escaping the fierce, freezing air and sinking into warm water among their countrymen."

Unfortunately, swimming pools and other social infrastructures with potential to facilitate sustained, intimate interaction across group lines can easily be used to segregate instead. Attractive places, after all, are only one element of good social infrastructure; programming, which can be inclusive or exclusive, welcoming or forbidding, is also important. The modern American history of municipal swimming pools, which is elegantly told in the historian Jeff Wiltse's *Contested Waters*, provides an object lesson in how to turn a community resource into an instrument of division. Swimming pools, Wiltse argues, have been key sites of cohesion and conflict "because they are places at which people build community and define the social boundaries of community life. . . . Swimming with others in a pool means accepting them as part of the same community precisely because the interaction is so intimate and sociable. Conversely, excluding someone or some group from a pool effectively defines them as social others."

In the late nineteenth century, northern cities like Boston and Philadelphia built austere pools, mainly in slums for immigrants and the poor. They were open to all working-class men and women, albeit on alternate days. "The facilities lacked showers," Wiltse writes, "because the pools themselves were the instruments of cleaning." But that didn't reduce their popular appeal, nor did their policy of ethnic and racial integration. By the end of the nineteenth century, Philadelphia's nine municipal pools attracted about 1,500 swimmers daily, and blacks and whites swam together in relative peace.

American municipalities built thousands of public pools during the 1920s and 1930s. They transformed from small bathing pools into massive spaces for communal leisure, often surrounded by lawns, decks, restaurants, and playing tables where the middle classes could spend an entire day. Millions of people flocked to these new hubs for social activity, and as social and sexual mores relaxed, they opened up across gender lines so that men and women could mix. With gender integration, Wiltse shows, came rising anxieties about intergroup contact, particularly between blacks and whites. Pools, after all, are places where large numbers of scantily dressed people come into close physical contact. Whites expressed concerns about contamination, sexual assault, and inappropriate relationships. City leaders responded with a policy tool that's usually associated with the South. They created segregated facilities, with racial divisions that were often enforced informally, but with unmistakable power.

By the 1950s, swimming pools had become flash points for racial segregation, and occasionally outright violence, throughout the North. (There were hardly any swimming pools for blacks in the South, and those that existed were formally segregated with official police enforcement.) Wiltse recounts the story of a Little League Baseball team in Youngstown, Ohio, that celebrated its city championship in 1951 at a beautiful municipal pool in South Side Park. The team had one African American player, Al Bright, and lifeguards refused to let him past the perimeter fence while the other players swam. When several parents protested, the supervisor agreed to let Al "enter" the pool for a few minutes, but only if everyone else got out and Al agreed to sit inside a rubber raft. While everyone watched, a lifeguard pushed Al around the pool, shouting, "whatever you do, don't touch the water!"

This was not an isolated incident, nor was it restricted to certain parts of the United States. Two years later, in 1953, the great African American film star Dorothy Dandridge dipped her toes in the swimming pool at the Last Frontier Hotel in Las Vegas, which welcomed her as a performer but banned her, and all other blacks, from the water. The hotel responded by draining the entire pool.

Civil rights attorneys challenged the legality of segregated swimming pools, but integrating social facilities proved just as difficult as integrating schools, if not more so. Shortly after *Brown v. Board of Education*, for instance, a federal judge in Baltimore ruled against the NAACP's demand that the city integrate its public swimming pools, on grounds that "pools were 'more sensitive than schools' because of the visual and physical intimacy that accompanied their use." The US Court of Appeals for the Fourth Circuit overruled this decision, forcing Baltimore to desegregate all public pools. But the city resisted and didn't give up its legal challenges until it lost the last one possible, when the US Supreme Court declined to review the case.

Baltimore was no outlier. Cities in the North and South responded to the desegregation orders by abandoning public facilities, building new private clubs, or closing down municipal pools altogether. Some cities were more creative. St. Louis reimposed sex segregation, so that black men and white women could never swim together. In Marshall, Texas, where the court ordered integration, city officials voted overwhelmingly to sell the city's recreational facilities. The public pool was subsequently purchased by the Lions Club, and operated as a white-only facility. Montgomery, Alabama, didn't merely shutter swimming pools. In 1959, local officials closed all public parks and the municipal zoo to head off a lawsuit. The local YMCA, however, remained segregated through the 1960s, and opened white-only swimming pools on the condition that the city provide tax exemptions, free water for its pools, and free park use. This secret deal went unchecked until 1970, when news of the arrangement leaked and courts forced the YMCA to end its segregationist practices.

In private, however, white families had another way to deal with forced desegregation: they retreated from public spaces and built pools in their own backyards. Between 1950 and 1975, the number of residential in-ground swimming pools in the United States increased from about twenty-five hundred to more than four million. Racism was obviously not the only factor in this building boom, but it played an unmistakably important role in the demise of public social infrastructures that supported collective life. Today, there are far fewer municipal swimming pools than there were during the mid-1900s. The resort-style pools, with decks and restaurants and other recreational facilities, have all but vanished. In the United States, they exist primarily in private clubs and resorts that are inaccessible to the middle and lower classes.

African Americans and civil rights activists protested this form of inequality well past the 1960s. In 1975, for instance, blacks in Pittsburgh (where in 1962 a sign posted outside one public pool stated "No Dogs or Niggers Allowed") fought against an order to close "Sully's Pool," a public pool used primarily by African Americans, arguing that the pool is "a way of life for us." In 1971, the Supreme Court had narrowly ruled that closing swimming pools in response to integration orders was not unconstitutional, even if the closure had discriminatory intent, because it affected whites and blacks equally. Perhaps sensing the fallout, the court specified that the decision would not apply to public schools, because it deemed swimming pools a "convenience or a luxury," whereas public schools are a "necessity." Of course, no one disputed that schools are necessary, but this reasoning failed to recognize how segregation in other public facilities would shape our civic life and culture. To this day, there are wide racial disparities in swimming ability in the United States, with whites twice as likely to know how to swim as blacks, and black children being three times more likely to die from unintentional drowning. Wiltse, the historian, argues that unequal access to pools meant that swimming never became a significant part of African American culture.

Pools, however, remain charged sites for discrimination and conflict. In June 2015, McKinney, Texas, gained the national spotlight after local police got involved in a conflict at a private community swimming pool. The interaction between the police and several black teenagers who had been attending a party at the pool was caught on phone cameras, and an uploaded YouTube video capturing a particularly forceful encounter between a police offer and a young girl amplified the national conversation about police abuse of African Americans. The swimming pool, while technically only accessible to members of a gated community, was being used by a neighborhood resident who was hosting a party. White residents approached a group of black teenagers who were there, accusing them of trespassing and telling them to go back to their "Section 8 homes." After receiving widespread media attention, the town placed the police officer involved in the incident on administrative leave. Soon after, residents posted a sign reading "Thank you McKinney Police for keeping us safe."

Stories like these help explain the popularity—or perhaps the necessity—of social infrastructures that serve as safe spaces for members of excluded groups that are subjected to prejudice, discrimination, and violence. Oppressed communities often endure extreme social and economic pressures that inhibit the formation of stable, enduring relationships. In the United States, as the Harvard sociologist Orlando Patterson has argued, the history of slavery, ghettoization, segregation, and mass incarceration has led to high levels of instability within the black community. "Afro-Americans are the most unpartnered and isolated group of people in America," Patterson writes, "and quite possibly in the world." Black Americans, and all other groups that face severe discrimination, need spaces that foster support and cohesion.

From ancient times, oppressed people—women, slaves, ethnic minorities, gays and lesbians, the working classes, and the like—have built special places and institutions where they can assemble to make sense of and plan responses to their situation, free from surveillance by the dominant group. The political theorists Nancy Fraser and Michael Warner call these social spaces "counterpublics," and argue that despite—and partly due to—their insularity they are essential tools for civic engagement in unequal societies, because they give marginalized groups the private forum they need before engaging other groups.

History offers countless examples of these protected social infrastructures. Many, from the *mikvahs* where observant Jewish women have long convened to provide mutual support to the bathhouses that anchored gay men's social life for much of the twentieth century, involve closed doors that facilitate safe intimacy. But most places that sustain counterpublics are out in the open, available for everyone to see.

In contemporary America, the black church and the black barbershop are among the most prominent social infrastructures that support a robust counterpublic. Black barbershops have been vital parts of African American culture and commerce since the first Africans arrived in North America, in part because whites knew little about how to style black hair and showed little interest in learning. In a context of racial discrimination, segregation, and inequality, argues Melissa Harris-Lacewell, the protected space of the black men's barbershop is a valuable resource that, counterintuitively, diversifies and enriches American civic life in the long run. "The barbershop is the black man's way station, point of contact, and universal home," write William Grier and Price Cobbs, in *Black Rage*. "Here he always finds a welcome—a friendly audience as he tells his story and a native to give him the word on local doings." In *Black Metropolis*, the landmark study of African Americans in Chicago, the sociologists St. Clair Drake and Horace Cayton report that, as of 1938, black hair salons were by far the most popular form of black-owned business, with 494 enterprises, compared with 257 groceries, 145 restaurants, and 70 taverns across the city.

Recent ethnographic studies depict precisely how black barbershops help to advance the race. Melissa Harris-Lacewell, who hired a male student to closely observe a Chicago barbershop where managers give exclusive access to black men, finds that insular salons allow people who are generally on the defensive to let their guard down, especially in discussions of racism. They also provide a common meeting ground to people in different generations, facilitating productive, if often contentious, exchanges between younger and older men. "The barbershops and beauty parlors, more than the churches, the schools, or the radio, exist as spaces where black people engage each other as peers," Harris-Lacewell writes, "where nothing is out of bounds for conversation, and where the serious work of 'figuring it out' goes on."

In one conversation Harris-Lacewell recounts, a young man blames police bias for high rates of traffic tickets given to African Americans, only to be challenged by an older customer, who says the man made himself a target by riding with the music blasting and the seat leaning way back. "Although deeply critical of whites and keenly aware of contemporary racism, [the men] were rarely willing to blame whites exclusively for the problems facing African Americans," Harris-Lacewell writes. "Even within the context of the deeply strained historical and contemporary relationship between Chicago police and Chicago's black residents, the men resisted blanket condemnation of police actions."

It also exercises the men's rhetorical muscles. Social exchange in the barbershop can be brutally honest, leading to heated exchanges between verbal combatants. It can also be extremely funny, as the blockbuster film series *Barbershop* shows. In one memorable scene, Eddie the barber, played by Cedric the Entertainer, tells his patrons: "Now, I probably wouldn't say this in front of white folk, but in front of y'all I'll speak my mind. . . . One, Rodney King shoulda got his ass beat for driving drunk and being grown in a Hyundai. Two, O.J. did it. And three, Rosa Parks ain't do nothing but sit her black ass down." Eddie, who's loudly challenged by nearly everyone around him as he makes these claims, is clearly not speaking on behalf of the film's writer or director. It's not the substance of the lines that matters. It's the fact that the barbershop allows patrons to articulate controversial ideas, and to argue them out until everyone has a better sense of who they are, why they're in their situation, and what they believe. When the barbershop closes, the men who spend time there feel a little less isolated and vulnerable. The bonds they form provide strength for the social bridging that comes later, making them better prepared to engage the world outside.

Bridging divisions in a highly segregated society is notoriously difficult, but, as we saw in industrial Chicago, some social infrastructures invite us to cross group lines. In recent years, social scientists have found surprisingly robust evidence of how community organizations and nonprofits bring neighbors together, increasing trust and civic engagement, and even reducing violent crime. Community organizations bolster civic and cultural life in every neighborhood fortunate enough to have them in abundance. They are critical parts of the social infrastructure, because they provide physical places where people can assemble, programs that bring people together on a regular basis, and local leaders who become advocates for the community. People usually do not volunteer in a community garden, teach children to read, attend a church picnic, or participate in a rally for better local air quality because they're trying to generate social cohesion. But, inevitably, the process of doing these activities creates or strengthens social bonds.

Consider the Elmhurst-Corona neighborhood in Queens, an area that was 98 percent white in 1960 but transformed dramatically in the following decades, becoming 45 percent Latin American, 26 percent Asian, and 10 percent black by 1990. The early stages of neighborhood change were predictably contentious. Both newcomers and old-timers harbored strong stereotypes and prejudices about their neighbors. During the 1960s and 1970s, distrust divided the community; conflicts and misunderstandings were common. The neighborhood had real problems to manage: Landlords started subdividing residential units to increase their profits as migrants entered the area and demand for housing increased. Blocks and buildings grew congested, as did local schools. Youth programs were disappearing. Parking was in short supply. Crime was rising, and the city, mired in a historic fiscal crisis, was cutting local services. Police response times slowed.

Most whites fled during this period, but many who remained were disoriented by the rapid changes in the neighborhood's commercial and religious establishments. Some insisted, vocally, that the Latinos and African Americans who were moving in were welfare recipients, although few in fact were. Blacks and whites often referred to Latinos as "illegal aliens," though most were not. In 1974, the chairman of the neighborhood community board referred to immigrants as "people pollution" during a public meeting, and said he hoped the INS would root them out. Ethnic slurs became standard features of the local parlance. Elmhurst-Corona was bursting at the seams. Many feared that it would explode.

Elmhurst-Corona survived the fiscal crisis of the 1970s, but residents still faced an abundance of social problems, from outdoor drug dealing and prostitution to illegal vending, garbage accumulation, and housing code violations. Some New York City neighborhoods buckled under these pressures, becoming sites of arson, abandonment, and blight. In Elmhurst-Corona, however, civic associations brought neighbors together to work on quality-of-life issues, small and large. Often, ordinary residents with no background in politics or activism started hyperlocal organizations to combat problems on their own block, and over time joined with neighbors on nearby streets to scale up their campaigns. A key to their success was getting access to the neighborhood's small public and semipublic places, including church basements, senior centers, and common rooms in large apartment buildings, where they hosted meetings and events.

Consider one typical example of a civic association that residents created to protest an announcement that their neighborhood police station would be relocated farther away, leaving them more vulnerable. Lucy Schilero, a freelance beautician who'd initially gotten involved in the neighborhood because of concerns about parking, took on the warden role, circulating a petition to keep the station nearby. She quickly learned that getting more signatures would require translating the document into all the local languages, and she called meeting after meeting to get the work done. "All the people on our block helped, 50 people," she told the anthropologist Roger Sanjek, who led an ethnographic research project in the neighborhood for thirteen years. "We had everything in Spanish, Greek, Italian, Chinese, Korean, [and] French. I met Iranians [and] Turkish [people], to help translate."

Schilero was so energized by the experience that she created the Coalition of United Residents for a Safer Community, an organization that grew to two thousand members, including residents of surrounding blocks and small business owners. The process of local collaboration, as sociologists like Robert Sampson explain, yielded more than a protest; it also changed the way neighbors thought about one another and helped them establish solidarity across group lines. "Now I have new ethnic friends: Hindu, Spanish—a lot—Chinese. My Ecuadorian neighbor . . . is a good friend, and in touch with Spanish residents. [White] friends in Maspeth and Middle Village [in southwest Queens] say to me, 'How can you live here? It's like Manhattan.' I tell them we have to live with one another or we won't survive."

During his extended fieldwork, Sanjek learned about all kinds of neighborhood organizations that helped the residents of Elmhurst-Corona live with one another and survive. In 1980, a Puerto Rican migrant named Haydee Zambrana created Ciudadanos Conscientes de Queens (Concerned Citizens of Queens) to advocate for better Spanish-language services in the neighborhood. But during that decade she grew frustrated that Latino groups in Elmhurst-Corona spent most of their time working on Puerto Rican national issues and not enough engaging on local problems. "My priority is to help the Hispanic community become part of the American political process," she told a city commission in 1986. The organization pivoted, promoting civic engagement in both formal and informal forums. Zambrana joined Community Board 4 (community boards are New York City's local political bodies), and within a year she'd recruited three other Hispanic members, doubling their level of representation.

The largest local campaigns Sanjek observed grew out of threats that touched everyone in the neighborhood, regardless of age, gender, or ethnicity. In 1986 and 1987, for instance, residents from different civic associations joined together to address a problem at the popular Lefrak City branch library. For years, the branch employed a security guard to oversee interactions in the building.

This was quite standard in New York City, where young children, teens, the homeless, freelance workers, the mentally ill, and the elderly, all with their own needs and codes of conduct, packed into branch libraries, competing for space every day. Inevitably, there were tensions, and librarians could not manage them while also performing their other duties. The security guards became important local actors, so the community was outraged when the city announced that, due to budget cuts, the guards would be fired.

At a community board meeting in early 1987, a coalition of concerned neighborhood groups protested the decision and demanded that the city retain the guards. A library official responded by blaming "latch key kids" from black families for the problems, and condemning their families for failing to supervise their children. A decade before, this argument might have resonated with white, Asian, and Hispanic residents and deepened the wedge between them. But after years of working together in neighborhood associations, Sanjek writes, the people who packed the community board jumped to the defense of local black families. Thousands of good parents in Elmhurst-Corona sent their kids to libraries after school, they argued, precisely because these places promised safe, positive, educational experiences for everyone. This argument, forcefully articulated by a community that stood together, proved difficult to counter. Library officials found the funds they needed to keep the guards on duty.

Although some large-scale social infrastructure projects are expensive, in general communities do not require massive funding to build places or institutions that bring diverse sets of people together for sustained interaction. Consider how, throughout the world, athletic facilities attract people of different backgrounds into a shared social space, allowing for competitive, playful, often joyous activity, and sparking relationships that would never have been formed off the field or court. Athletic fields can be sacred places, set aside for community purposes, where categories and hierarchies that matter so much for social and political life often lose their significance. The great anthropologist Victor Turner referred to such places as "anti-structural," because they allow people who might otherwise be hostile to one another play together in an experience that he calls *communitas*: a liminal moment when all participants have the same social status and forbidden social bonds are suddenly encouraged. In some cases, these special interactions have lasting significance, helping divided groups recognize their common humanity, and paving the way for more meaningful relationships off the field.

In *Netherland*, Joseph O'Neill's elegant novel about dislocation in New York City after September 11, a cricket field in Brooklyn plays a starring role. "Bald Eagle Field" is the place where Hans van den Broek, the Dutch banker who narrates *Netherland*, rediscovers the America he'd lost, and himself as well, after his anxious wife takes their young child to London, leaving him alone in New York. The field has been leased and carefully cultivated by Chuck Ramkissoon, a charismatic, entrepreneurial Indian from Trinidad who insists that cricket is "the first modern team sport in America . . . a bona fide American pastime," and makes himself president of the New York Cricket Club. Before he meets Chuck, Hans appears unmoored. He rents an apartment in the Chelsea Hotel and floats around the boroughs with a flaneur's eye, taking in the lights, the commerce, the colorful characters, but always at a distance. The city is not his.

That changes once Chuck invites Hans to join his cricket club. A wealthy, white European, Hans is an outlier on a field full of brown people from Asia and the Caribbean who are trying to establish legitimacy in the United States. For such men, the *New Yorker* book critic James Wood writes, cricket is "an immigrant's imagined community, a game that unites, in a Brooklyn park,

Pakistanis, Sri Lankans, Indians, West Indians, and so on, even as the game's un-Americanness accentuates their singularity." For Hans, Bald Eagle Field becomes the sacred ground where he must prove himself as "a real American," by which he means an aspiring immigrant who's trying to find secure footing. The games he plays test not only whether he belongs on the field, but whether he belongs. Eventually he passes, and only then does he find his place.

In real life, the social action on athletic fields is usually less poetic than it is in good fiction, but it's no less consequential for our relationships and sense of identity. Consider how many young people meet their closest friends—and also get to know themselves a lot better—while playing in a ballpark. Consider how many parents forge lasting relationships on the sidelines while their children practice and compete on the diamond, field, or court.

As a young child in Chicago, I spent countless afternoons on a makeshift soccer pitch near the Lincoln Park Zoo, where a neighborhood organization called the Menomonee Club ran practices. In the 1970s, the Menomonee Club was a meeting place for kids from Old Town, which was quickly gentrifying, and the housing projects immediately to the south. The director, a garrulous soccer fanatic named Basil Kane, charged something like $6 per season, so that everyone could afford to play. As a result, the experience I had playing "the beautiful game" was unlike most of the other experiences I had in the grotesquely unequal and segregated city.

My neighborhood public school, for instance, had a playground basketball court that was popular among kids from Old Town as well as the housing projects nearby. My friends and I used it often, but one year, when I was around ten, vandals took the hoops off the backboards so that no one could play there. When the city installed new ones, the vandals removed them again. I was furious, and I'd heard so many people complain about crimes committed by poor African Americans from the projects that I presumed they were responsible for destroying the basketball courts too. But one day, when I was visiting a white neighbor who lived in one of the nicest houses in the area, he asked if I wanted to know a secret. His teen-age brother and his friends had been taking down the hoops, he explained, because they didn't want black kids from the projects in our neighborhood. I'd never considered that possibility.

In retrospect, I probably should have. Nearly everything in Chicago was segregated: neighborhoods, schools, social clubs, re-ligious institutions. But on the soccer field, at least, I got to know people whose race and social class—and therefore homes, cars, and meals—made them different from the people I met in other circles. And yet, during the season we were on the same team. Playing to-gether was hardly enough to form deep and lasting friendships, but it provided an opening, a chance to connect.

Now that I'm a parent, the time I spend on athletic fields—albeit on the sidelines—is once again shaping my family's so-cial and community life. During the week my wife and I shuttle between our offices at the university and our children's school, squeezing in an occasional date night, dinner party, work event, or show. On weekends our schedules are less constricted, but since our son joined his first soccer team they've revolved around his games and tournaments, some of which take us far from home. Friends whose children don't play on travel teams are puzzled by our commitment to this lifestyle and the impositions it poses. To be honest, sometimes I am too! But then I remember what makes the experience so valuable and compelling: the relationships we build with the families who share our commitment, and with our own child as well.

The community we've built around the soccer field has been a significant part of our life since our son was seven, but when my family moved to Stanford University for a sabbatical in 2016, it proved especially important. My wife and I knew only a few people there when we arrived, and they were primarily friends from work. My children had no friends, and, naturally, they were anxious about the change. But on our first day in Palo Alto our son was invited to play on the travel team of a large local soccer club, and his teammates quickly became pals. After a few weekends of games around the Bay Area, other parents had invited our whole family to barbecues, beach trips, and holiday meals. Our daughter befriended the players' sisters. We got advice about local schools, doctors, grocery stores, and after-school programs. We formed car pools, so that everyone could help each other get through the week.

No one would mistake our team for a fully integrated community. Silicon Valley is astronomically expensive, and—as is too often the case in modern American youth sports programs—so was participating on the region's travel team. But about 20 percent of the players lived in poor or working-class neighborhoods like East Palo Alto, a primarily minority community that's physically separated from prosperous Palo Alto by a large highway. Because the club offered financial support, the team had more class and ethnic diversity than other local social groups. There were a few soccer parents who worked in the tech industry and drove Teslas or Mercedes, but most had Nissans, Subarus, and more conventional professional or middle-class jobs. There were families from Canada, Mexico, Brazil, India, Israel, Tunisia, France, and Germany. There were Democrats, Republicans, independents, and progressives. Our team formed during the most heated moments of the 2016 presidential election, and occasionally we suspended the debate over Messi vs. Ronaldo to argue Clinton vs. Trump. We didn't agree or change each other's minds, but we liked and trusted each other enough to listen to opposing positions. Through face-to-face interactions, we came to understand where people with different viewpoints were coming from; on the sidelines, our social distance narrowed.

It turned out to be a hard year of politics but a sensational year of soccer, with the boys developing individually and gradually gelling into the division champion, one of the strongest teams in California. My son, who might otherwise have struggled with the transition to a new school in a distant state, had never felt more confident or socially connected. My wife and I found ourselves looking forward to the long weekend tournaments in small towns like Manteca and Davis, and to the long afternoons and evenings that we'd spend with families who were unlike our academic colleagues and friends. The end of the season was more emotionally difficult than the end of our dreamy fellowships at Stanford—not because the games were over, since there are always more games, but because the team was moving on and we were moving back.

When we returned to New York City in 2017, finding the right soccer club became a major family project. We knew we weren't just choosing a sports team for our child, but a community for our family as well. There's a terrific neighborhood soccer program not far from our apartment, and we had every reason to send our son there—except one. He was invited to try out for Metropolitan Oval, a legendary club located in Maspeth, Queens, on a gorgeous field built by German and Hungarian immigrants in the 1920s. They designed the field to be a community center, and it has remained exactly that for the past ninety years. Naturally, the club's composition has changed along with the city, and today the coaches, players, and families reflect the diversity of Queens. We fell in love with the organization, and the fact that they played beautiful soccer didn't hurt. My son was overjoyed when he was offered a spot in their academy, but all of us have benefited from being around the club.

Our experience is typical. Sociologists have consistently found that participating in organized sports teams increases social capital and leads to more participation in non-sports-related collective activities as well. A recent British study, for instance, reports "substantial correlations between measures of social capital and measures of sporting participation, both at the national level and, within Britain, at the individual level." Eighty percent of people who play an organized sport have friends in the organization, considerably higher than the rate for those who participate in humanitarian, environmental, or consumer organizations. That's not surprising, since the latter groups typically "require a more passive, often subscription based, involvement" rather than the deeply physical, interpersonal engagement required by athletics. What is surprising, though, is the finding that, after people who regularly attend church, people who play organized sports are more likely than others to volunteer in other civic and associational projects. The authors argue that learning to lead or work with teammates on the field helps players develop skills that transfer to other domains of social life. "This is not only beneficial to the individual," they conclude, "it can also make a valuable contribution to the civil renewal process by providing skills that can also be employed elsewhere in the community."

A recent study by the anthropologist Eric Worby shows how this happens. In the 2000s, Worby conducted ethnographic fieldwork on neighborhood soccer pitches around Johannesburg. When Worby and his family moved there, friends and colleagues offered lots of advice on how to protect and defend themselves, but little on how to build relationships. He and his daughter discovered that on their own, in pickup soccer matches played on "dusty, flat soccer pitches . . . with solitary cement trash bins as targets for goals." In postapartheid South Africa, Worby discovered, fields like these were sites of "urban social freedom," places where people could open themselves to encounters that had long been feared or forbidden. Playing soccer across racial and class lines did not make the entrenched divisions disappear, of course, but it helped South Africans "rehumanize" one another, a modest yet necessary step in the nation's attempt to integrate and democratize a deeply divided society.

Because, in so many modern societies, athletic fields are quasi-sacred sites for playful social integration, acts of violence committed on them take on special symbolic significance. In June 2017, for instance, a lone assailant shot several people on a baseball diamond where Republican members of Congress were practicing for their annual ritualistic game against the Democrats. Mass shootings are always horrific, but commentators noted that this one was especially offensive. "Baseball and softball provide common ground in political Washington," declared the *New York Times*. On National Public Radio, congressional officials attested that the field provided an important break from everyday life in the Capitol, where too many partisan members have come to see one another one-dimensionally, as enemies. Debbie Wasserman Schultz, the former head of the Democratic National Committee, cofounded a softball game so that women in Congress could have that same experience. "I have sponsored and passed laws with colleagues who I likely wouldn't have spoken to, let alone gotten to know, without this team" she said.

Establishing meaningful connections with people we conceive as different is not only a challenge in historically divided places like South Africa and politically contentious cities like Washington, DC. Scholars such as Sherry Turkle, Cass Sunstein, and Jonathan Haidt argue that the rapid rise of the Internet has changed the ways that people everywhere view and treat one another, creating vast terrains of social distance, even between friends.

There's no doubt that parts of the Internet bring out the worst in human behavior, but does it actually cause polarization? Sunstein and Haidt believe it does. "As a result of the Internet, we live increasingly in an era of enclaves and niches—much of it voluntary, much of it produced by those who think they know, and often do know, what we're likely to like," Sunstein claims. "So long as we are all immersed in a constant stream of unbelievable outrages perpetrated by the other side," Haidt writes, "I don't see how we can ever trust each other and work together again." But other research casts doubt on the causal relationship between political polarization and use of the Internet or social media. Drawing on data from the American National Election Studies, one team of economists finds that, surprisingly, "the increase in polarization is largest among the groups least likely to use the internet and social media." For instance, polarization has risen far more among people over the age of seventy-five, who are avid consumers of cable television news channels such as Fox, than among those between the ages of eighteen and thirty-nine, who are the heaviest users of online media. This simple fact "rules out what seem like the most straightforward accounts linking the growth in polarization to the internet," the authors write. Social media may well contribute to our widening ideological divisions, but if the Internet doesn't explain changes in the group that has grown the most polarized, it cannot be entirely to blame.

In some ways it has been a force for good, allowing people to develop relationships with those they might never have otherwise met. A recent study shows that Americans and Germans who find their romantic partner online are significantly more likely than those who search through friends, family, or school to couple up with a person who has a different education level, ethnic identity, or religious affiliation. And, following the divisive US election of 2016, a number of socially engaged entrepreneurs are using the Internet to help people with opposing political viewpoints start conversations about the sources of their disagreement. One project, LivingRoomConversations.org, allows anyone who's interested to join a civil dialogue on contentious topics with strangers through a group video chat. Another, HiFromTheOtherSide.com, matches two individuals with conflicting perspectives, verifies their identities on Facebook, and sends them an introductory e-mail—along with links to a conversation guide—so that they can get to know each other in real life.

In some cases, such as gay and lesbian teenagers who live in small towns or conservative communities, dissidents who live under repressive political regimes, and refugees fleeing war zones, the Internet isn't just a way to get to know someone, but a lifesaving source of support and connection. Facebook, for all its problems, helps people see that they're not alone in their struggle, and provides a forum where they can exchange ideas about how to make things better, or even escape. In recent years, thousands of Syrian refugees in Europe have used Facebook for all kinds of information, from which gear to purchase before traveling to the names of affordable hotels on the trail. They've also used Facebook to find old friends or townsmen in their new country, to build communities in foreign places, and, once they're settled, to get news from home.

At the most mundane level, websites like Nextdoor facilitate connections between neighbors who lack a convenient way to meet each other or start group conversations, whether about important civic matters or parochial concerns. On college campuses, students who are heavy users of Facebook are more likely than light users to develop weak—but nonetheless meaningful—social ties with a diverse set of peers. When I did fieldwork in New York City libraries, I got to know a group of immigrants—from China, Russia, Mexico, and Poland—who met one another in English or citizenship classes and formed an active social group on WhatsApp. They remain connected, years later, in part because the technology makes it so easy to stay in touch.

There are countless other instances when people use the Internet to build more unlikely social bridges. Often, they involve conversations about issues such as health, music, or sports that have limited or indirect connections to political or ideological matters. These topics allow people who might be divided by their convictions to establish common ground.

Recently, for instance, I learned about an anonymous chat room for people with HIV who are unwilling or unable to attend traditional support groups. One relationship that developed there involved a trans woman of color who helped a rural white Trump supporter get through his recovery from addiction. That's by no means anomalous. People with difficult health problems routinely use the Internet to give and get support from others who are unlike them in every way except the one that is suddenly most relevant. They know from experience: if we use the Internet wisely, or design it with our common humanity rather than our differences in mind, the technology we so often blame for polarizing us can be palliative instead.

Social distance and segregation—in physical space as well as in lines of communication—breed polarization. Contact and conversation remind us of our common humanity, particularly when they happen recurrently, and when they involve shared passions and interests. In recent decades, we've lost the factories and industrial towns where different ethnic groups once formed blue-collar communities. We've made our neighborhoods more segregated by class. We've seen private companies organize competitive, professionalized sports programs for affluent children, and left most low-income kids to play in leagues of their own. We've watched cable news programs and listened to radio talk shows that tell us what we already believe.

These conditions facilitate social bonding within certain groups but make social bridging difficult. They foster polarization, and divided we fall. There's no easy way to restore the sense of common purpose and shared humanity that makes civic life possible. But the hard work that lies before us will be impossible if we don't build better social infrastructure. The future of our democracy is at stake.

CHAPTER SIX

Ahead of the Storm

Paul and Shelle Simon have lived in Houston long enough to know that rain can be dangerous. In a typical year, the nation's fourth-largest city gets about fifty inches of rainfall, and it's prone to torrential downpours and the occasional hurricane or tornado. Although Houston is not one of the wettest American cities, its hard infrastructure and physical plan were designed to facilitate private automobiles and nearly limitless growth, without much regard for storm water management. The sprawling, six-hundred-square-mile metropolis has massive amounts of impermeable paved surfaces and scores of residential communities in the flood-plain. When the rain is heavy, drainage channels, sewers, and detention ponds fill up quickly. Water courses through the city's vital arteries, inundating roads and, on occasion, hospitals, homes, and businesses as well. When a major storm hits, floodwaters can breach the oil refineries and chemical plants that saturate Houston, turning what might otherwise be a weather disaster into an uncontrollable toxic event.

In late August 2017, the Simons, a middle-class African American couple in their late thirties, saw a news story warning that a tropical storm named Harvey had formed over the Caribbean and was gradually making its way toward the Gulf of Mexico. It had been an unusually hot summer—though so many summers have been unusually hot that it was probably just usual—and the water in the Gulf and the Bay of Campeche was warm. Harvey picked up energy as it moved toward Texas. On Wednesday, August 23, scientists at the National Hurricane Center predicted that it would become a strong tropical storm, or even a Category 1 hurricane, by the time it made landfall. They were mistaken. Harvey continued to strengthen as it approached the coastline, and on Thursday meteorologists forecast that it would likely hit America's fourth-largest city as a Category 3 or 4 hurricane, with fierce winds topping 115 miles per hour and biblical precipitation. More ominously, Harvey seemed poised to stall over southern Texas and stay awhile, possibly for days. Houston officials didn't order a mandatory evacuation, but they advised all residents to prepare for a deluge.

The Simons decided to hunker down in the house they own in Richmond, a working-class, predominantly Hispanic area in the southwest part of Houston. They live in West Oaks Village, a landscaped community with a mix of modest single-family homes, small apartment buildings, and generous collective amenities, including a playground and a large swimming pool. The Simons have two young sons, an eight-month-old and a two-year-old, and their extended families live in the area as well. They remembered 2005, when 2.5 million people tried to flee Houston as Hurricane Rita approached. Shelle was one of them, and her drive to Austin, which is ordinarily a two-hour journey, took more than seventeen hours. Rita wasn't as bad as everyone feared—not nearly as bad as Katrina, which had hit New Orleans weeks before—but the highways were jammed and overheated, and more people died in the botched evacuation than in the city center. With Harvey, Paul and Shelle figured they'd be better off at home.

This time, though, the storm proved even more severe than anyone anticipated. The rain started on Friday, but on Saturday it became torrential. In church, a few days later, Shelle told her fellow congregants what happened: "My sister, Sheraine, she and her [twenty-one-month-old] son came to stay with us so we could go through the storm together. She didn't want to go through it alone." Once they arrived, the tornado warnings started. "Paul came up with a plan. We would clear out all the closets, move the clothes. And Paul kept saying, 'If this happens we go in this closet, if that happens we go in that closet.' We were doing that."

Ordinarily, hard rain lets up after awhile. The clouds empty, the sky opens, the sun or the stars reappear. "Everyone knows that Houston floods," Paul told me. "But I've lived here fifteen years and this neighborhood has never had any problems. We've never had water in this house. Nothing even close. I figured that we'd be okay." The Simons listened as the wind howled and the storm roared. They looked outside and saw that the streets were drowning. They were stressed, exhausted. And soon there was nothing to do except go to bed.

But who could sleep in those conditions?

They woke up before dawn and went straight to the windows. "The rain was up to our driveway," Shelle said. "And the water was rising, higher and higher." Her pulse quickened. The walls weren't going to save them if the rain kept coming. The closets weren't going to, either. They needed another plan.

"I'm going out there," Paul said. "I'm gonna drive around and see if we can get out."

"Don't do it," Shelle shot back. "Because I don't want you to get separated from us, not from the kids."

But the water kept rising through the day, and by early afternoon Paul and Shelle realized that they couldn't leave even if they wanted to. The driveway was a river, the streets running rapids. Their house was about to be inundated. Their children, Shelle's family, and everything they owned was inside.

"I was on the phone with my mother [who's also in Houston]," Shelle recalled, when she, Paul, and I spoke a few weeks after the storm hit. "And she asked me to send her a picture of what was happening outside. I went to the door, and there was so much water I couldn't believe it. I was just wide-eyed, in shock. And just then, at that very moment, our neighbors came walking right by our door. The water was so high that they had to stay close to the houses. They were carrying plastic garbage bags with their belongings, and they were with their cousin, TJ, who'd driven there in a truck. I was just standing there. I had clips in my hair, I had a baby on my hip, and I was just looking at them, like, 'What are you guys doing?' And they said, 'We're getting out of here! Do you want to come with us? Do you need help?' And I said yes, yes!"

She screamed for Paul and he rushed over. TJ said he'd parked a few blocks away because the streets around the Simons' house were impassable. He told Paul that he didn't have room for all of them in his truck, but he took Paul's number and promised he'd return soon. Paul, Shelle, and Sheraine raced through the house to pack up the essentials: diapers, formula, water, food, clothes for the children. "I'm not really that good with emergency situations," Shelle admitted. "I kind of break down. But then TJ came back for us. And, you know, we walked through that water."

The Simons made it, children hoisted in their arms. They wanted to go to Shelle's father's place, but the roads leading there were inaccessible. "God had different plans," Paul said. "We drove around, and all our access points were closing or shutting down." At one point TJ got to a flooded street where the median looked like a roadway. He tried to drive along it, but the truck went off the edge and, suddenly, they were stuck. "That was definitely the scariest moment," Paul told me. "It was dark. The rain was just pouring down on us. The radio was broadcasting tornado warnings. And there we were, with three little kids in the truck, no car seats even, totally exposed."

This time Shelle really did break down. "I was bawling in there. I was scared. My baby was premature and when he was born he'd had trouble breathing. When I looked at him he was totally still. I didn't know if something was wrong. I couldn't reach my phone so I took my sister's, got on her Facebook, and posted that we were stranded. I sent out a message saying 'Please pray for us.' I honestly didn't know if we'd make it."

Another truck came by, and the driver stopped and used cables to pull them off the median. TJ found a way out of the flooded area, but now he was late and needed to help his own family, so they drove to a gas station where emergency workers had congregated, and the Simons got out. The baby was fine, just exhausted, but now there was a new problem: they had nowhere to go. "We thought the EMS workers would be able to help us," Paul recalled. "But it turned out they were waiting for emergency calls only. So we were pretty much stranded." A group of men had gathered inside the station, and one of them was explaining that he'd found a safe driving route to an area that had escaped flooding. "When I heard him," Paul said, "I realized that the route went right by the subdivision where my parents live. He was going to show the others the way, and I asked if I could go with him. My father was out of town, and I had the keys to his truck with me. I told Shelle and Sheraine that I could get us out of there." For a moment, the Simons couldn't believe their luck.

The feeling didn't last long. The floodwater had breached the front door of Paul and Shelle's home, probably soon after they left. And it kept coming, in greater and greater volumes, because Harvey really did settle over Houston for another three days. By Tuesday, when the storm clouds finally dispersed, more than fifty-one inches of rain had fallen on parts of the city—breaking the record for the most precipitation from a single storm or hurricane on the continental United States. (The National Weather Service, a cautious scientific organization that typically uses dry, descriptive language, wrote that the rainfall figures were "simply mind-blowing.") For the Simons, and for thousands of other Houston residents, the numbers were academic. What mattered was that their homes were underwater, and that they'd lost nearly everything they'd left behind.

The following Sunday, when Shelle and Paul went to the place where they always go on Sunday mornings, the Wilcrest Baptist Church, they told everyone assembled that what happened during the storm only deepened their faith in the community. First there was TJ, the neighbor's cousin who suddenly became their "first responder" and risked his life to rescue them. And then, when the challenge turned to recovery and rebuilding, there was the community that has always been primary but never before so important, the one they'd built through the church.

Wilcrest Baptist is a small church in Alief, a lower-middle-class area in Southwest Houston. It has about five hundred active members with roots in about fifty nations, and they're a fairly even mix of whites, Latinos, and African Americans, some urban, some suburban, some rural, and mostly but not all conservative. Such diversity is unusual in American churches, which have long been among the nation's most ethnically and racially segregated institutions, and it didn't happen at random. Until recently, Wilcrest was a mostly white congregation. Michael Emerson, an eminent sociologist of religion who both joined and wrote about Wilcrest, reports that the church used to keep a supply of cards with the names and addresses of churches that served primarily black, Latino, and Asian communities. When someone from one of those groups came to Wilcrest, church leaders would politely hand them a card and suggest they find a place where they'd feel more at home.

That changed in the 1980s, when whites began moving out of the area and blacks and Latinos moved in. Nearly all of Wilcrest's leaders wanted to move the church to the outlying suburbs where their congregants were going, but the bylaws required a unanimous vote from the board to do that, and one member insisted that they stay and adapt. Wilcrest began to expand its community, first slowly and then with a strong, deliberate push. In the early 1990s, the church hired Rodney Woo to be the new pastor. Woo was part of a rising religious movement in the American evangelical community—fueled by multiculturalism and the influx of new Christian immigrants—to make the congregation a place of cross-racial, multiethnic integration. He began doing outreach around Southwest Houston, and led congregants on missionary trips around the world. Paul told me that "the first time I went there Pastor Woo was preaching the Gospel in a way that just touched me. I was with my twin sister. We looked around and we just felt welcome. It was multicultural, which was big for us. There were flags in the sanctuary, each one representing a country where a member is from or where the church has done work. We felt like we belonged."

The Simons are active churchgoers. Paul, who first joined in 2007, is a deacon and the head usher. Shelle, who joined when they got married, in 2012, hosts home groups and sings in the choir. But they never imagined that their family, and their home, would one day get so much help. Wilcrest canceled services on the Sunday of the storm, but church leaders began organizing a relief effort before the rain stopped. Jonathan Williams, the energetic young pastor who replaced Woo in 2011, posted a video prayer and message of hope on Facebook and offered thanks that the congregation was looking after one another. Several families, including the Simons, had suffered severe flood damage and were displaced from their homes. Church members had volunteered to house them, kids and all.

On Thursday, August 31, Wilcrest used social media to post a list of the supplies that its families needed: "Boys clothes, sizes 9–12 months, 2T, 3T. Baby wipes and diapers sizes 4 and 5 and formula.

Car seats. Tee-shirts. Men's jeans. Socks." Jonathan requested that congregants bring these items to the church as soon as possible. On Friday, five of Paul's friends from church met him at his house and scoped out the situation. About four feet of water had covered the first floor, and almost everything it touched—floorboards, cabinets, sheet rock, tiles and laminate—had to be ripped out and replaced. Paul's friends told Jonathan, who called for everyone in the congregation who could get to church to come back on Saturday morning. They'd transform the religious center into a relief operation for anyone, member or not, with hot food, fresh clothing, cleaning supplies, and prayer. It would also be a staging ground, from which teams of congregants would carpool to flooded neighborhoods and help clean out damaged homes. They'd start at the Simons. If time permitted, they'd extend outward and help other families, even those who didn't belong to the church.

Despite the widespread flood damage, on Saturday morning more than eighty people arrived at Wilcrest for the relief effort. Some got there early to prepare a hot breakfast, and the day began with a shared meal and a prayer. Jonathan told everyone that the hurricane was a reminder that our lives on earth were temporary, as was our hold on our material possessions. He urged congregants to recognize that they were part of a church body, and part of the body of Christ. He promised that the church would be there to help anyone who needed assistance, physical, emotional, or spiritual. Today, and for the hard months to come, their most immediate challenge would be to attend to one another here on earth.

After breakfast, most people, including nearly all of the men, went to the Simons' house, parking in a nearby elementary school and walking over because the streets were still coated in dirty water and there was no place for cars. Others formed small groups to help with other projects at the church: preparing food in the cafeteria, organizing supplies in the donation center, delivering relief packages to congregants who'd requested specific items, taking care of children whose parents were out taking care of neighbors and friends. Repairing the Simons' house required grueling manual labor, but with more than forty people pitching in the work went quickly. Once they'd finished, everyone stuck around for group photos and a prayer. And then nearly all of them went to help the Simons' next-door neighbors, an elderly couple, as well as Laverne and Brittney, who lived across the street. The two women had been thinking of joining a church but hadn't yet decided on one. Their choice soon became clear.

On Sunday, Laverne and Brittney joined the Simons and the Ayalas, a family with four children that had also been flooded out of their home, for services at Wilcrest. It was an emotional day for everyone in the congregation, but especially for the Ayalas. They'd been anxious because their relatives, with whom they'd been staying since the storm hit, had other displaced family members to house and couldn't fit everyone much longer. But Leasa and Guy Cantwell, two longtime Wilcrest members whom they barely knew, had invited the Ayalas to move in with them for as long as they needed. The Cantwells were white empty nesters with a large home and a swimming pool, and although the Ayalas' young children were nervous about staying with strangers, they were also excited, for the first time in days. The chapel was crowded, and Jonathan opened the service by acknowledging what the community had accomplished: "I'll tell you what a joy it is to look at the group that was there yesterday and know that if it was my house, they would be there. If it was your house, they would be there. I know. I know if my house was flooded, Paul would be there. Shelle would be there. Laverne and Brittney better be there. I will call you. I know where you live. That's my prayer."

In the following days, as people and communities throughout Houston prayed for their own miraculous recoveries, scientists announced that, according to current weather models, Harvey was a "500-year flood." In other words, there is a one in five hundred chance of a storm that strong happening each year. Of course, that didn't mean that citizens, governments, or relief agencies could rest easy. The United States had already experienced twenty-four five-hundred-year storms since 2010, and with climate change, it could expect many more. What no one anticipated, though, is that the next monstrous hurricane, Irma, would arrive on the US mainland about ten days later, and yet another, Maria, would cause catastrophic destruction in Puerto Rico, including months of disrupted power and water service to millions of people and more than one thousand deaths, about ten days after that.

Irma, which tore through the Caribbean, the Florida Keys, and the western side of Florida, was a Category 5 hurricane with sustained wind speeds of 185 miles per hour at its peak, and a Category 4 storm when it hit the mainland. In Florida, as in Texas, runaway development on low-lying land meant that millions of people were living in places that are likely to flood often and be uninhabitable by the end of the twenty-first century. Irma knocked out power to 6.7 million households across two-thirds of the state, caused between $42.5 and $65 billion of property damage, and took at least seventy-five lives, including twelve residents of a nursing home that overheated when the power went out. That's actually a lower toll than experts expected, because the hurricane's path changed and weakened at the last minute. But 2017 wound up setting an American record for costs from extreme weather events, with $306 billion in total damage. And it's only a matter of time before the next wave of hurricanes and superstorms arrives.

Today, cities and nations throughout the world are beginning to face up to the existential security challenges posed by global warming: rising seas, stronger storms, hotter and longer heat waves, droughts, migration, and conflicts over basic resources like water, food, and land. We have a narrow window to reduce global greenhouse gas emissions and prevent the climate from changing so dramatically that countless species, including our own, will no longer be able to live in places where they currently flourish. For that reason, there's no environmental project more urgent than climate mitigation, which means radically reducing our use of fossil fuels, converting to renewable sources of energy, and building new infrastructures to support these systems and sustain new ways of life much sooner than most governments are currently planning.

But much of the carbon dioxide we've already emitted will remain in the atmosphere for centuries, heating the oceans and raising the seas. If, through some unfathomable invention, scientists managed to stop all greenhouse gas emissions tomorrow, the process of global warming would continue for centuries, and sea levels would keep rising for thousands of years. We must mitigate, but we also have no choice but to adapt.

In coming decades, the world's most affluent societies will invest trillions of dollars on new infrastructure—seawalls, smart grids, basins for capturing rainwater—that can withstand twenty-first-century challenges, including megastorms like Harvey and Irma. But no investment in hard infrastructure will be sufficient to "climate-proof" the densely populated cities and suburbs that modern societies have built in coastal areas, river deltas, deserts, and plains. Engineered systems can be more or less responsive to the emerging climate, but history shows that they are never infallible. Breakdowns often occur for unanticipated reasons. Social infrastructure is always critical during and after disasters, but it's in these moments that it can truly mean the difference between life and death.

Social infrastructure can be built into traditional megaprojects, so that expensive climate security systems like seawalls and water basins function as parks or public plazas where people congregate on a regular basis and develop the informal support networks that we need during crises. It can also come from community organizations and religious groups, whose physical facilities and programs are staging grounds for all variety of collective life, regardless of the weather.

In the United States, religious organizations like Wilcrest play a vital role in helping their communities get through extreme weather. One reason that sites of worship are such important social infrastructures is that they are ubiquitous. Today, there are more than three hundred thousand religious congregations in the United States. "To put that number in context," writes one group of sociologists, "religious congregations are more common than Subways, McDonald's, Burger Kings, Wendy's, Starbucks, Pizza Huts, KFCs, Taco Bells, Domino's Pizzas, Dunkin' Donuts, Quiznos, and Dairy Queens combined and multiplied by three."

Another reason religious organizations are so important is that they are not merely houses of worship but key sites for community building. Religious institutions are driven by moral and spiritual concerns and are deeply engaged in the lives of their congregants. Although they vary dramatically by size and resources, churches, mosques, and synagogues tend to offer all kinds of social programs in their facilities: education and study groups, athletic leagues, childcare, elder support, and the like. Some engage people outside their congregation and try to build bridges; others are self-segregating and focus on the needs of the group. But in either case, their significance as social infrastructure is beyond dispute.

Not everyone belongs to a religious organization, however, and not every religious organization has the capacity to provide the kind of disaster relief that places like Wilcrest offer. There are, fortunately, many other places and organizations that serve as social infrastructures for secular or religiously unaffiliated people, including libraries, schools, and community groups. But most need resources to thrive.

Increasingly, governments and disaster planners are recognizing the importance of social infrastructure as part of climate security. Nicole Lurie, a scholar at Rand who previously served as

President Obama's assistant secretary for preparedness and response, told me that when she was in the federal government her team understood "how much better people do in disasters, how much longer they live, when they have good social networks and connections. And we've had a pretty big evolution in our thinking, so promoting community resilience is now front and center in our approach."

Barack Obama worked as a community organizer during the late 1980s, learning firsthand why social ties matter. He must have been thinking of the impoverished communities he'd gotten to know so well in Chicago when, as a US senator in 2005, he connected the effects of Hurricane Katrina to the slow-motion disaster that New Orleans's vulnerable neighborhoods endured every day. "I hope we realize that the people of New Orleans weren't just abandoned during the hurricane," he said. "They were abandoned long ago." Katrina, Obama continued, should "awaken us to the great divide that continues to fester in our midst" and inspire us to "prevent such a failure from ever occurring again."

During his first term, President Obama introduced a new National Health Security Strategy that emphasized preparedness and resilience, calling for the participation of the "whole community"—government agencies, civic organizations, corporations, and citizens—in all aspects of the security plan. After March 2011, when Obama issued a directive on national preparedness, FEMA began to embrace a similar approach to community resilience. "Community-engagement" programs funded by the Centers for Disease Control and Prevention have been launched in Los Angeles, Chicago, New York City, and Washington, DC. "There's always been a big focus on classic infrastructure in mitigation," Alonzo Plough, a former director of emergency preparedness and response for the County of Los Angeles, says. "But it's not just engineering that matters. It's social capital. And what this movement is bringing to the fore is that the social infrastructure matters, too."

Today, a growing network of policy makers and designers recognize the advantages of building social infrastructure into larger vital system upgrades. Their goal is to carry out "multipurpose projects" so that public investments in security don't just mitigate disaster damage but also strengthen the networks that promote health and prosperity during ordinary times.

Hurricane Sandy marked a turning point in the way government and civic groups think about climate security. The "superstorm" of 2012 covered an area more than one thousand miles in diameter, making it one of the largest hurricanes in American history. Its winds were both punishingly severe and painfully slow, and like Harvey, Sandy seemed to pause so that it could inflict extra damage on nearly everything in its path. Sandy hit the Atlantic coast on October 29—the worst possible moment. Not only was there a full moon with high tides, there was also an early winter storm with arctic air moving into the Northeast from the other direction, and the two systems collided to form what journalists called a hybrid "Frankenstorm."

As the primary target of the attacks on September 11, New York City had spent billions of dollars, over the course of a decade, shoring up its security systems and preparing for a catastrophe. Terrorism was not its only concern. Under Mayor Michael Bloomberg, the city also became a leader in planning for climate change, issuing high-profile reports about adaptation and mitigation and beginning the process of making the city more weather-resistant. In August 2011, New York City braced itself for the arrival of another severe storm system, Hurricane Irene, but was largely spared when the storm spun off to the north and west. The experience was something like a dress rehearsal for city officials and emergency managers, but it also gave residents a false sense of security, and only bolstered the collective confidence that has historically served Gotham so well.

Sandy laid waste to New York City's spirit of invulnerability, and to much of the city's vital infrastructure as well. The storm surge, which reached fourteen feet, toppled the city's flood protection systems. Subway tunnels filled up like bathtubs. The sewage system flooded and eleven billion gallons of soiled water overflowed into rivers and streets. The communications system broke down, leaving more than one million residents and businesses without phone or Internet service. The power grid failed, massively, with outages lasting nearly a week in Lower Manhattan and much longer in parts of Brooklyn, Staten Island, and Queens. Several hospitals and nursing homes were evacuated. Tens of thousands of residents were displaced from their homes, some permanently. Officials estimated the economic toll at around $60 billion. Miraculously, only around 150 people died in the United States, and fewer than 100 died across the Caribbean.

Sandy was neither the most deadly nor the most expensive storm in recent US history, and in global terms, its impact was far less severe than other twenty-first-century disasters, from the Indian Ocean tsunami in 2004 (which killed more than two hundred thousand people) to the pan-European heat wave of 2003 (which killed around seventy thousand people). But Sandy was important for other reasons: Not only did it reveal the surprisingly fragile physical and social infrastructure of one of the world's wealthiest and best-protected metropolitan areas, but it also directly affected the political, economic, and media elite of the United States. The fossil fuel industry has had great success promoting climate change denial and policy stagnation on all variety of environmental matters, but Sandy forced many of America's most powerful institutions to begin reckoning with global warming. A wide range of people and institutions that have the capacity to shape public opinion, social policy, and urban planning see the world

differently today than they did before Sandy hit. They are looking for new ideas—about how to reduce greenhouse gas emissions,
how to protect vulnerable people and places, how to rebuild cities,
communities, and critical infrastructures so that the systems we
depend upon don't fall apart when we need them most.

Sandy revealed serious flaws in all forms of infrastructure in
the New York area. When I visited Rockaway Beach and Staten Island in mid-November 2012, residents complained about the slow
pace of recovery. The power was out. The gas was off. Phone service was spotty. Trains weren't running. Sewage water from the
flooding covered the streets.

Still, there were some surprising reserves of strength. Consider
Staten Island, which suffered more fatalities than any other borough in New York City, and endured flooding so destructive that
the state helped relocate residents in several coastal neighborhoods
to higher ground. In the New Dorp neighborhood, a branch library
housed in a modest building escaped major damage, but homes
nearby took in as much as sixteen feet of water and residents
needed all kinds of assistance. There are schools and senior centers
in the area, but when people are in serious trouble they want to go
to a place that's familiar and comfortable, where they are likely
to find neighbors and friends. In New Dorp, as in so many New
York City neighborhoods, that place was the local library. Old and
young, they came in droves.

At first the library offered basic resources: food, hot water,
clean bathrooms, phones, power, cleaning supplies, companionship. Within days it was doing much more: helping residents apply
for FEMA funds online, connecting them with the Red Cross, and
hosting volunteers from civic organizations that were mounting
their own relief efforts. In New Dorp, the library staff worked like
the religious leaders in Houston. They knew their patrons well
enough to do their own emergency outreach, checking in with
regulars whom no one had heard from and making sure someone

visited those who were alone or vulnerable and in need of extra support.

Something similar happened at the Rockaway Beach Surf Club in Queens, which had opened in a converted auto-repair shop beneath the El on Beach Eighty-Seventh Street a few months before Sandy hit. The club transformed itself into a temporary relief agency when two of its founders returned there after the storm, posted Facebook updates inviting friends to join them, and watched more than five thousand volunteers come to help. Along with some local churches that, as in Houston, quickly transformed their chapels into relief centers, the surf club became one of the Rockaways' main community organizations, providing food, cleaning supplies, camaraderie, and manual labor for nearby residents. The club's neighbors, including blue-collar families and poor African Americans who, months before, had worried about how the club would fit into the community, joined in and benefited from the organization.

Unfortunately, thousands of people whose homes were damaged by Sandy live in neighborhoods that lack strong support networks or community organizations capable of mounting a large relief effort. They tend to be poorer and less educated than typical New Yorkers, with weaker ties to their neighbors as well as political power brokers.

After Sandy, Michael McDonald, who heads Global Health Initiatives in Washington, DC, and worked in Haiti after the 2010 earthquake, coordinated relief efforts by volunteer groups, government agencies, corporate consultants, health workers, and residents in vulnerable areas, particularly in the Rockaways. McDonald calls the network the New York Resilience System, and he's convinced that civil society will ultimately determine which people and places withstand the emerging threats from climate change. "What's actually happening on the ground is not under an incident command system," he told me. "It's the fragile, agile networks that make a difference in situations like these. It's the horizontal relationships like the ones we're building that create security on the ground, not the hierarchical institutions. We're here to unify the effort."

The island nation of Singapore—where 5.6 million people are packed into 277 square miles of land, much of which is perilously close to sea level—has combined physical and social infrastructure in several exemplary projects. Singapore began adapting to dangerous weather thirty-five years ago, after a series of heavy rains during monsoon seasons caused repeated flooding in the low-lying city center. The country has always had a difficult relationship with water: its geography makes it vulnerable to heavy seasonal rains and frequent flooding, but there is never a sufficient supply of potable water, and in recent years Singapore's dependency on Malaysian resources has led to political conflict. Climate change, with its rising sea levels and increase in heavy rains, threatens the city-state's stability. But Singapore's government also sees this moment as an opportunity.

The Marina Barrage and Reservoir, which opened in 2008, is at the heart of Singapore's $2 billion campaign to improve drainage infrastructure, reduce the size of flood-prone areas, and—through better social infrastructure—enhance the quality of city life. It consists of nine operable crest gates, a series of enormous pumps, and a ten-thousand-hectare catchment area that is roughly one-seventh the size of the country. The system not only protects low-lying urban neighborhoods from flooding during heavy rains but also eliminates the tidal influence of the surrounding seawater, creating a rain-fed supply of freshwater that currently meets 10 percent of Singapore's demand. Moreover, by stabilizing water levels in the Marina basin, the barriers have produced better conditions for water sports. The Marina's public areas, which include a sculpture garden, a water-play space, a green roof with dramatic skyline vistas, and the Sustainable Singapore Gallery, bolster the city's tourist economy. They've become vital parts of the social environment, and models for other cities that want their investment in climate security to pay off every day.

Rotterdam, which has a long history of flooding, is another model for climate planning that incorporates social infrastructure. After enduring a devastating storm surge in 1953, Rotterdam began building a series of dams, barriers, and seawalls as part of a national project called Delta Works, and in the early 2000s, when the United States was investing so many resources in homeland security, the Dutch government provided funds for an upgrade, the Rotterdam Climate Proof Program. Arnoud Molenaar, who manages it, said his team realized that they could convert the water that comes into the city from the skies and the sea into "blue gold." "Before, we saw the water as a problem," Molenaar told me. "In the Netherlands, we focused on how to prevent it from coming in. New York City focused on evacuation, how to get people out of the way. The most interesting thing is figuring out what's between these approaches: what to do with the water once it's there."

In 2005, Rotterdam hosted the Second International Architecture Biennale. The theme was "The Flood." Designers from around the world presented plans for how cities could cope with water in the future, and when the exhibition ended Molenaar's team set out to implement those that would have immediate practical value. Rotterdam is now a global leader in what climate designers consider the architecture of accommodation: Rather than simply attempting to block out heavy precipitation, the city is creating attractive, usable physical places that let the water in. There's a floating pavilion in the city center made of three silver half spheres with an exhibition space that's equivalent to four tennis courts; a floodable terrace and sculpture garden along the city's canal; and buildings whose facades, garages, and ground-level spaces have been engineered to be waterproof.

The most exciting social infrastructure that Rotterdam has built for climate security is Waterplein Benthemplein (the Benthemplein Water Square), designed by the Dutch architectural group De Urbanisten. The square, near the city's Central Station, in a formerly drab open space surrounded by large buildings, consists of three basins—two shallow, one deep—whose primary ecological purpose is to collect rainwater during the city's heavy storms. Ordinarily, flood management projects like these are buried underground as invisible infrastructure, so that the water disappears from view without anyone knowing how much there is, where it's going, or how the urban system works. Waterplein Benthemplein takes the opposite approach: the basins are not merely exposed; they are the most prominent architectural features of the plaza, places that attract different groups of people and offer a wide range of social and recreational activities.

On dry days, the deep basin doubles as a sport court, and people of all ages sit around the tiered seating area that surrounds it, taking in the action. The two shallow basins have different everyday functions. One contains an island with materials resembling a dance floor; the other is designed for skaters and the people who watch them. The square has other amenities. The site had long been a healthy habitat for trees, but the designers filled in open areas with wild flowers, tall grass, and small benches, which together create a series of pocket sanctuaries for rest and conversation. There's a large fountain, a dramatic water wall, and a rain well that feeds into an oversize, stainless steel gutter. There's always a pleasant flow of water in the square, but when there's precipitation, the full system rushes into operation. It sounds like a powerful waterfall, and looks exactly like what its designers intended: a dramatic work of urban art that doubles as critical infrastructure for a city where rain can be deadly.

Projects like Waterplein Benthemplein and the Singapore Marina Barrage and Reservoir are not inexpensive; but as storms mount and their costs, both human and financial, add up, governments will have no choice but to dedicate the kinds of resources to climate change that we've devoted to the war on terror. Unfortunately, governments in the world's poorest and most vulnerable nations do not have the kinds of resources that are necessary to build high-tech infrastructure systems that protect people from extreme weather while also improving the quality of everyday life. They've lobbied for adaptation funds during negotiations for every major international climate treaty, and although they've gained some concessions from the affluent societies whose carbon emissions are responsible for most global warming, the pool of money available to help developing nations fend off ecological ruin is a fraction of what they need.

Consider Bangladesh, a geographically small nation of 165 million people densely packed onto a delta formed by the confluence of several large rivers, and one of the most ecologically vulnerable places on earth. Bangladesh has a long history of catastrophic flooding that predates global warming: tsunamis, cyclones, and rainstorms arrive with frightening regularity, and each storm surge sends salinated water into the agricultural regions, ruining the crops that residents rely on for income and nourishment. In 1991, a tropical cyclone killed roughly 138,000 Bangladeshis, including a disproportionate number of women, old people, and children, who were trapped in the water and didn't know how to swim. In 1998, monsoon rains flooded two-thirds of the country, destroying some three hundred thousand houses, killing livestock, contaminating drinking water, and devastating local farms. In some nations, dealing with global warming remains a low priority, but in Bangladesh it's already a matter of grave national significance, part of every major policy debate.

In Bangladesh, as in most of the world's poor nations, international development agencies tend to dictate the terms of new infrastructure investments. Malcolm Araos, an NYU graduate student and one of my research assistants, did fieldwork in Dhaka to examine how adaptation projects unfold on the ground. He found, predictably, that hard infrastructure like embankments, sluice gates, and drainage systems were often placed around command centers where the nation's elites clustered rather than in the crowded, low-income neighborhoods where residents are most at risk. Not only did most climate security projects neglect social infrastructure; in some cases, they required demolishing the informal settlements and busy marketplaces where poor people gathered.

But Araos also discovered exciting projects where communities unable to secure conventional flood protection developed new ideas for staying above water. Throughout the country, grassroots organizations have been collaborating with nonprofits and local governments on social infrastructure projects that enhance resilience during weather disasters and dramatically improve residents' everyday lives too.

One particularly effective initiative is the "floating schools and libraries" program, led by Shidhulai Swanirvar Sangstha, a nonprofit that's addressing climate change, access to education, human rights, health care, and the digital divide with buoyant social infrastructure—in this case, boats. Shidhulai operates a fleet of fifty-four vessels in flood-prone areas in northwest Bangladesh, where recurrent flooding, even from routine rain events, regularly renders schools, hospitals, and libraries inaccessible. The boats, which are tethered to particular places and function as local institutions, are large and steady enough to host classrooms and health clinics during all but the stormiest weather. Children are not their only beneficiaries. The boats are staging grounds for all kinds of adult education, including courses for literacy, sustainable agriculture, and, more urgently, disaster survival. They're places where women build closer ties to one another, learn when and where to evacuate with their children, and even how to swim. Traditional security experts don't always appreciate the value of these programs, but scholars and international relief agencies believe they're among the most effective ways to help women and children survive the region's dangerous monsoons and floods.

Poor, developing nations are not the only places experimenting with "floating infrastructure." In 2017, several leading international design firms proposed building floating work and residential space in the bay water that runs along Silicon Valley. That same year, the *New York Times* reported on the rise of "seasteading" in areas threatened by rising sea levels—"Floating Cities, No Longer Science Fiction, Begin to Take Shape," teased one headline—and high-profile investors including PayPal founder Peter Thiel are betting on the concept.

Leaders in the international development field may not yet appreciate the importance of these climate-driven programs, but Bangladeshi leaders credit grassroots education projects like floating schools with dramatically reducing mortality during extreme weather crises. Social infrastructure is not a substitute for well-designed hard infrastructure, but it's just as important. In Bangladesh, as in so many low-lying, developing nations facing dire threats from climate change, it's the best way for communities to protect themselves.

In recent years, as ferocious hurricanes, searing heat waves, and raging wildfires have threatened life and destroyed valuable property in the world's most affluent societies, governments that long denied or delayed action on global warming have begun to act more like Bangladesh. It was easy to ignore remote and abstract ecological transformations like sea-level rise and warmer temperatures. But today, climate change is coming to mean something specific, and scary. "Even on a clear day a hundred years from now, the water will be where it is today under storm-surge conditions," says Klaus Jacob, a geophysicist at Columbia University whose 2009 report on climate risks to New York City contains eerily accurate predictions about what would happen to the city's infrastructure during a major storm surge. Sandy, for instance, seemed to be following Jacob's script. "We can't just rebuild after every disaster," Jacob told me. "We need to pro-build, with a future of climate change in mind."

After Sandy, President Barack Obama created a special initiative to support such pro-building in new infrastructure projects, an international design competition called Rebuild by Design. The competition was managed by then–HUD secretary Shaun Donovan and funded with more than $1 billion from a federal disaster relief bill. It attracted applications from 148 multidisciplinary teams from around the world, 10 of which were selected to participate in an intensive nine-month process of research, outreach, and design. I served as the research director for the competition, and by doing this job I came to appreciate both the inadequacy of our current infrastructure systems and the social benefits that rebuilding them could create.

I also got to work closely with leaders in an emerging field of practice that links climate science, social science, urban planning, engineering, and design, all in service of mitigating climate hazards and protecting vulnerable people in an ever-warming world. These individuals are not just changing the conversation about climate change; they're changing the systems we need to become more resilient to all variety of threats.

Of all Sandy's targets, none was more densely packed with human, economic, and cultural activity than Lower Manhattan, and none had such vulnerable infrastructure either. The compact but crowded area below Forty-Second Street includes some of New York City's most impoverished and most affluent neighborhoods, headquarters for several of the world's largest corporations, thousands of public housing units, and scores of community organizations that serve those in need. It hosts global financial institutions near the Battery, large hospitals near the East River, prestigious art galleries in Chelsea and the West Village, and thousands of small businesses throughout. It also has dozens of subway stops and an electrical substation in the East Village that supplies power to most of downtown.

All of this flooded during Sandy, when fourteen-foot storm surges topped the river's edges in southern Manhattan, inundating the Lower East and Lower West Sides. There was damage everywhere, but the East Side, where there are thick concentrations of poor people in aging public housing projects, and a cluster of large medical institutions, proved especially vulnerable. Water from the East River poured into the lobbies and basements of major hospitals, destroying years of research materials, forcing emergency evacuations, and, after the storm, disrupting the region's chronic care network for more than a year. The surge destroyed systems that provide power and communications to housing projects up and down the Lower East Side, and it left thousands of vulnerable people stranded, without water, electricity, or elevator service, on high floors of apartment buildings. And, for good measure, the surge dumped wastewater and debris onto the beaten-down asphalt that dominates the area's public spaces, including the South Street Seaport and the East River Greenway.

Safeguarding Lower Manhattan from future hurricanes and sea-level rise is a major priority for New York City, but so too is improving the quality of everyday life on the Lower East Side. The Rebuild by Design competition yielded an extraordinary, multibillion-dollar proposal for doing this, from Bjarke Ingels and the BIG Group. The plan, initially called the BIG U because it wraps around Lower Manhattan in a U-shape, but now known as the East Side Coastal Resiliency Project, relies on a series of protective walls that double as sloped parklands and recreational facilities, such as athletic fields, bike paths, and walkways. The project is divided into three sections, each called a compartment, and the design ideas for each site grew out of extensive consultations with local residents, businesses, and community organizations.

The compartment on the Lower East Side, which is, for now, the only funded part of the project, features lushly planted berms that protect neighborhoods, infrastructure, and institutions near the river, while also bridging them over the FDR Drive (an elevated highway that carries lots of traffic up and down the East Side of Manhattan and currently cuts off pedestrian access to the waterfront) to new gathering places and commercial outlets on the water's edge. The berms would block and absorb storm surges when necessary, but their everyday function, as parklands and recreational areas for inhabitants of an especially gray and unpleasant part of an especially gray city, is at least equally as important.

Deployable walls, camouflaged as a series of murals that hang from strong hinges on the ugly underside of the FDR Drive, are another key part of the proposal. Most of the time, the structures, which will be designed by local artists, operate as decorative ceiling panels that enhance the experience of walking beneath the highway, which, lacking good alternatives, thousands of residents do each day. Occasionally the walls will flip down for other functions, such as blocking out wind and framing space for a protected seasonal food market. And when hurricanes hit, the walls become hard barriers, reducing the odds that floodwaters will devastate the area again.

Staten Island, a sprawling barrier island at the mouth of the Hudson River and directly exposed to the Atlantic, also needs better protection. Residents there have endured repeated, occasionally devastating flooding since the late 1950s, when the government began building the Verrazano-Narrows Bridge, expanding infrastructure, and encouraging people to settle there. Although Staten Island has a smaller population than any other New York City borough, it had the greatest number of fatalities during Sandy. Tremendous waves crashed into its low-lying neighborhoods, eviscerating homes, carrying cars off the roads, and penetrating communities blocks from the ocean, where no one expected a deluge.

You can't wall off an ocean, but you can reduce the energy of its waves and protect against catastrophic flooding. Doing this, while also promoting social life and encouraging collective climate action in vulnerable waterfront communities, is the core goal of Living Breakwaters, a creative plan to build natural infrastructure—rocky sloped walls full of finfish, shellfish, and lobsters—that cuts the risk of flood damage and erosion on the south shore of Staten Island. The landscape architecture firm Scape, which is directed by the pioneering designer Kate Orff, leads the project. But it also includes a team of climate scientists, marine ecologists, educators, and advocates for social infrastructure.

Instead of building a massive barrier, Scape's plan acknowledges the inescapable fact that water is coming and uses nature's tools to protect vulnerable people and places from dangerous floods. It also does something bigger: since a robust climate policy agenda will require citizens, and not just scientists, to understand the risks of global warming, Living Breakwaters includes an ambitious educational program to teach how ecological citizenship can mitigate future climate threats.

Scape's way of shoring up Staten Island's social infrastructure involves using environmental educational hubs as everyday cultural centers, promoting social cohesion around a shared set of projects and concerns. The plan, which also introduces a curriculum codesigned with the New York Harbor School and the Billion Oyster Project, is designed to bring thousands of students into marine restoration projects and, through them, help families and communities see how our fate is linked to the fate of our oceans. It also links people in the area to one another through cultural programs and beachfront activities—such as planting oyster reefs and observing local wildlife—so that they'll know who needs support, and how to help them, when the next big storm hits.

Both Living Breakwaters and the East Side Coastal Resiliency Project await final environmental reviews and regulatory approvals, and there's much that could go wrong. Living Breakwaters requires working in or around areas where the city, the state, and the US Army Corps of Engineers have other water projects, and it could get tangled in a web of conflicting priorities and jurisdictional disputes. From the beginning, critics have warned that cutting costs to meet a budget in the final stages of the East Side Coastal Resiliency Project implementation process could reduce the verdant bridging berms into an ugly and imposing seawall, exactly the kind of project that Rebuild by Design was supposed to reject.

But at this stage the federal, state, and city governments continue to support the innovative projects, and other cities, in the United States and around the world, have already taken inspiration from the plans. If the East Side Coastal Resiliency Project and Living Breakwaters are built close to their designs, they will change the way we conceive of climate adaptation, putting social infrastructure at the core.

Unless we dramatically reduce greenhouse gas emissions, however, climate adaptation will be nothing more than a temporary survival strategy, one fated to make environmental injustice a more serious problem within and across nation-states. Consider, again, Houston: Many of its neighborhoods already benefit from social infrastructure that fosters cohesion and support in disasters.

Since it's one of the world's wealthiest cities, embedded in one of the world's wealthiest and most powerful nations, it has resources to build better hard infrastructure for flood protection too. But as long as Houston continues its current trajectory, with an economy rooted in oil and gas and a city plan that promotes continuous sprawl, single-family homes, and dependence on private automobiles, the great metropolis will wind up fueling global warming and increasing its own risk. Houston, like all the world's cities, needs to become more compact, dense, and amenable to walking and biking, which means building taller, multiunit residential towers in central places. It needs more trees to absorb carbon and cool the air, more urban parks and greenways where people can enjoy themselves without using their cars. It needs to replace its seemingly endless span of paved, impermeable roadways that channel floodwater to low-lying areas. All of this means building better social infrastructure, which is no easy project in a city that famously lacks zoning ordinances, and rebuilding after Harvey is the ideal moment to begin.

For inspiration, Houston can look to a nearby city that's also recovering from a catastrophic hurricane: New Orleans. In 2010, city leaders developed *New Orleans 2030*, a master plan that went far beyond what people urgently wanted in the wake of Katrina: flood protection, adaptation, and climate security. The city faced major challenges. Its population, 455,000 before Katrina hit in 2005, had fallen to 208,000 in 2006 and was only 348,000 in 2010. (It was 391,000 as of 2016.) With far fewer children, New Orleans had no choice but to close some of its public schools. The new plan called for repurposing and redeveloping the large institutional buildings as community centers, art studios, small business incubators, and apartments. That wasn't the only major change. Before the flood, in 1999, the city plan promised support for regional commercial development on major roadways and intersections, places where big-box stores could fit comfortably and parking would be abundant. After Katrina, as citizens and civic groups grew more concerned about climate change, that idea was discarded in favor of pedestrian-friendly, mixed-use commercial and residential developments that encouraged local social activity on sidewalks and streets. New Orleans was already famous for its ebullient, neighborhood-based public culture. Now it would double down.

In highly segregated cities, social polarization is a potential downside of intense neighborhood culture, and although New Orleans has a long, unique history of ethnic and racial mixing, its residential areas are sharply divided by race and class. To combat that problem, *New Orleans 2030* features a social infrastructure that facilitates pedestrian circulation across the city, and helps with climate mitigation and flood protection too. The Lafitte Greenway, which opened in 2015 around the historic Carondelet Canal, is a three-mile, multiuse trail and park linking six diverse neighborhoods, including affluent areas like Mid-City and Lakeview, the African American Tremé, a cluster of Section 8 housing buildings, the bustling French Quarter, and the bayou. The path is lined with bioswales (plants that absorb storm water, silt, and pollution) and native trees, and walkways run into a string of neighborhood parks. In just a few years, the greenway has become one of the city's most popular sites for leisure and recreation. It has also helped revive a formerly moribund cycling culture. New Orleans had 11 miles of bikeways when Katrina hit; today it has 115. Since the greenway opened, New Orleans has shot into the top American cities for bike commuters. It currently ranks fifth in the per capita population that cycles to work, and it promises to move further up the list once it launches its bike-share program. If political officials need evidence that social infrastructure can entice people out of their cars and into transit options that reduce our carbon footprint and curb global warming, New Orleans is a fine place to look.

The Lafitte Greenway is a modest project, with an initial budget of $9 million, but it has already expanded to incorporate new playgrounds, dog runs, community gardens, and athletic fields that branch off the pathway. Today, community groups in neighborhoods just beyond its reach are pushing to build new paths into the corridor. Commercial establishments, including bars and restaurants, are opening on the trail and all around the periphery. Real estate development is following, and in the process helping New Orleans become more walkable and compact. If there's a downside to this infrastructure project, it's that too much upscale development could generate additional waves of gentrification and displacement. But the early signs are that residents all along the greenway are embracing the project. It makes their daily lives healthier and more enjoyable, and it makes the city more sustainable too.

More important, the Lafitte Greenway, with its storm protection systems and clean transit networks, exemplifies the kind of new infrastructure project that we will need to survive climate change. It blends climate adaptation with mitigation while also improving the quality of urban life, regardless of the weather, and giving the people fortunate enough to be near it a way to connect. The water is coming. With the right kind of social infrastructure, we may well get through it without building an ark.

Before We Lift the Next Shovel

In February 2017, Facebook founder and CEO Mark Zuckerberg posted a six-thousand-word open letter on the site he created. It's addressed "To our community," and within a few sentences Zuckerberg asks his company's two billion or so users a straightforward question: "Are we building the world we all want?"

The answer was self-evident.

If there's a core principle in Zuckerberg's worldview, it's that human beings make progress when we break down social and geographic divisions and form larger, more expansive moral communities. "History is the story of how we've learned to come together in ever greater numbers—from tribes to cities to nations," he claims. "At each step, we built social infrastructure like communities, media and governments to empower us to achieve things we couldn't on our own."

As CEO of one of the world's most profitable and fastest-growing corporations, Zuckerberg is generally cautious about making explicitly partisan statements. But in the 2016 campaign he had denounced the "fearful voices calling for building walls and distancing people they label as others," and a few weeks before posting his letter, he condemned Trump's executive order to ban immigrants from selected Middle Eastern nations: "We should . . . keep our doors open to refugees and those who need help. That's who we are." Zuckerberg's letter, released during this unusually public conflict with the new president, was meant to be Facebook's new mission statement as well as its blueprint for how to rebuild society in a tumultuous, potentially authoritarian age.

"In times like these, the most important thing we at Facebook can do is develop the social infrastructure to give people the power to build a global community that works for all of us," he explained. Facebook, as Zuckerberg sees it, is uniquely capable of bridging our social divisions. He recognizes that, where they remain popular, churches, sports teams, unions, and other civic groups deliver the social benefits that he wants Facebook to generate: "They provide all of us with a sense of purpose and hope; moral validation that we are needed and part of something bigger than ourselves; comfort that we are not alone and a community is looking out for us; mentorship, guidance and personal development; a safety net; values, cultural norms and accountability; social gatherings, rituals and a way to meet new people; and a way to pass time." Yet he also argues that, in these dark times marked by the "striking decline" of group membership since the 1970s, "online communities are a bright spot." At Facebook, Zuckerberg writes, "our next focus will be developing the social infrastructure for community—for supporting us, for keeping us safe, for informing us, for civic engagement, and for inclusion of all."

Zuckerberg's first promise is to develop better algorithms for predicting which kinds of "very meaningful" Facebook communities (those that "quickly become the most important part of our social network experience") would benefit its users, and to "help connect one billion people with meaningful communities, that can strengthen our social fabric." His second promise is to "expand groups to support sub-communities," people who care about the same sports teams, television shows, video games, and the like. His third is to "reinforce our physical communities by bringing us together in person to support each other."

Zuckerberg tells readers how Facebook's social infrastructure will promote health and safety, and again it involves getting people to do more things online. Using artificial intelligence, the company will "help our community identify problems before they happen." He says that Facebook has "built infrastructure to show Amber Alerts," that it has "built infrastructure to work with public safety organizations," and "built infrastructure like Safety Check so we can all let our friends know we're safe and check on friends who might be affected by an attack or natural disaster."

Zuckerberg wants to reinvigorate democracy. He sees Facebook as a tool for helping people vote, speak out, and organize. He envisions it generating new ways for people around the world to participate in collective governance, new ways to achieve openness, transparency, and, more ambitiously, a renewed commitment to the common good.

Zuckerberg's rhetoric is as grandiose as we'd expect from a man whose company has billions of active users and a market value around $500 billion. But the vision of social infrastructure that he endorses is flimsy. Social media, for all their powers, cannot give us what we get from churches, unions, athletic clubs, and welfare states. They are neither a safety net nor a gathering place. In fact, insider accounts from Silicon Valley tech companies establish that keeping people on their screens, rather than in the world of face-to-face interaction, is a key priority of designers and engineers.

Facebook can, and occasionally does, help us find people with whom we build relationships in real life, and perhaps someday it will improve. In early 2018, Zuckerberg posted an acknowledgment that Facebook "is crowding out the personal moments that lead us to connect more with each other," and he pledged to change the site even if it meant that "the time people spend on Facebook and some measures of engagement will go down." But no matter how the site's designers tweak Facebook content, the human connections we need to escape danger, establish trust, and rebuild society require recurrent social interaction in physical places, not pokes and likes with "friends" online.

It was disingenuous for Zuckerberg to claim that Facebook, like the social organizations that he sees declining, promotes the kinds of values, cultural norms, and systems of accountability that democracy requires. Because when Zuckerberg wrote his open letter he already knew what Facebook would not acknowledge until the US Congress effectively forced a confession: During the most divisive and consequential presidential election in recent history, Russian propagandists had used Zuckerberg's so-called social infrastructure to buy more than three thousand fake news ads that reached at least ten million people. Thanks to Facebook's technology, the Russians—as well as alt-right organizations intent on spreading misinformation inside the United States—could target their campaign to swing-state voters. The organizations behind these ads did not merely want to manipulate citizens and suppress turnout in communities likely to support the Democratic candidate, Hillary Clinton. They also aimed to sow social divisions that would undermine Americans' faith in democracy, and they made similar efforts to wreak havoc in open societies around the world. Facebook, whose algorithms amplify extreme, emotional messages that stoke polarization and downplay more nuanced, deliberative posts, was ideally suited for the job.

Since the 2016 election, Facebook and other tech companies have made major investments in a lobbying campaign to stave off regulations that would require them to disclose who is purchasing political advertising. Zuckerberg's team has portrayed the Russians' ability to manipulate social media for their political project as a technical problem that can be fixed with engineering. More fundamentally, however, the election and the subsequent congressional hearings with high-tech leaders revealed that the companies that manage large-scale, for-profit communications infrastructures are set up to prioritize generating revenue above delivering public goods. Publicly traded corporations, including Facebook, are legally required to maximize shareholder value, and while some CEOs define value expansively, most focus on the bottom line.

Zuckerberg surely didn't want his company to facilitate malevolent intervention into the democratic process; and yet, as investigative reporters discovered, Facebook's advertising salespeople and engineers made great efforts to help domestic political advocacy groups, including the anti-Clinton, anti-Islam organization Secure America Now, reach their targeted audiences. No matter their political preferences, Facebook employees had a simple reason for doing this: Winning advertisers is their job. Promoting democracy isn't. During the 2016 campaign, Facebook made a negligible profit from accepting paid political ads from groups associated with the Russian government and the alt-right. American democracy, and the global community that Zuckerberg says he is committed to building, suffered a devastating loss.

There is another community that has suffered devastating losses since Facebook and other big tech companies began setting up shop in the Bay Area: poor, working-class, and middle-class residents of the region, who have been steadily priced and crowded out. Gentrification hardly seems like a strong enough word to describe what's happened in the Bay Area during the historic tech boom. Housing costs in San Francisco are so outrageously high that few members of the middle class can afford to live there. Research by the University of California's Urban Displacement Project shows that 47 percent of all the region's census tracts, and 60 percent of low-income households, are in neighborhoods at risk of or already experiencing displacement or gentrification pressures. San Francisco's African American population is declining sharply, while low-income and middle-class families are moving farther from urban centers and spending ever more time on long commutes. The impact is apparent everywhere. There's heavy traffic on local roads and freeways, insufficient parking on city streets and at malls. A few decades ago, Silicon Valley was full of pristine suburbs that provided a high quality of life; today it is terribly congested and on the brink of being overrun.

For all their emphasis on software engineering, there's no question that companies like Facebook, Google, and Apple appreciate the value of real social infrastructure: the physical places that shape our interactions. Their campuses are stunning, with verdant gardens, juice bars and gourmet restaurants, manicured athletic fields and exercise facilities, hair salons, day care centers, theaters, libraries, cafés, and ample space for social gatherings, both indoors and out. These are private social infrastructures, there for the pleasure and convenience of first-tier staff members whose color-coded badges grant them access, but, crucially, not for the low-level temps and contractors who cook and clean in the same organization, and not for neighboring residents or visitors. These expensive, carefully designed social infrastructures work so well for high-level tech employees that they have little reason to patronize small local businesses—coffee shops, gyms, restaurants, and the like—that might otherwise benefit far more from the presence of a large employer.

Some companies have made modest efforts to improve the surrounding social infrastructure. Google, for instance, built new soccer fields, gardens, and bike paths around its headquarters in Mountain View, and Sergey Brin, a cofounder, subsidizes leases for proprietors of small shops that cater to families in properties he owns nearby. In July 2017, Facebook, facing pressure from employees who were exhausted from long commutes and from neighbors in East Menlo Park who'd grown fed up with congestion around its growing campus, proposed developing a campus extension. The "village," designed by star architect Rem Koolhaas's firm, OMA New York, would link new offices with housing, retail outlets, parkland, and, crucially, a grocery store for an area that, despite Facebook's massive presence, remains a food desert. Zuckerberg hopes to open the extension by 2021, but—if the comments they've made in public forums and news articles are any indication—residents of East Menlo Park would prefer that the municipal government slow down and address their concerns first. Why, they ask, should the city approve Facebook's expansion without securing funds to renovate their dilapidated schools, parks, and fields? How will the city mitigate the traffic and pollution that seem certain to increase as thousands more employees come into the area? What can Facebook do to make sure that its plans are good for the community, and not just the company? Does Facebook really care?

Facebook's attempt to win over local support for its new developments has been unsuccessful in part because the company has done so little to improve the local social infrastructure since it moved into Menlo Park. Although people who purchased houses before the tech companies arrived would surely profit if they wanted to sell and move out of the region, rising real estate prices don't do anything to improve the lives of residents and workers. For them, the biggest daily impact of being close to corporations like Facebook is being stuck in traffic, often behind the private buses that shuttle workers to and from campus. The buses, perhaps more than Facebook's famous blue and white logo, have become the most potent symbol of what tech leaders are doing all over the

Bay Area: building private social infrastructures that help their companies prosper on top of public ones that urgently need repair, and telling everyone in "the community" to trust that it's for the common good.

It's not surprising that Silicon Valley titans are so intent on persuading the public that the things they do to advance their corporate interests are actually meant to make the world more peaceful, just, and humane. The executives who run oil, finance, and automobile companies have said the same kinds of things for decades. But it's off-putting to see Zuckerberg doing it so brazenly, since he built Facebook on the idea that social media require openness and transparency. At this point, we all know what the game is, and it's insulting to be told that each new revenue-generating Facebook product—the messaging app for children under age thirteen, for instance—is really on offer because the company wants society to flourish.

I don't doubt that, in addition to his interest in accumulating more wealth and power, Zuckerberg has good intentions. He has championed experiments that provide a "universal basic income" in communities where decent-paying jobs are becoming scarce. In 2015, he and his wife, Priscilla Chan, set up the Chan Zuckerberg Initiative (a limited liability company rather than a traditional foundation, which requires owners to give away 5 percent of the endowment every year and cannot invest in profit-seeking ventures). The couple has pledged to donate 99 percent of their shares in Facebook to the charity; at the time of the announcement, analysts estimated the value of these shares at $45 billion over their life span. Chan and Zuckerberg have also pledged to give $3 billion in the next decade to a project that aims to "cure all disease" by the end of the twenty-first century. They've already opened the Chan Zuckerberg BioHub, a research center in San Francisco where engineers, computer scientists, chemists, biologists, and other scientists from Stanford, the University of California, Berkeley, and the University of California, San Francisco, are collaborating on a variety of health-related projects. They've given $24 million to a start-up that trains software developers in Africa and made a $50 million investment in a learning app designed to help children in India.

These are admirable projects, and together they may well save or improve millions of lives. But today, as Zuckerberg's open letter to Facebook users acknowledges, there are urgent problems in the world—from isolation and polarization to runaway inequality in health, education, and the capacity to deal with climate change— and many of them are visible in Silicon Valley's own backyard. It's naive to claim that better algorithms and meaningful Facebook community groups will help us make any real advances on these issues. Despite—or maybe precisely because of—the fact that we spend so much time on screens and the Internet, we desperately need common places where people can come together, participate in civil society, and build stronger social bonds. Unless we invest in real social infrastructures, the answer to Zuckerberg's question—"Are we building the world we all want?"—will remain decidedly no.

Neither Zuckerberg nor any other twenty-first-century corporate leader bears individual responsibility for the sorry state of our social infrastructure. But it's worth noting that in earlier historical moments, when a small number of business leaders made enormous fortunes while much of society struggled to satisfy basic human needs, great philanthropists used their wealth and power to build places that created opportunities for everyone and that didn't double as profit-seeking ventures. Consider the railway and steel magnate Andrew Carnegie. He was a true "robber baron," who allowed managers to hire hundreds of armed Pinkerton detectives and violently suppress unionized workers during the Homestead strike, and lobbied fiercely against the income tax and other government efforts to address inequality. Yet Carnegie gave away so much of his fortune that the Philanthropy Roundtable, the leading network of charitable donors in the United States, says he "may be the most influential philanthropist in American history." His contributions, they write, are "without peer."

Entrepreneurs have amassed vast fortunes in the new information economy, and yet no one has come close to doing what Carnegie did between 1883 and 1929, when he funded construction of 2,811 lending libraries, 1,679 of which are in the United States. Today, the Carnegie libraries are set in ordinary residential neighborhoods throughout the world, and they continue to be powerful sources of uplift. Carnegie's extraordinary commitment to American cities and communities is worth recalling, as are the principles that motivated him. An immigrant himself, Carnegie believed that anyone who had access to culture and education could achieve success in the United States. He knew firsthand that not everyone could be a student here. As a child in Pittsburgh, he had no choice but to work instead of going to school. But a local merchant who lent books to children in his neighborhood changed his life. "It was from my own early experience that I decided there was no use to which money could be applied so productive of good to boys and girls who have good within them and ability and ambition to develop it, as the founding of a public library in a community," Carnegie wrote. He funded libraries to provide books, courses, social activities, and relief from the pressures of daily life. He also wanted them to inspire people, which is why so many of the original Carnegie libraries have high windows, vaulted ceilings, and ornate designs. Building libraries "is but a slight tribute," Carnegie explained, "and gives only a faint idea of the depth of gratitude which I feel."

I appreciate the appeal of "moon shots," the projects with goals like space colonization and immortality that today's leading philanthropists, particularly those in the tech industry, pursue with such passion. But too many of these initiatives seem motivated by hubris and narcissism rather than concern for "boys and girls who have good within them and ability and ambition to develop it."

It's hard to find Carnegie's sense of goodwill and civic-mindedness in today's Silicon Valley, where the entire industry depends on a technology developed by the government—the Internet—and a publicly funded communications infrastructure. Like Zuckerberg, corporate leaders are always happy to experiment with projects that promote the common good while raising their market capitalization. But there are limits to how much they can accomplish by giving while taking. How much more wealth do they need to accumulate before they are ready to help?

It's particularly puzzling that so few corporate leaders from the information economy, including those in technology and finance, have supported the library, the primary institution promoting literacy and providing Internet access to those who would otherwise have no way to get online. There are exceptions. In the 1990s, Microsoft and the Gates Foundation, which stands out for its investments in schools, health centers, and other vital social infrastructures, donated $400 million to help libraries across the United States establish Internet connections. In 2008, Stephen Schwarzman, the Wall Street financier and CEO of the Blackstone Group, gave $100 million to the New York Public Library, which in turn named its landmark building on Fifth Avenue after him. And in 2017, the Stavros Niarchos Foundation gave $55 million to renovate Manhattan's major circulating library, just across from the Schwarzman building. These are extraordinary contributions, but they're just a drop in the bucket compared with what cities around the world need in order to rebuild the woefully outdated branch libraries that, despite their old age, still uphold neighborhoods and communities, helping those who aspire to a better life or just need companionship to get through the day.

Today, as cities and suburbs reinvent themselves, and as cynics claim that government has nothing good to contribute to that process, it's important that institutions like libraries get the recognition they deserve. After all, the root of the word "library," *liber*, means both "book" and "free." Libraries stand for and exemplify something that needs defending: the public institutions that—even in an age of atomization and inequality—serve as bedrocks of civil society. Libraries are the kinds of places where ordinary people with different backgrounds, passions, and interests can take part in a living democratic culture. They are the kinds of places where the public, private, and philanthropic sectors can work together to reach for something higher than the bottom line.

Not everyone believes this. In recent decades, political leaders driven by the logic of the market have proclaimed that institutions like the library don't work any longer, that we'd be better off investing in new technologies and trusting our fate to the invisible hand.

The influence of these arguments is reflected in the way we treat what was once a sacred public institution. Today, libraries in most places are starved for resources. Across the country, branch libraries have reduced their hours and days of operation despite rising attendance and circulation, leaving those with weekday obligations like work and school with fewer opportunities to visit. They've downsized staff, cutting back on librarians as well as on basic services like sanitation and information technology. They've decreased the budget for new books, periodicals, and films.

In most municipalities, neighborhood libraries are in old, worn-down facilities that don't meet twentieth-century standards, let alone twenty-first-century needs. In some cities, including affluent ones like Denver, the situation is so dire that local governments have been shutting down entire branches. In San Jose, just down the road from Facebook, Google, and Apple, the public library budget is so tight that system leaders recently prohibited users with overdue fees above $10 from borrowing books or using computers. When the fees reach $50, the library sends the case to a debt collection agency. Instead of lifting up patrons, the library becomes yet another institution that's holding them down.

In New York City, global epicenter of culture and finance, the fight over what to do with branch libraries has much higher stakes.

The current battle pits the library's executive leadership, which is anxious about the system's declining fortunes, against local patrons who fear they'll lose neighborhood branches and specialized services if the system consolidates.

They have good reason to fear. According to the Center for an Urban Future, the New York Public Library system has more than $1.5 billion in construction needs—just for repairs and maintenance on existing facilities. In Manhattan, the city sold land and air rights to the beloved Donnell Library, across from the Museum of Modern Art on Fifty-Third Street, in 2007, for $59 million, promising to open a new facility within the new luxury hotel and condo building there by 2011. It opened in summer 2016, and while some appreciated its twenty-first-century design, both users and critics complained that it felt soulless, more like an Apple Store than a community hub.

In Brooklyn, where estimates for repairing the borough's sixty branch buildings top $300 million, the public library board tried to sell the historic, heavily used Pacific Library branch in Boerum Hill to real estate developers, only to withdraw the offer because of fierce neighborhood protests. Soon after, the board voted to sell the land rights to the Brooklyn Heights Library for $52 million, so that another developer could build a thirty-six-story, mixed-use tower that, as in Manhattan, would include a new library, considerably smaller than the current one. Once again, neighbors protested, but this time for naught. The Brooklyn Borough Board approved the sale in early 2016.

The fiscal crisis in the New York Public Library has had more immediate consequences too. Between 2008 and 2013, New York City cut the library system's operating funds by $68 million, resulting in a 24 percent drop in staff hours. A century ago, most branch libraries were open seven days a week; today, most are closed on Sundays, which have always been popular days for immigrants, blue-collar workers, and families to visit. No other institution can fill the void.

Sometimes the market provides partial substitutes. In the Bronx, for instance, the Baychester Barnes & Noble long served as the borough's only bookstore, open seven days and eighty-eight hours a week (from 9 a.m. to 10 p.m. Monday through Saturday, 10 a.m. to 8 p.m. on Sunday), with ample time for working parents who could come only on evenings and children who could come only on weekends. The store opened in 1999 and immediately began to operate as a crucial social infrastructure, a place where people were welcome to linger and enjoy one another's company even if they didn't make a purchase.

Bookstores, large and small, have always been more than just retailers. For centuries—and in the United States, since 1745, when the Moravian Book Shop opened in Bethlehem, Pennsylvania—they've served as vital gathering places where we can reliably find other people who love good stories and new ideas, as well as shop owners or clerks who delight in helping patrons find literature that they'll love. They often provide special programs for children and families, sponsor reading groups for grown-ups, host author lectures and signings, and get involved in all variety of civic affairs. They facilitate conversations among strangers, not only by providing safe places but also by giving us so much to discuss.

As a professor and onetime graduate student, I surely rank among the most dedicated bookstore customers. Yet I know people in a variety of professions with fond and vivid memories of the time they spent in local bookshops, and I'm hardly the only one who can track the course of my life through the bookstores that I visited regularly. In Chicago, my parents and I spent countless hours reading children's books together at Barbara's Bookstore on Wells Street, and when I got old enough I went there solo, seeking books (like Judy Blume's *adult* fiction) that they might not have approved. In Berkeley, where I went for graduate school in sociology, I filled entire afternoons reading my way through the musty used books stacks on the second and third floors of Moe's on Telegraph Avenue. I was never alone, either. A small world of students congregated there, using the books as conversation starters, just as they do in small bookshops in Hyde Park, Cambridge, Ann Arbor, and college towns around the world. Fortunately, my girlfriend, and now wife, shared my passion for extended browsing, and since she had enough income to buy new books, we spent plenty of nights up the block at Cody's as well.

We moved to New York City around the time my first book was published, and I'll never forget the pleasure of seeing it on the shelves of the Barnes & Noble stores that saturated our neighborhood: the chain operated four shops within a half mile of us, two on Avenue of the Americas, one on Union Square, and the flagship, on Fifth Avenue and Eighteenth Street. We were somehow regulars in all of them, and at the time my wife told everyone that she could tell that, after so many years of graduate student wages, I finally felt some financial security, because it was the first time she'd seen me buy hardcover books. When our children were little we made a habit of taking them to a place in the Flatiron District called Books of Wonder, which, for good or ill, sold cupcakes and coffee along with every picture book we wanted. As they got older we took them on outings to places where they couldn't help but notice that the world is full of people who love books—and bookshops—as much as we do: the Strand in Greenwich Village, McNally Jackson in SoHo, Kepler's during our sabbatical year in Menlo Park. The visits could be expensive, but there aren't many more worthwhile ways of spending what we have.

These days, of course, there are cheaper and more efficient ways to buy books (and everything else), and my family is hardly immune to their appeal. No matter how much we love bookshops, we often opt to make purchases on the Internet when we're in a hurry or looking for a better price. But inevitably, as ever more people choose online vendors over brick-and-mortar establishments, bookshops close and social infrastructures disappear. It happened in our neighborhood, when both of the Barnes & Noble shops on Avenue of the Americas closed within a few years of each other. One building became a chain grocery, but the other, on Eighth Street, quickly went from being a vibrant community center to the site of a homicidal hate crime, which took place in front of the shuttered building just months after it closed. In late 2016, Barnes & Noble, facing a steep rent increase, announced that it would close its Baychester operation too, to be replaced by a Saks Off 5th discount outlet. The change left 1.5 million people, in a borough whose former residents include the celebrated writers Mark Twain, Edgar Allan Poe, Cynthia Ozick, and Richard Price, without a social infrastructure that the community had enjoyed for as long as anyone can remember. A Barnes & Noble executive pledged that the company was "committed to working diligently with local officials to reopen a store in the Bronx in the future." I very much hope they do.

In an era characterized by urgent social needs and gridlock stemming from political polarization, it is tempting to give up on government and reach almost desperately for new solutions—many in our time tech-driven, experimental, and privatized, based on faith that the market will deliver what we want and need. For communities without grocery stores, there's Amazon and Fresh-Direct. For communities without enough corner stores, two former Google employees have created Bodega, pantry boxes stocked to meet local demand and programmed so that customers can make all their purchases with a smartphone. "Eventually, centralized shopping locations won't be necessary," says Paul McDonald, a co-founder, "because there will be 100,000 Bodegas spread out, with one always 100 feet away from you." This kind of ambition helped McDonald and his business partner, Ashwath Rajan, secure angel investors at Google, Facebook, Twitter, and Dropbox, as well as venture funding from some of Silicon Valley's leading firms. It's not yet clear how many Bodegas will ultimately open, but no matter the number, it's worth noting that their proposal did not merely offend Latinos and threaten the ethnic entrepreneurs whose industry they hope to "disrupt"; it also sparked a backlash in communities throughout the United States, because most people enjoy living near a small shop run by human beings who can engage in occasional interaction or, when we're in a hurry, just smile and hand over our change.

Today, as our unending interactions with screens threaten to eclipse the moments we share with other real people, communities everywhere are voicing frustration with the limits of life online. Across the planet, people are gaining a new appreciation for the physical places where they gather, and it's instructive to see the extraordinary things that can happen when coalitions of citizens and philanthropic agencies commit to rebuilding the kinds of social infrastructure that meet our contemporary needs.

Consider Columbus, Ohio, an emerging model for cities that are using the library to help bridge social divisions and reanimate civic life. As the state capital and home to the flagship Ohio State University, Columbus is a fairly liberal city surrounded by conservative counties. Although it has high levels of income and education overall, there are also pockets of deep poverty. One recent study found that about 35 percent of preschoolers in the city were "unready for kindergarten," because they didn't have age-appropriate literacy skills, and another showed that 20 percent of households lacked Internet access.

When the Great Recession of 2008 hit, Ohio state legislators cut spending so deeply that Columbus city leaders feared their library system was in jeopardy. Local branches reduced their hours and eliminated some programs. They introduced a referendum and gave voters the chance to decide whether to issue a property tax levy that would add $56 million per year to the library's budget. There aren't many things that American voters like less than property taxes, but the citizens of Columbus had become passionate about their libraries. Nearly two hundred volunteers canvassed the city to rally support for the initiative, leading town hall meetings, running phone banks, and visiting civic groups. As it turned out, Columbus voters didn't need to be persuaded. By a two-to-one margin, they opted to raise their own taxes. Soon after, the city restored full service in the main building and all the local branches.

In 2016, the city renovated several branch libraries and the main library as well, adding a wall of windows that looks over its seven-acre Topiary Park, building new children's rooms, improving the restroom facilities, and creating better connections between the library and the park. That year, as prosperous cities like San Jose cracked down on users with late fees, Columbus took the opposite approach. As of January 1, 2017, the metropolitan library stopped issuing fines for overdue books. "Removing barriers to get more materials into the hands of more customers brings us closer to achieving our vision of a thriving community where wisdom prevails," said Patrick Losinski, the library system's CEO. So too do the library's numbers for circulation and in-person visits, which remain among the highest in the nation per capita. The fact that the library recorded ninety-five thousand visits to its homework help centers and nearly sixty thousand participants in its summer reading groups is equally impressive. The people of Columbus pay a price to get such strong social infrastructure, about $86 per year for a $100,000 home. But their behavior, at the ballot box and in their libraries, shows how much they value what they get in return.

Libraries are only one form of vital social infrastructure. As we've seen, many other public places and institutions play a pivotal role in the daily lives of our neighborhoods and communities. On good days, they can determine how many opportunities we have for meaningful social interactions. On bad days, especially during crises, they can mean the difference between life and death.

Although some important social infrastructures—the church, the café, the bookstore, and the barbershop, among others—arise from the nonprofit sector or the market, most of the vital places and institutions that we need to rebuild are either funded or administered by the state. For decades, antitax ideology has whittled down the public funds we need to build and maintain all kinds of critical infrastructures. Generations ago, Americans took great pride in the power and resilience of our ultramodern systems: majestic dams and bridges, sprawling railways, reliable electric grids, clean waterworks, verdant parklands from coast to coast. Today, these public goods are in shambles. Instead of lifting us to reach for something greater, infrastructure is now a source of shame and embarrassment. Our roads are crumbling. Our trains are slow. Our airports, President Trump says, are "like third world countries." Dozens of cities, including Boston, Chicago, and Philadelphia, were recently caught cheating on water-quality tests to conceal potential contaminants. Other cities, such as Flint, Michigan, have water so poisonous that its dangers proved impossible to deny or conceal. Countless cities and suburbs have social infrastructures that are comparably toxic, and although the problems they generate unfold in slow motion, they put the entire body politic at risk.

Debates about infrastructure innovation to better protect the public tend to focus exclusively on technology, but designers throughout the world are also innovating at a more fundamental level, transforming the key concepts and building typologies that have long dictated what we develop. Take, for instance, the "Polis Station," the architect Jeanne Gang's attempt to transform the police station, a potent site and symbol of the racially divisive security state, into an inclusive social infrastructure that fosters interaction across group lines. Gang, who lives in Chicago and has deep ties to the city, had observed fierce conflicts and rising distrust between the Chicago Police Department and the minority communities they patrol so aggressively. Her firm, Studio Gang, began conducting one-on-one and group interviews with civic leaders and local officials in the neighborhoods where residents and police were most estranged, and over time they organized gatherings where youths, neighbors, community groups, and police officers could share their concerns and desires. The process wasn't easy. For more than two decades, the police department had targeted, abused, and, as the city formally acknowledged in 2015, secretly tortured suspects from the neighborhoods where Gang was working. Officers were not the only ones with blood on their hands. Although the city was hardly a war zone, violent crime remained a major problem in many of its poor and segregated neighborhoods. All of this made bringing the police and the people together a difficult, sensitive task.

When the different sides came together, however, they expressed more sympathy for each other's predicament than Gang had expected, and more interest in fixing things too. No one harbored fantasies that designing a new building would solve the underlying problems of gun violence and racist police abuse in Chicago, but there were other, more practical ways to improve conditions on the streets. All of them involved enhancing the social infrastructure. In neighborhood after neighborhood, both community leaders and the police complained that there weren't enough safe places where teenagers and adolescents could play after school. The result was that too many young people spent their afternoons milling around the sidewalks, and though they usually weren't causing trouble, the police had a hard time figuring out how to maintain order and keep things safe. Gang and her collaborators had been brainstorming design ideas that could help heal the fractured social body, and in one of the gatherings they pitched something novel: What if the police station became a community center, with recreational facilities that young people could use without fear?

The concept was mind-bending: the station house has always been a space of detention, inquisition, and intimidation—all the more so in Chicago, where the threat of violence suffused the criminal justice system. But Gang, a MacArthur "genius" whose accomplishments include building the world's tallest skyscraper designed by a woman (Aqua Tower, in Chicago), was known for big, ambitious ideas. She's also something of a local celebrity, with a good relationship with Mayor Rahm Emanuel. Emanuel, for his part, was eager to signal his commitment to police reform, and officers were hoping to get residents involved in community engagement. With interests aligned, they decided to build a prototype. As it happens, the site they selected is in North Lawndale, whose social infrastructure had not improved much since I spent time there studying the effects of the heat wave, and where so many frail and vulnerable people remained at risk of being isolated at home.

By the time Gang got approval to work in North Lawndale she'd already developed the Polis Station concept, both in her practice and in her architecture studios for students. In her grand vision, the Polis Station would include many of the social infrastructures whose benefits we've seen in previous chapters: a barbershop, a café and restaurant, a well-groomed park and playground, a community garden, a gymnasium, and a communal lounge with free Wi-Fi, all of which would be open to police officers and citizens alike. In places with more land available, Gang's designs include police housing, libraries and computer labs, counseling centers, and places of worship as well. The scope of the pilot project in North Lawndale was far more limited. Gang had only a portion of a parking lot to play with, and after listening to the people who lived in the area, she and her team decided to transform it into a basketball court, set off from the street by a line of trees and a handsome black metal fence. It's a modest but successful project. The court, painted green with an orange key, is well maintained, with features like a smooth surface and an intact net that are hard to find on the dangerous and dilapidated playgrounds nearby.

The station house basketball court is far from the most popular hangout in North Lawndale, but it's a place that local youths use often, and each time they visit, the officers who work there become a little more familiar, a little less threatening. Hopefully, the proximity will have the same effect on police officers too. Chicago has not yet committed to developing any larger Polis Station projects, yet other cities, including Baltimore, where Gang redesigned the aquarium, are interested in experimenting with a more expansive version of the concept, and New York City is discussing ways to do something similar with fire stations. As in Chicago, civic leaders in these municipalities recognize that architecture alone will not resolve the roiling conflicts between the police and people of color. But it's hard not to believe that turning station houses into social infrastructures would be a productive first step.

The president of the United States has pledged to rebuild the nation's infrastructure, and he's left no question about his preferred first step: a wall. There's no simpler design idea, nothing easier to erect. But a wall is both symbol and agent of the very divisiveness that weakens us. And, as many of the political officials who are deeply concerned about illegal border migration argue, it doesn't even work.

Building walls is as unwise for climate policy as it is for immigration, but unfortunately, the recent spike in deadly and expensive megastorms like Sandy, Harvey, Irma, and Maria has inspired calls for crude coastal defenses that aim to keep the water out. It's true that, in some places, the irreversible threat of rising seas and towering storm surges requires protecting vulnerable people and places from inundation. But walls, as Kate Orff and the team that designed Living Breakwaters for Staten Island understood, can generate just as many problems as they prevent. They create a false sense of security among those who live beyond them, and when they fail—as the levees did in Hurricane Katrina, and the storm walls did in Superstorm Sandy—few are ready for the deluge. Worse, sea gates and barriers are limited tools that cannot be deployed in every area threatened by global warming. They're prohibitively expensive in most places, and often futile. No matter how much we invest in efforts to block out the sea and its tributaries, we will, inevitably, leave most of humanity exposed to the elements.

In the densely populated, richly developed places where walls are necessary—including cities like London, New Orleans, Rotterdam, and Venice—policy makers and engineers are beginning to understand that they're by no means sufficient for climate resilience. That's why Bjarke Ingels and the group that proposed the East Side Coastal Resiliency Project for Lower Manhattan rejected conventional designs for riverfront barriers and invented "bridging berms" and parklands that bring people together as effectively as they keep the water out. Like the Polis Station, it's a radical concept: a wall that includes rather than excludes, by inviting diverse communities into a shared social space. Ingels's design is an infrastructure that is at once hard and soft, social and physical, meant to improve life for everyone, every day, and also to protect against the deluge that all of us fear.

Unfortunately, building hard and social infrastructure for climate security is extraordinarily expensive, and most of the people and places that are already being threatened by global warming lack the resources that cities like New York, London, and Rotterdam have at their disposal. Without substantial financial assistance from the wealthy nations whose consumption has induced climate change, far more than they agreed to give under the landmark Paris Agreement of 2016, poor and developing societies will remain vulnerable to the lethal storms on the way. Today, this degree of financial investment seems unlikely, but if it doesn't happen soon environmental inequalities will grow deeper and more consequential. The injustice will spark anger and outrage that, like the changing climate and treacherous weather, may well prove impossible to contain.

For now, at least, we can still control our destiny, and the infrastructure we build will help determine how long that power lasts. Infrastructures, as the eminent Princeton engineer David

Billington writes, have a way of symbolizing historic periods and expressing dominant ideas about how to organize economy and society. Our railroads, highways, parks, and power grids reveal who we were and what we aspired to become at the time that we built them. The systems we build in coming years will tell future generations who we are and how we see the world today. If we fail to bridge our gaping social divisions, they may even determine whether that "we" continues to exist.

Today, nations around the world are poised to spend trillions of dollars on vital infrastructure projects that we need to get through the twenty-first century and beyond. In the coming decades, as the systems we rely on to support modern life become outdated and dysfunctional, the United States will have no choice but to invest hundreds of billions of dollars in new projects. In the decades after, it will spend even more. Before we lift the next shovel, we should know what we want to improve, what we need to protect, and, more important, what kind of society we want to create.

Political officials often claim that infrastructure projects are too technical for citizens and civic groups to understand, let alone debate meaningfully in a democratic forum. They ask that we trust engineers and experts to manage things, which ultimately means letting authority flow from the top down. But no president or cabinet member should have the power to make unilateral decisions about how to rebuild the critical systems that sustain us, and history shows that when this happens people rarely get what they want. What we need, now more than ever, is an inclusive conversation about the kinds of infrastructure—physical as well as social—that would best serve, sustain, and protect us. We need a democratic process that, like Rebuild by Design, solicits the active participation of people and communities whose lives will be affected by the projects our public dollars will support, one that respects local knowledge and wisdom as well as technical expertise.

Rebuilding the infrastructure that can help solve the wicked problems unfolding before us requires harnessing all kinds of collective intelligence about the emerging vulnerabilities and possibilities in different cities and regions. We need smart civil engineering to fix the critical networks that are failing, no doubt, but we also need to engineer civility in societies—including our own—that are at risk of breaking apart. It's an enormous undertaking, and, given our current conflicts and fissures, it's going to be a long-term project. But we cannot put it off any longer. The question is when and where we will begin.

ACKNOWLEDGMENTS

It's been more than fifteen years since I moved out of Chicago, but I attribute my interest in social infrastructure to the experience of growing up and, later, doing immersive fieldwork in a great city of neighborhoods. My childhood home in Old Town was directly across the street from the original Menomonee Club, a nonprofit community organization that offered daily after-school programs at virtually no cost. Old Town was gentrifying during the 1970s and 1980s. The neighborhood, which was adjacent to both the opulent Gold Coast and the impoverished Cabrini-Green housing projects, was a site of conflict and occasional violence. I spent several afternoons per week at both the club and the local park where its charismatic director, Basil Kane, taught soccer to a diverse if not especially talented group of city kids. For years I took for granted all the things I learned in this special community center. Now I understand how much it shaped me.

If the ideas for this book come from Chicago, they developed in New York City, and particularly at New York University. Since 2012, I've had the great privilege of directing NYU's Institute for Public Knowledge, which is as real a community as any I've known in the academy, and a rare place where scholars are rewarded for engaging in civic life. I thank Craig Calhoun, IPK's founding director, for creating such a special environment and entrusting me with its future; Katy Fleming, the provost, and Cybele Raver, the senior vice provost, for supporting it; and Jessica Coffey, Siera Dissmore, and Gordon Douglas for sustaining it. I've also been fortunate to work with a wonderful group of IPK fellows and students, including Hillary Angelo, Max Besbris, Daniel Aldana Cohen, David Grazian, Max Holleran, Liz Koslov, Caitlin Petre, Eyal Press, Alix Rule, Malkit Shosan, and Matthew Wolfe. All of them contributed to this project.

So too did my collaborators in the Rebuild by Design competition. I thank Henk Ovink, our visionary principal; Amy Chester, our indomitable managing director; Tara Eisenberg, Lynn Englum, Juliet Gore, Idan Sasson, and Raka Sen, from the RBD staff; and Judith Rodin, Nancy Kete, and Sam Carter at the Rockefeller Foundation, our major funder. I'm equally grateful to the architects, engineers, scientists, and designers whose brilliant ideas for mitigating and adapting to climate change remain sources of inspiration. Among the many whose work taught me what we can do with infrastructure, and what infrastructure can do for us, are Matthijs Bouw, Pippa Brashear, Bjarke Ingels, Klaus Jacob, Ellen Neises, Kate Orff, Richard Roark, Laura Starr, Marilyn Taylor, David Waggonner, Claire Weisz, and Gena Werth.

I owe a special debt to Carrie Welch and the staff of the New York Public Library, who always kept their doors open and allowed me to camp out in the Seward Park branch far longer than even the most dedicated patron.

I wrote most of this book in one of academia's sacred spaces: Stanford University's Center for Advanced Study in the Behavioral Sciences. As a social infrastructure, CASBS has just about everything, including private writing studios, seminar rooms, miles of walking paths, bottomless cups of Peet's Coffee, and dining tables where the conversation has been nourishing important books in the social sciences for more than sixty years. I thank the Hewlett Foundation for helping to support my fellowship; Margaret Levi, the brilliant director who has rebuilt CASBS for the twenty-first century; and her dynamic staff. I'm grateful for the intellectual companionship of the 2016–17 fellows, including Brooke Blower, Ruth Chang, Mark Greif, Andrew Lakoff, Deborah Lawrence, Terry Maroney, Allison Pugh, Jack Rakove, Jesse Ribot, Brenda Stevenson, and Barry Zuckerman. I'm lucky to have spent a year in their presence.

I'm also lucky to have met Julie Sandorf, president of the Charles H. Revson Foundation and a fierce champion of public libraries. In early 2016, Julie came to IPK and pitched a small, collaborative project on the state of New York City's branch libraries. I raised the bid, and came back to the foundation with a proposal for what ultimately became a wide-ranging project on libraries, social infrastructure, and civic life. Julie and her team have been all in ever since, and I thank them for their tremendous support.

I'm humbled by the generosity of family, friends, and colleagues who took time to read and comment on drafts of this manuscript. Thanks to Gabriel Abend, Sasha Abramsky, Hillary Angelo, Aziz Ansari, Eric Bates, Craig Calhoun, Daniel Aldana Cohen, Andrew Deener, Shamus Khan, Andrew Lakoff, Margaret Levi, Sharon Marcus, Harvey Molotch, Eyal Press, Patrick Sharkey, Rona Talcott, Iddo Tavory, Fred Turner, and Matt Wray.

I owe a special debt to my research assistants from NYU, especially Delaram Takyar, who collaborated on all aspects of this project, and Matt Wolfe, who helped with the sections on social isolation and opioid addiction. After I finished writing, Delaram, who's now studying law and social science, and Matt, who's a sociologist as well as a journalist, teamed up to fact-check the entire document. I can't say I enjoyed that process, but Delaram and Matt saved me from writing things I'd later regret. I hope more social scientists subject their work to such scrutiny; it pays. Kiara Douds, a Houston native, joined Delaram on a trip home immediately after Hurricane Harvey. She connected us with the community at Wilcrest Baptist Church so we could track their emergency relief efforts. Liz Koslov, Xiang Lu, and Katie Donnelly spent countless days observing the social life of neighborhood libraries. I couldn't have written this book without their hard work.

The same is true of the team at Crown Publishing. Amanda Cook, my ace editor, began helping me see the potential in this book the moment she read the proposal and didn't stop offering smart, incisive suggestions until the day we went to press. What a privilege it has been to work with her, and what a pleasure it is to collaborate with someone who often understands your ideas better than you do yourself. Zachary Phillips and Emma Berry pitched in with helpful editorial feedback throughout the process. Maureen Clark gave the manuscript a brilliant polish. Molly Stern's enthusiasm helped me through the final push. I couldn't ask for more from a publishing group. Thank you.

Tina Bennett and her assistant, Svetlana Katz, have always delivered more than I could ask for from literary agents. They're the best in the business, and I'm lucky they're in my corner, wherever I go.

It's a good thing that my parents, Rona Talcott and Edward Klinenberg, their spouses, Owen Deutsch and Anne McCune, and my mother-in-law, Carolyn Grey, love spending time with their grandchildren. I'm grateful for the endless support they offered while I worked on this book project. And I know that, now that it's finished, the kids will still rather hang out with them.

Kate Zaloom somehow manages to make time for all of us, and to help me think through all things worth discussing, including each idea in this book. Kate has always had a dazzling mind, but since she launched *Public Books* a few years ago, she's also developed a brilliant editor's eye. Spending my life with Kate makes everything I do better.

So too does spending time with my children, Lila and Cyrus, for whom my love knows no limits. I dedicate this book to them. They deserve a better world, and there's nothing I want more than to help them build one.

We can only do it together.

NOTES

INTRODUCTION: THE SOCIAL INFRASTRUCTURE

1 **"think cool thoughts":** The quotes here are from Eric Klinenberg, *Heat Wave: A Social Autopsy of Disaster in Chicago* (Chicago: University of Chicago Press, 2002).

2 **"We're overwhelmed":** The quote is from Dirk Johnson, "Heat Wave: The Nation; In Chicago, Week of Swelter Leaves an Overflowing Morgue," *New York Times,* July 17, 1995.

5 **dozens of articles:** James House, Karl Landis, and Debra Umberson, "Social Relationships and Health," *Science* 241, no. 4865 (1988): 540–45.

8 **they already believe:** The quotes in here are from Emanuela Campanella, "We All Live in a Bubble. Here's Why You Step Out of It, According to Experts," *Global News,* February 4, 2017, https://globalnews.ca/news/3225274/we-all-live-in-a-bubble-heres-why-you-step-out-of-it-according-to-experts/; Sreeram Chaulia, "Why India Is So Unhappy, and How It Can Change," *TODAYonline,* April 3, 2017, https://www.todayonline.com/commentary/why-india-so-unhappy-and-how-it-can-change; "Class Segregation 'on the Rise,' " *BBC News,* September 8, 2007, http://news.bbc.co.uk/2/hi/uk_news/6984707.stm; Rachel Lu, "China's New Class Hierarchy: A Guide," *Foreign Policy,* April 25, 2014, https://foreignpolicy.com/2014/04/25/chinas-new-class-hierarchy-a-guide/; "Private Firms Filling Latin America's Security Gap," *Associated Press Mail Online,* November 24, 2014, http://www.dailymail.co.uk/wires/ap/article-2847721/Private-firms-filling-Latin-Americas-security-gap.htm.

10 **soaring urban condominium towers:** Martin Filler, "New York: Conspicuous Construction," *New York Review of Books,* April 2, 2015.

10 **prepare for civilization's end:** Evan Osnos, "Doomsday Prep for the Super-Rich," *New Yorker,* January 30, 2017.

12 **"and its home is the neighborly community":** John Dewey, *The Public and Its Problems* (1927; repr., University Park: Pennsylvania State University Press, 2012), 157.

12 **"Everything that makes America exceptional":** Charles Murray, *Coming Apart: The State of White America, 1960–2010* (New York: Crown Forum, 2012), 12, 22, 283.

13 **fairly steady since the 1970s:** Peter Marsden, ed., *Social Trends in American Life* (Princeton, NJ: Princeton University Press, 2012).

13 **"across persons of all levels of educational attainment":** On the decline of volunteering, see the Bureau of Labor Statistics, "Volunteering in the United States, 2015," https://www.bls.gov/news .release/volun.nr0.htm.

13 **alienation from public life:** Claude Fischer, *Still Connected: Family and Friends in America Since 1970* (New York: Russell Sage Foundation, 2011), 93.

14 **"It is by definition invisible":** Susan Leigh Star, "The Ethnography of Infrastructure," *American Behavioral Scientist* 43, no. 3 (1999): 380–82.

15 **"allows a people to choose their own way":** Ashley Carse, "Keyword: Infrastructure—How a Humble French Engineering Term Shaped the Modern World," in *Infrastructures and Social Complexity: A Companion,* ed. Penny Harvey, Casper Bruun Jensen, and Atsuro Morita (London: Routledge, 2016).

16 **produce the material foundations for social life:** The classic text about how small businesses and commercial operators shape daily social life is Jane Jacobs's *The Death and Life of Great American Cities* (New York: Vintage, 1961). In recent years, the eminent sociologist Elijah Anderson has been writing about what he calls "the cosmopolitan canopy," places where people from different backgrounds "not only share space but seek out each other's presence," and occasionally forge relationships as well. Anderson has conducted ethnographic fieldwork in several exemplary sites of cross-group interaction, including Philadelphia's Reading Terminal Market and Rittenhouse Square, as well as in places marked by surveillance, suspicion, and social segregation. See Elijah Ander-

son, *The Cosmopolitan Canopy: Race and Civility in Everyday Life* (New York: W. W. Norton, 2011).

17 **"A levee":** Marshall Brain and Robert Lamb, "What Is a Levee?," https://science.howstuffworks.com/engineering/structural/levee .htm.

18 **quickly return to their private lives:** Mario Small, *Unanticipated Gains: Origins of Network Inequality in Everyday Life* (New York: Oxford University Press, 2009).

19 **largest and most heterogeneous public space:** Stéphane Tonnelat and William Kornblum, *International Express: New Yorkers on the 7 Train* (New York: Columbia University Press, 2017).

20 **"participator rather than spectator":** MassObservation, *The Pub and the People* (1943; repr., London: Cresset Library, 1987), 17.

20 **people in public can feel like they're at home:** Ray Oldenburg, *The Great Good Place: Cafés, Coffee Shops, Bookstores, Bars, Hair Salons and Other Hangouts at the Heart of a Community* (Cambridge, MA: Da Capo Press, 1989).

22 **the air that pedestrians breathe a little cleaner:** See Vanessa Quirk, "The 4 Coolest 'High Line' Inspired Projects," *ArchDaily,* July 16, 2012, https://www.archdaily.com/254447/the-4-coolest -high-line-inspired-projects.

23 **an unrelated concern:** Several recent books champion infrastructure investment, including Rosabeth Moss Kanter's *Move: How to Rebuild and Reinvent America's Infrastructure* (New York: W. W. Norton, 2016), Henry Petroski's *The Road Taken* (New York: Bloomsbury, 2016), and Gretchen Bakke's *The Grid* (New York: Bloomsbury, 2016); yet none call attention to the value of social infrastructure.

24 **"palaces for the people":** Not long after Andrew Carnegie began investing in libraries, Joseph Stalin started his own campaign to build "palaces for the people" in Russia. The most significant legacy of this project is a set of magnificent subway stations in Moscow, each decorated with marble, grand chandeliers, mosaics, and sculptures, as well as a number of housing complexes and social clubs for Soviet workers.

CHAPTER ONE: A PLACE TO GATHER

26 **strong incentives to stay away:** A study by New York University's Rudin Center for Transportation ranks East New York last

in Brooklyn for public transit access to jobs within one hour, and among the worst in all of New York City. See Sarah Kaufman, Mitchell Moss, Jorge Hernandez, and Justin Tyndall, "Mobility, Economic Opportunity and New York City Neighborhoods," November 2015, https://wagner.nyu.edu/files/faculty/publications /JobAccessNov2015.pdf.

26 **studies of isolation have found as well:** See Neal Krause, "Neighborhood Deterioration and Social Isolation in Later Life," *International Journal of Aging and Human Development* 36, no. 1 (1993): 9–38.

28 **they lack compelling places to go:** For the demographic data on aging, see Administration on Aging, *A Profile of Older Americans, 2015,* https://www.acl.gov/sites/default/files/Aging%20and% 20Disability%20in%20America/2015-Profile.pdf/; and Renee Stepler, "Smaller Share of Women Ages 65 and Older Are Living Alone," Pew Research Center, February 18, 2016, http://www.pewsocial trends.org/2016/02/18/smaller-share-of-women-ages-65-and -older-are-living-alone/. On the historic rise of older people who live alone, see Eric Klinenberg, *Going Solo: The Extraordinary Rise and Surprising Appeal of Living Alone* (New York: Penguin Press, 2012).

32 **health hazards, including obesity and smoking:** See Lisa Berkman and Thomas Glass, "Social Integration, Social Networks, Social Support, and Health," in *Social Epidemiology,* ed. Lisa Berkman and Ichiro Kawachi (New York: Oxford University Press, 2000), 137–73, and John Cacioppo and William Patrick, *Loneliness: Human Nature and the Need for Social Connection* (New York: W. W. Norton, 2008).

32 **social infrastructure that we have:** It's worth noting that Robert Putnam includes a chapter on branch libraries in a coauthored book about people and organizations that are creating social capital. See Robert Putnam and Lewis Feldstein, with Don Cohen, *Better Together: Restoring the American Community* (New York: Simon & Schuster, 2003).

33 **"major impact on their community":** See John Horrigan, "Libraries 2016," Pew Research Center, September 9, 2016, http://www .pewinternet.org/2016/09/09/libraries-2016/.

33 **number of hours that people spend in libraries is up too:** The data on library usage come from David Giles, *Branches of Opportunity,* Center for an Urban Future, January 2013, https://nycfuture .org/pdf/Branches_of_Opportunity.pdf. Giles reports that between

2002 and 2011, New York City library program attendance was up 40 percent and program sessions were up 27 percent.

33 **San Francisco Public Library:** Ibid.

33 **"and first responders":** The Pew report is quoted in Wayne Wiegand, *Part of Our Lives: A People's History of the American Public Library* (New York: Oxford University Press, 2015), 1.

39 **"are also spaces for interaction":** Mario Small, *Unanticipated Gains: Origins of Network Inequality in Everyday Life* (New York: Oxford University Press, 2009), 115–16.

40 **sense of where we belong:** On the school as a social institution, see John Dewey, *The School and Society* (1900; repr., Chicago: University of Chicago Press, 2013), and *The Child and the Curriculum* (1902; repr., Chicago: University of Chicago Press, 2013), and Anthony Bryk and Mary Erina, *The High School as Community: Contextual Influences and Consequences for Teachers and Students* (Madison, WI: National Center of Effective Secondary Schools, 1988).

41 **affect child development far more than parents do:** See, for instance, Judith Rich Harris, "Where Is the Child's Environment? A Group Socialization Theory of Development," *Psychological Review* 102, no. 3 (1995): 458–89.

41 **search for and find their spouse:** John Cacioppo et al., "Marital Satisfaction and Break-ups Differ Across On-line and Off-line Meeting Venues," *Proceedings of the National Academy of Sciences* 110, no. 25 (2013): 10135–40.

41 **more isolated than ever:** In a May 2012 *Atlantic* cover story, "Is Facebook Making Us Lonely?," Stephen Marche offers an unusually extreme claim about the state of our disunion: "We suffer from unprecedented alienation," he writes. "We have never been more detached from one another, or lonelier. In a world consumed by ever more novel modes of socializing, we have less and less actual society. We live in an accelerating contradiction: the more connected we become, the lonelier we are."

41 **before the Internet existed:** Claude Fischer, *Still Connected: Family and Friends in America Since 1970* (New York: Russell Sage Foundation, 2011).

42 **diversity of people's personal networks:** Keith Hampton, Lauren Sessions, and Eun Ja Her, "Core Networks, Social Isolation, and New Media," *Information, Communication, and Society* 14, no. 1 (2011): 130–55.

42 **"continue throughout life"**: Sherry Turkle, *Reclaiming Conversation: The Power of Talk in a Digital Age* (New York: Penguin Press, 2015), 3.

43 **"physically stuck at home"**: danah boyd, *It's Complicated: The Social Lives of Networked Teens* (New Haven, CT: Yale University Press, 2014), 21.

CHAPTER TWO: SAFE SPACES

55 **American public housing:** The classic sociological account of Pruitt-Igoe is Lee Rainwater, *Behind Ghetto Walls: Black Families in a Federal Slum* (New Brunswick, NJ: AldineTransaction, 1970). According to Rainwater, "Pruitt-Igoe condenses into one 57-acre tract all of the problems and difficulties that arise from race and poverty and all of the impotence, indifference and hostility with which our society has so far dealt with these problems" (3).

56 **90 percent of all units were occupied:** The occupancy rate of 91 percent in 1957 is reported in Roger Montgomery, "Pruitt-Igoe: Policy Failure or Societal Symptom," in *The Metropolitan Midwest: Policy Problems and Prospects for Change*, ed. Barry Checkoway and Carl Patton (Champaign: University of Illinois Press, 1985), 229–43.

56 **"The corridors, lobbies, elevators, and stairs were dangerous":** Oscar Newman, *Creating Defensible Space* (Washington, DC: US Department of Housing and Urban Development, Office of Policy Development and Research, 1996), 10.

56 **occupancy rate was 35 percent:** Colin Marshall, "Pruitt-Igoe: The Troubled High-Rise That Came to Define Urban America," *Guardian*, April 22, 2015.

56 **"Walking through Pruitt-Igoe":** Newman, *Creating Defensible Space*, 11.

57 **"neat and well maintained":** Ibid.

57 **"Across the street from Pruitt-Igoe":** Ibid.

57 **"eyes on street":** Jane Jacobs, *The Death and Life of Great American Cities* (New York: Vintage, 1961), 35.

57 **"With social variables constant":** Newman, *Creating Defensible Space*, 11.

58 **"an accord about acceptable behavior":** Ibid., 25, 11–12.

58 **1972 report, *Defensible Space*:** The report was not limited to St. Louis. In New York City, Newman found that residents of a low-

rise public housing complex in Brownsville experienced 34 percent fewer overall crimes and 74 percent fewer indoor crimes than their neighbors in the nearby high-rise Van Dyke projects. He attributed this difference solely to architecture, but subsequent research shows that the families who lived in the two projects were not at all identical. The Van Dyke complex had far more single mothers with multiple children, which meant there were more unsupervised young people, an established risk factor for crime. See Fritz Umbach and Alexander Gerould, "Myth #3: Public Housing Breeds Crime," in *Public Housing Myths: Perception, Reality, and Social Policy*, ed. Nicholas Dagen Bloom, Fritz Umbach, and Lawrence Vale (Ithaca, NY: Cornell University Press, 2015), 64–90.

59 **"is the real and final villain":** Oscar Newman, *Defensible Space* (New York: Macmillan, 1972), 25.

59 **"environment where crimes occur":** C. Ray Jeffery, *Crime Prevention Through Environmental Design* (Beverly Hills, CA: Sage Publications, 1971), 177, 19.

60 **"to curb crime":** John MacDonald, "Community Design and Crime: The Impact of the Built Environment," *Crime and Justice* 44, no. 1 (2015): 333–383.

61 **"That muggings will occur":** James Q. Wilson and George Kelling, "Broken Windows," *Atlantic*, March 1982.

61 **"the blueprint for community policing":** Quoted in Bernard Harcourt, *Illusion of Order: The False Promise of Broken Windows Policing* (Cambridge, MA: Harvard University Press, 2001), 3.

61 **"If you take care of the little things":** Joseph Goldstein, "Street Stops Still a 'Basic Tool,' Bratton Says," *New York Times*, March 4, 2014.

61 **a work of empirical science:** In one fascinating study, a team of Dutch social scientists led by Kees Keizer conducted a series of experiments to test whether adding graffiti and litter to a small urban place would lead to more rule breaking. Although, as they concede, "so far there has not been strong empirical support" for the broken windows theory, signs of disorder did lead to more criminal behavior in their experiments. They have called for more research to test the broken windows effect in other sites, but it's not easy to get permission to create disorder in real places, and to date we still have only weak evidence that the theory holds. See Kees Keizer, Siegwart Lindenberg, and Linda Steg, "The Spreading of Disorder," *Science* 322, no. 5908 (2008): 1681–85.

61 **"the theory is probably not right":** Harcourt, *Illusion of Order,* 8.

62 **with the policies it inspired:** See Robert J. Sampson and Stephen W. Raudenbush, "Seeing Disorder: Neighborhood Stigma and the Social Construction of 'Broken Windows,'" *Social Psychology Quarterly* 67, no. 4 (2004): 319–42, and Franklin Zimring, *The City That Became Safe: New York's Lessons for Urban Crime and Its Control* (New York: Oxford University Press, 2012).

62 **"Pedestrians are approached by panhandlers":** Wilson and Kelling, "Broken Windows."

63 **two hundred more are injured:** See Kevin Quealy and Margot Sanger-Katz, "Comparing Gun Deaths by Country: The U.S. Is in a Different World," *New York Times,* June 13, 2016. For useful synopses of the data on gun violence, see https://everytownresearch.org /gun-violence-by-the-numbers/#DailyDeaths.

64 **Kees Keizer in the Netherlands:** Keizer, Lindenberg, and Steg, "The Spreading of Disorder."

65 **high-poverty and extreme-poverty areas:** William Spelman, "Abandoned Buildings: Magnets for Crime?," *Journal of Criminal Justice* 21, no. 5 (1993): 481–95, and Lance Hannon, "Extremely Poor Neighborhoods and Homicide," *Social Science Quarterly* 86, no. S1 (2005): 1418–34. Both articles are summarized in John MacDonald, "Community Design and Crime: The Impact of Housing and the Built Environment," *Crime and Justice* 44, no. 1 (2015): 333–83.

65 **two natural experiments in Philadelphia:** Charles Branas, Michelle Kondo, Sean Murphy, Eugenia South, Daniel Polsky, and John MacDonald, "Urban Blight Remediation as a Cost-Beneficial Solution to Firearm Violence," *American Journal of Public Health* 106, no. 12 (2016): 2158–64.

69 **grass if the police drive by:** Branas and his colleagues hypothesize that the utility of abandoned property for those hiding guns is why the remediation project reduced gun-related homicides but not other violent crimes; see ibid.

69 **other crime reduction programs:** Ibid.

70 **"are exposed on a daily basis":** Ibid., 2163.

70 **"for every dollar invested":** Ibid., 2162.

71 **"a 10% reduction in homicides":** Ciro Biderman, João M. P. De Mello, and Alexandre Schneider, "Dry Laws and Homicides: Evidence from the São Paulo Metropolitan Area," *Economic Journal* 120, no. 543 (2010): 157–82.

72 **"individuals under the age of 18":** World Bank, *Making Brazilians Safer: Analyzing the Dynamics of Violent Crime*, 78, http://documents.worldbank.org/curated/en/252761468015010162/pdf/707640ESW0REVI0ics0of0Violent0Crime.pdf.

72 **São Paulo's great crime drop:** Ibid., chap. 3.

73 **"from those considered dangerous":** Teresa Caldeira, *City of Walls: Crime, Segregation, and Citizenship in São Paulo* (Berkeley: University of California Press, 2000), 1–2.

73 **luxurious residential developments:** Karina Landman, "Gated Communities in South Africa: The Challenge for Spatial Planning and Land Use Management," *Town Planning Review* 75, no. 2 (2004): 158–59.

74 **"Many people object to a restriction of access":** Ibid., 162.

74 **"demanded full citizenship":** João Costa Vargas, "When a Favela Dared to Become a Gated Condominium: The Politics of Race and Urban Space in Rio de Janeiro," *Latin American Perspectives* 33, no. 4 (2006): 49–81.

75 **imperil local residents:** See Vincent Carroll, "The Mindless Roasting of ink!," *Denver Post*, December 1, 2017, https://www.denverpost.com/2017/12/01/unfair-roasting-of-ink-coffee-for-gentrification-sign/.

76 **remain in their broiling homes:** My finding on the protective effects of commercial density during the heat wave came from observational research, but was subsequently verified by a quantitative study. See Christopher Browning, Danielle Wallace, Seth Feinberg, and Kathleen Cagney, "Neighborhood Social Processes, Physical Conditions, and Disaster-Related Mortality: The Case of the 1995 Chicago Heat Wave," *American Sociological Review* 71, no. 4 (2006): 661–78.

76 **restrict their development:** Shlomo Angel, "Discouraging Crime Through City Planning," Working Paper 75, Institute of Urban and Regional Development, University of California, Berkeley, 1968.

76 **more protective than Angel realized:** The criminologist James Wo, for instance, studied the long-term impact of retail outlets on neighborhood crime rates and found that while alcohol-related shops and banks led to more crime, "third places," such as coffee shops and restaurants, made places safer. James Wo, "Community Context of Crime: A Longitudinal Examination of the Effects of Local Institutions on Neighborhood Crime," *Crime & Delinquency* 62, no. 10 (2016): 1286–312.

77 **informal surveillance to deter crime:** Andrew Papachristos, Chris Smith, Mary Scherer, and Melissa Fugiero, "More Coffee, Less Crime? The Relationship Between Gentrification and Neighborhood Crime Rates in Chicago, 1991 to 2005," *City & Community* 10, no. 3 (2011): 215–40.

78 **feels at home:** The quotes about the ink! controversy are from Jean Lotus, "Gentrification Gaffe: Denver Coffee Shop and Ad Agency Apologize," *Denver Patch*, November 25, 2017, https://patch.com /colorado/denver/gentrification-gaffe-denver-coffee-shop-ad -agency-apologize/.

78 **"displacement of Cabrini residents":** Papachristos et al., "More Coffee, Less Crime?," 228–29.

79 **high-poverty residential development:** The research of Kuo and Sullivan, along with many other studies that document the health benefits of nature, is nicely summarized in Florence Williams, *The Nature Fix: Why Nature Makes Us Happier, Healthier, and More Creative* (New York: W. W. Norton, 2017).

80 **building height, and vacancy rates:** Frances Kuo and William Sullivan, "Environment and Crime in the Inner City: Does Vegetation Reduce Crime?," *Environment and Behavior* 33, no. 3 (2001): 343–67.

80 **feelings of ownership and control:** In a paper cowritten with Rebekah Levine Coley, Sullivan and Kuo argue that the lack of green spaces can mean diminished opportunities for social interaction. Using observational data from trees and vegetation at both Ida B. Wells and the Robert Taylor Homes, they find that people are more likely to be present in outdoor areas with trees than in those without trees, concluding that natural elements in outdoor spaces can draw people outdoors and make them feel more ownership over their surroundings. Rebekah Levine Coley, William Sullivan, and Frances Kuo, "Where Does Community Grow?: The Social Context Created by Nature in Urban Public Housing," *Environment and Behavior* 29, no. 4 (1997): 468–94.

CHAPTER THREE: LEARNING TOGETHER

88 **"solve every one of these critical issues":** Deborah Meier, "In Education, Small Is Sensible," *New York Times*, September 8, 1989.

88 **"violence or other antisocial behavior":** Ibid.

89 **graduation rate reached 80 percent:** Julie Bosman, "Small Schools Are Ahead in Graduation," *New York Times*, June 30, 2007.

90 **his book *Small Victories*:** Samuel Freedman, *Small Victories: The Real World of a Teacher, Her Students, and Their High School* (New York: Harper & Row, 1990).

90 **"Are you ashamed to go to Seward?":** Ibid., 20.

90 **"a security guard said":** InsideSchools, "Seward Park Educational Campus," October 2011, https://new.insideschools.org/component /schools/school/93.

91 **feelings about the school climate:** See National Education Association, "Research Talking Points on Small Schools," http://www.nea .org/home/13639.htm; Jonathan Supovitz and Jolley Bruce Christman, "Small Learning Communities That Actually Learn: Lessons for School Leaders," *Phi Delta Kappan* 86, no. 9 (2005): 649–51; and Craig Howley, Marty Strange, and Robert Bickel, "Research About School Size and School Performance in Impoverished Communities," ERIC Digest (Charleston, WV: ERIC Clearinghouse on Rural Education and Small Schools, December 2000).

91 **attend selective universities:** The MDRC research on small schools is summarized in the report "Frequently Asked Questions About MDRC's Study of Small Public High Schools in New York City," October 2014, https://www.mdrc.org/publication/frequently-asked -questions-about-mdrc-s-study-small-public-high-schools-new-york -city.

92 **"diversity in discourse and vision":** Richard Dober, *Campus Design* (New York: John Wiley & Sons, 1992), 280, 8. Dober viewed higher education as "the common ground for acculturation" in contemporary societies, and in recent years universities have grown more central. Today, more than 20.4 million students (roughly 7.3 million in two-year schools and 13.4 million in four-year schools), totaling about 6 percent of the US population, enroll in American universities each academic year; more than 2 million, or 3.5 percent of the population, attend universities in the United Kingdom; and about 1.7 million, or 5 percent of the population, go to college in Canada. Their experiences are usually consequential, and often pivotal. For US college enrollments, see the report *Fast Facts* from the National Center for Education Statistics, https://nces.ed.gov/fast facts/display.asp?id=372. For the United Kingdom, see http://www .universitiesuk.ac.uk/policy-and-analysis/reports/Documents /2014/patterns-and-trends-in-uk-higher-education-2014.pdf. For Canada, see http://www.univcan.ca/universities/facts-and-stats/.

92 **otherwise never form families together:** See Michael Rosenfeld, *The Age of Independence: Interracial Unions, Same-Sex Unions, and*

the Changing American Family (Cambridge, MA: Harvard University Press, 2007).

92 **the Stanford professor Paul Turner recounts that the first universities:** Paul Venable Turner, *Campus: An American Planning Tradition* (Cambridge, MA: MIT Press, 1984), 9–10.

94 **"world outside the college":** Ibid., 12.

94 **"the distractions of civilizations":** Ibid., 17.

94 **"many spirited resolves":** Ibid., 47. Surprisingly, Turner writes, in addition to their goal of teaching future leaders from settler families, the first colleges were often "motivated by the goal of training Indians for missionary work" (18).

96 **parties and social events:** See Jordan Friedman, "11 Colleges Where the Most Students Join Fraternities," *US News & World Report,* October 25, 2016, https://www.usnews.com/education/best -colleges/the-short-list-college/articles/2016-10-25/11-colleges -where-the-most-students-join-fraternities.

97 **sleep deprivation, and sex acts:** Elizabeth Allan and Mary Madden, *Hazing in View: College Students at Risk,* March 11, 2008, https://www.stophazing.org/wp-content/uploads/2014/06/hazing _in_view_web1.pdf.

97 **Northern Illinois University, and Fresno State:** See John Hechinger and David Glovin, "Deadliest Frat's Icy 'Torture' of Pledges Evokes Tarantino Films," Bloomberg News, December 30, 2013, https://www.bloomberg.com/news/articles/2013-12-30/deadliest -frat-s-icy-torture-of-pledges-evokes-tarantino-films. Also see Richard Pérez-Peña and Sheryl Gay Stolberg,"Prosecutors Taking Tougher Stance in Fraternity Hazing Deaths," *New York Times,* May 8, 2017, https://www.nytimes.com/2017/05/08/us/penn-state -prosecutors-fraternity-hazing-deaths.html.

97 **perpetrate sexual assault than those who are not:** See Catherine Loh, Christine Gidycz, Tracy Lobo, and Rohini Luthra, "A Prospective Analysis of Sexual Assault Perpetration: Risk Factors Related to Perpetrator Characteristics," *Journal of Interpersonal Violence* 20 (2005): 1325–48, and Leandra Lackie and Anton de Man, "Correlates of Sexual Aggression Among Male University Students," *Sex Roles* 37, no. 5 (1997): 451–57.

97 **controlling for background factors:** Jeffrey DeSimone, "Fraternity Membership and Binge Drinking," *Journal of Health Economics* 26, no. 5 (2007): 950–67.

98 **"secrecy and self-protection":** Lisa Wade, "Why Colleges Should Get Rid of Fraternities for Good," *Time*, May 19, 2017, http://time .com/4784875/fraternities-timothy-piazza/.

98 **perceived as dangerous:** A recent academic study found that many of America's most famous university towns—including Berkeley, Chapel Hill, Ann Arbor, and Evanston—top the nation's list of communities with wide racial achievement gaps. See Sean Reardon, Demetra Kalogrides, and Ken Shores, "The Geography of Racial/Ethnic Test Score Gaps," CEPA Working Paper No. 16-10, Center for Education Policy Analysis, Stanford University, 2017.

100 **"and rebuild our neighborhood":** Arnold Hirsch, *Making the Second Ghetto: Race and Housing in Chicago, 1940–1960* (1983; repr., Chicago: University of Chicago Press, 2009), 147.

100 **they'd be targets of crime:** For a firsthand report on the experience of being told not to cross out of the university's safe space, see Loïc Wacquant, *Urban Outcasts: A Comparative Sociology of Advanced Marginality* (Cambridge: Polity Press, 2008).

101 **avoid neighboring communities:** See https://arts.uchicago.edu /arts-public-life/arts-block.

102 **grown up with at home:** Ibid.

105 **people from 190 countries enrolled:** Jeremy Selingo, "Demystifying the MOOC," *New York Times*, October 29, 2014.

106 **four-year college programs:** John Horrigan, "Lifelong Learning and Technology," Pew Research Center, March 22, 2016, http://www.pewinternet.org/2016/03/22/lifelong-learning-and -technology/.

106 **"receive a credential":** Chen Zhenghao, Brandon Alcorn, Gayle Christensen, Nicholas Eriksson, Daphne Koller, and Ezekiel Emanuel, "Who's Benefiting from MOOCs, and Why," *Harvard Business Review*, September 22, 2015.

106 **college experience so rich:** Dhawal Shal, "By the Numbers: MOOCS in 2016," Class Central, December 25, 2016, https://www .class-central.com/report/mooc-stats-2016/.

109 **"Minerva's performance is unique":** Stephen Kosslyn, "Minerva Delivers More Effective Learning. Test Results Prove It," Medium, October 10, 2017, https://medium.com/minerva-schools /minerva-delivers-more-effective-learning-test-results-prove-it -dfdbec6e04a6.

CHAPTER FOUR: HEALTHY BONDS

117 **their miserably low scores:** American Society of Civil Engineers, *2017 Infrastructure Report Card,* https://www.infrastructurereport card.org/americas-grades/.

118 **street drugs like heroin:** US Centers for Disease Control and Prevention, "Vital Signs: Overdoses of Prescription Opioid Pain Relievers—United States, 1999–2008," *Morbidity and Mortality Weekly Report* 60, no. 43 (2011): 1487.

118 **have been devastating:** Katherine Keyes, Magdalena Cerdá, Joanne Brady, Jennifer Havens, and Sandro Galea, "Understanding the Rural-Urban Differences in Nonmedical Prescription Opioid Use and Abuse in the United States," *American Journal of Public Health* 104, no. 2 (2014): 52–59.

118 **almost $80 billion:** Curtis Florence, Chao Zhou, Feijun Luo, and Likang Xu, "The Economic Burden of Prescription Opioid Overdose, Abuse, and Dependence in the United States, 2013," *Medical Care* 54, no. 10 (2016): 901–6.

118 **linked to opioid abuse:** German Lopez, "How to Stop the Deadliest Drug Overdose Crisis in American History," Vox, August 1, 2017, https://www.vox.com/science-and-health/2017/8/1/15746780 /opioid-epidemic-end.

118 **the entirety of the Vietnam War:** Josh Katz, "Drug Deaths in America Are Rising Faster Than Ever," *New York Times,* June 5, 2017.

118 **the next decade alone:** Max Blau, "STAT Forecast: Opioids Could Kill Nearly 500,000 Americans in the Next Decade," STAT, June 27, 2017, https://www.statnews.com/2017/06/27/opioid-deaths -forecast.

119 **social cohesion and social support:** Another is the massive increase, pushed by pharmaceutical companies, in the prescription of these painkillers. See, for example, Sam Quinones, *Dreamland: The True Tale of America's Opiate Epidemic* (New York: Bloomsbury, 2015).

119 **white Americans dying in middle age:** Anne Case and Angus Deaton, "Rising Morbidity and Mortality in Midlife Among White Non-Hispanic Americans in the 21st Century," *Proceedings of the National Academy of Sciences* 112, no. 49 (2015): 15078–83.

119 **"deaths of despair":** Anne Case and Angus Deaton, "Mortality and Morbidity in the 21st Century," *Brookings Papers on Economic Activity,* Spring 2017, 397–443.

119 **"Durkheim-like recipe for suicide":** Ibid., 429–30.

119 **naturally occurring opioids:** Tristen Inagaki, Lara Ray, Michael Irwin, Baldwin Way, and Naomi Eisenberger, "Opioids and Social Bonding: Naltrexone Reduces Feelings of Social Connection," *Social Cognitive and Affective Neuroscience* 11, no. 5 (2016): 728–35.

120 **"cause there ain't shit else to do":** Katherine McLean, "'There's Nothing Here' Deindustrialization as Risk Environment for Overdose," *International Journal of Drug Policy* 29 (2016): 19–26.

120 **comparatively fragile communities:** Michael Zoorob and Jason Salemi, "Bowling Alone, Dying Together: The Role of Social Capital in Mitigating the Drug Overdose Epidemic in the United States," *Drug and Alcohol Dependence* 173 (2017): 1–9.

120 **to find them and call 911:** In a stunning article on opioid addiction in West Virginia, the journalist Margot Talbot reports a spike in people taking drugs and overdosing in public spaces, including parks and athletic fields, in part because they want other people to find them and call 911 if they overdose. See Margot Talbot, "The Addicts Next Door," *New Yorker,* June 5, 2017.

120 **become addicted to heroin:** My account of the Swiss experiment comes from Joanne Csete, "From the Mountaintops: What the World Can Learn from Drug Policy Change in Switzerland," Open Society Foundations, 2010.

122 **elements of "recovery capital":** William Cloud and Robert Granfield, "Conceptualizing Recovery Capital: Expansion of a Theoretical Construct," *Substance Use & Misuse* 43, no. 12–13 (2008): 1971–86.

122 **overdose deaths in Switzerland dropped by 50 percent:** Jürgen Rehm, Ulrich Frick, Christina Hartwig, Felix Gutzwiller, Patrick Gschwend, and Ambros Uchtenhagen, "Mortality in Heroin-Assisted Treatment in Switzerland 1994–2000," *Drug and Alcohol Dependence* 79, no. 2 (2005): 137–43.

122 **not a single person died:** Salaam Semaan, Paul Fleming, Caitlin Worrell, Haley Stolp, Brittney Baack, and Meghan Miller, "Potential Role of Safer Injection Facilities in Reducing HIV and Hepatitis C Infections and Overdose Mortality in the United States," *Drug and Alcohol Dependence* 118, no. 2 (2011): 100–10.

122 **heroin-related property crimes:** Csete, "From the Mountaintops," 4.

122 **program made an immediate impact:** Francie Diep, "Inside North America's Only Legal Safe Injection Facility," *Pacific Standard,* August 30, 2016.

123 **deaths dropped less than 10 percent:** Brandon Marshall, Michael Jay Milloy, Evan Wood, Julio Montaner, and Thomas Kerr, "Reduction in Overdose Mortality After the Opening of North America's First Medically Supervised Safer Injecting Facility: A Retrospective Population-Based Study," *Lancet* 377, no. 9775 (2011): 1429–37.

123 **there than in comparable places:** Chloé Potier, Vincent Laprévote, Françoise Dubois-Arber, Olivier Cottencin, and Benjamin Rolland, "Supervised Injection Services: What Has Been Demonstrated? A Systematic Literature Review," *Drug and Alcohol Dependence* 145 (2014): 48–68.

123 **particularly women, from assault:** Susan Zalkind, "The Infrastructure of the Opioid Epidemic," CityLab, September 14, 2017, https://www.citylab.com/equity/2017/09/methadone-mile /539742/.

124 **"IDs hanging around their necks":** Ibid.

126 **presence of gangs and guns:** The USDA classifies food deserts as urban areas in which at least five hundred people or one-third of the population lives more than half a mile from a supermarket, supercenter, or large grocery store. In rural areas, the distance must be greater than ten miles. Delaram Takyar, an NYU graduate student and research assistant for this book, calculated the percentage of low-income census tracts by using data from the USDA Food Access Research Atlas.

128 **fortunate enough to live near them:** See the interactive map at the Chicago Urban Agriculture Mapping Project, http://cuamp .org/#/searchGardens?q=-1&q=-2&community=-1&ward=-1& boardDistrict=-1&municipality=-1.

128 **overheated urban environments:** American Public Health Association, *Improving Health and Wellness Through Access to Nature*, November 5, 2013, https://www.apha.org/policies-and-advocacy /public-health-policy-statements/policy-database/2014/07/08 /09/18/improving-health-and-wellness-through-access-to-nature.

128 **many more small-scale green spaces:** See Robert Channick, "4,000 Empty Lots on Sale for $1 to Chicago Homeowners," *Chicago Tribune*, November 28, 2016.

128 **thousands of dollars per month:** See the report "Chicago City Hall Green Roof" at the Conservation Design Forum website, https:// www.cdfinc.com/Chicago-City-Hall-Green-Roof. There's some disagreement about the energy savings that the green roof generates. One report claims that it reduces costs by up to $10,000 per month, while another says it's closer to $5,000 per year.

131 **"neighborhood redevelopment projects":** The APHA report *Improving Health and Wellness Through Access to Nature* is just one of several recent studies to show that treating vulnerable places by developing accessible public green spaces and other social infrastructure can do more to improve a community's health and well-being than targeting vulnerable individuals or groups. In the past decade, reams of published research have established scientific evidence for long-standing and widely held beliefs about the benefits of spending time in natural settings: It promotes social cohesion. It encourages physical activity and makes people feel more energetic. It lowers the risk of obesity and reduces stress, anxiety, anger, and sadness. It helps prevent attention disorders in children. It quickens the pace of recovery in people who are sick.

132 **"nation forward at too slow a pace":** According to Charles Branas and John MacDonald: "Electric power grids, water treatment plants, building codes, and roadway redesign did more to enhance the health of the public than many (maybe any) other programs, including medical care." See Charles Branas and John MacDonald, "A Simple Strategy to Transform Health, All Over the Place," *Journal of Public Health Management and Practice* 20, no. 2 (2014): 157–59.

133 **"persons repeatedly exposed":** Eugenia South, Michelle Kondo, Ross Cheney, and Charles Branas, "Neighborhood Blight, Stress, and Health: A Walking Trial of Urban Greening and Ambulatory Heart Rate," *American Journal of Public Health* 105, no. 5 (2015): 909–13.

133 **"difficult urban problems":** Ibid., 913.

133 **"almost half of women living independently":** United Nations, *World Population Ageing 2013,* 38, http://www.un.org/en /development/desa/population/publications/pdf/ageing/World PopulationAgeing2013.pdf.

134 **16 percent of the global population, by 2050:** World Health Organization, National Institute on Aging at the National Institutes of Health, *Global Health and Aging,* NIH Publication 11-7737, October 2011, http://www.who.int/ageing/publications/global_health .pdf.

135 **important to understand how they work:** Anastasia Loukaitou-Sideris, Lené Levy-Storms, and Madeline Brozen, *Placemaking for an Aging Population,* UCLA Luskin School of Public Affairs, June 2014, https://www.lewis.ucla.edu/wp-content/uploads/sites /2/2015/04/Seniors-and-Parks-8-28-Print_reduced.pdf.

135 **and the United States is thirty-first, at 79.3:** The life expectancy data come from the World Health Organization's Atlas, which uses 2015 data. See http://gamapserver.who.int/gho/interactive_charts /mbd/life_expectancy/atlas.html.

137 **eat together whenever they choose:** See the conclusion of Eric Klinenberg, *Going Solo: The Extraordinary Rise and Surprising Appeal of Living Alone* (New York: Penguin Press, 2012).

138 **playground is on the nearest lot:** All of these examples are from the case studies presented in Loukaitou-Sideris et al., *Placemaking for an Aging Population*, chap. 4.

139 **more than a minute to seventeen seconds:** David Sillito, "Finns Open Playgrounds to Adults," BBC News, February 8, 2006, http:// news.bbc.co.uk/2/hi/4691088.stm.

140 **skills that will help them in civic life:** See, among Roger Hart's many excellent papers on childhood and play, *Children's Participation: From Tokenism to Citizenship* (Florence: UNICEF International Child Development Center, 1992) and "Containing Children: Some Lessons on Planning for Play from New York City," *Environment and Urbanization* 14, no. 2 (2002): 135–48.

141 **"peering out their tenement windows":** Pamela Wridt, "An Historical Analysis of Young People's Use of Public Space, Parks and Playgrounds in New York City," *Children, Youth and Environments* 14, no. 1 (2004): 100–20.

142 **"I text message on my cell phone":** Ibid., 99–100.

143 **"regional park system":** The City Project, *Olmsted Report Parks, Playgrounds, and Beaches for the Los Angeles Regions, 1930s and Today*, 2015, https://www.cityprojectca.org/blog/archives/39416.

144 **"improve parks in every neighborhood":** The City Project, *Healthy Parks, Schools and Communities: Green Access and Equity for Los Angeles County, 2011*, http://www.mapjustice.org/images /LosAngelesENGLISH.pdf.

144 **census wards across the United Kingdom:** Jamie Pearce, Elizabeth Richardson, Richard Mitchell, and Niamh Shortt, "Environmental Justice and Health: The Implications of the Socio-Spatial Distribution of Multiple Environmental Deprivation for Health Inequalities in the United Kingdom," *Transactions of the Institute of British Geographers* 35, no. 4 (2010): 522–39.

145 **environmental deprivation matters, period:** There's a nice account of how Richard Mitchell's scholarship on nature evolved in Florence Williams, *The Nature Fix: Why Nature Makes Us Hap-*

pier, Healthier, and More Creative (New York: W. W. Norton, 2017), chap. 7.

145 **access to all of Hyde Park:** Indeed, the life expectancy for men in Islington is nearly three years lower than for men in the rest of England, and for women it's one year lower. See "Introduction to Islington," a report from the National Health Service, http://www.islingtonccg.nhs.uk/jsna/Introduction-and-The-Islington -Population-JSNA-200910.pdf.

CHAPTER FIVE: COMMON GROUND

148 **"similarity begets friendship":** The classic account of "primary" and "secondary" groups comes from Charles Cooley, *Social Organization* (New York: Charles Scribner's Sons, 1909), chap. 3. The quotes from Aristotle and Plato are from a classic sociological article on homophily: Miller McPherson, Lynn Smith-Lovin, and James Cook, "Birds of a Feather: Homophily in Social Networks," *Annual Review of Sociology* 27 (2001): 415–44.

149 **social dynamics worked:** William Kornblum, *Blue-Collar Community* (Chicago: University of Chicago Press, 1974).

150 **"competition among peers":** Ibid., 66.

150 **"switchyards of the steel industry":** Ibid., 37, 18.

151 **segregated by race and class:** See William Julius Wilson, *The Truly Disadvantaged* (Chicago: University of Chicago Press, 1987), and Douglas Massey and Nancy Denton, *American Apartheid* (Cambridge, MA: Harvard University Press, 1993).

151 **most major policy matters:** The leading text on polarization from the 2000s is Morris Fiorina, Samuel Abrams, and Jeremy Pope, *Culture War?* (New York: Pearson Longman, 2005). In 1996, the sociologists Paul DiMaggio, John Evans, and Bethany Bryson showed that there was little evidence to support widespread assertions that Americans were growing more polarized. Why, then, did so many people perceive rising fragmentation? They suggested several possible reasons, including that Americans might be developing more intense political beliefs, that the media might be airing more polarized opinions, and that people tended to romanticize the past and forget how conflicted they used to be. See Paul DiMaggio, John Evans, and Bethany Bryson, "Have Americans' Social Attitudes Become More Polarized?," *American Journal of Sociology* 102, no. 3 (1996): 690–755.

152 **that confirm their beliefs:** On inequality and class segregation, see Sean Reardon and Kendra Bischoff, "Income Inequality and Income Segregation," *American Journal of Sociology* 116, no. 4 (2011): 1092–153. On the filter bubble, see Eli Pariser, *The Filter Bubble* (New York: Penguin Press, 2011).

152 **"discrimination based on race":** Shanto Iyengar and Sean Westwood, "Fear and Loathing Across Party Lines," *American Journal of Political Science* 59, no. 3 (2015): 690–707.

152 **"threaten the nation's well-being":** Pew Research Center, "Partisanship and Political Animosity in 2016," June 22, 2016, http:// www.people-press.org/2016/06/22/partisanship-and-political -animosity-in-2016/.

153 **forms of group mixing that are uncommon today:** The data on labor unions come from Gerald Mayer, *Union Membership Trends in the United States* (Washington, DC: Congressional Research Service, 2004). The quote is from Peter Bearman and Delia Baldassarri, "Dynamics of Political Polarization," *American Sociological Review* 72 (October 2007): 787. On the rise of marriage within a social class (or "assortative mating"), see Robert Mare, "Educational Homogamy in Two Gilded Ages," *Annals of the American Academy of Political and Social Science* 663 (2016): 117–39.

153 **"met with plausible counterarguments":** Cass Sunstein, *#Republic: Divided Democracy in the Age of Social Media* (Princeton, NJ: Princeton University Press, 2017), 91–92.

154 **It's urgent that we understand them:** See Elijah Anderson, *The Cosmopolitan Canopy: Race and Civility in Everyday Life* (New York: W. W. Norton, 2011).

155 **"they all meet up":** Hafstein is quoted in https://www.cnn.com /2017/03/20/health/iceland-pool-culture/.

155 **"among their countrymen":** Dan Kois, "Iceland's Water Cure," *New York Times Magazine*, April 19, 2016.

156 **"defines them as social others":** Jeff Wiltse, "America's Swimming Pools Have a Long, Sad, Racist History," *Washington Post,* June 10, 2015.

156 **swam together in relative peace:** Jeff Wiltse, *Contested Waters: A Social History of Swimming Pools in America* (Chapel Hill: University of North Carolina Press, 2007), 1.

157 **"don't touch the water!":** Ibid., 2.

157 **draining the entire pool:** Rachaell Davis, "This Tweet Perfectly Sums Up Why Simone Manuel's Olympic Win Is So Important,"

Essence, August 12, 2016, https://www.essence.com/2016/08/12 /simone-manuels-why-olympic-win-so-important.

157 **declined to review the case:** Wiltse, *Contested Waters*, 156.

158 **could never swim together:** "Swimming Pool Clash Reported in St. Louis," *Atlanta Daily World*, July 21, 1950.

158 **as a white-only facility:** Yoni Appelbaum, "McKinney, Texas, and the Racial History of American Swimming Pools," *Atlantic*, June 8, 2015, https://www.theatlantic.com/politics/archive /2015/06/troubled-waters-in-mckinney-texas/395150/.

158 **head off a lawsuit:** Rose Hackman, "Swimming While Black," *Guardian*, August 4, 2015, https://www.theguardian.com/world /2015/aug/04/black-children-swimming-drownings-segregation.

158 **to end its segregationist practices:** Ibid.

158 **twenty-five hundred to more than four million:** Appelbaum, "McKinney, Texas."

158 **inaccessible to the middle and lower classes:** Ibid.

158 **pool is "a way of life for us":** See Robert Flipping Jr., "Blacks Demand Re-opening of Sully's Pool," *New Pittsburgh Courier*, June 7, 1975, and Wiltse, "America's Swimming Pools."

159 **whereas public schools are a "necessity":** "The Court's Swimming Pool Ruling," *Los Angeles Times*, June 16, 1971.

159 **die from unintentional drowning:** Hackman, "Swimming While Black."

159 **part of African American culture:** National Public Radio, "Public Swimming Pools' Divisive Past," May 28, 2007, https://www.npr .org/templates/story/story.php?storyId=10495199.

159 **go back to their "Section 8 homes":** Wiltse, "America's Swimming Pools."

159 **"Thank you McKinney Police for keeping us safe":** Appelbaum, "McKinney, Texas."

160 **"and quite possibly in the world":** Orlando Patterson, *Rituals of Blood: The Consequences of Slavery in Two American Centuries* (New York: Basic Books, 1998), 4.

160 **before engaging other groups:** The classic texts on counterpublics are Nancy Fraser, "Rethinking the Public Sphere," *Social Text* 25, no. 26 (1990): 56–80, and Michael Warner, "Publics and Counterpublics," *Public Culture* 14, no. 1 (2002): 49–90.

161 **American civic life in the long run:** Melissa Harris-Lacewell, *Barbershops, Bibles, and BET: Everyday Talk and Black Political Thought* (Princeton, NJ: Princeton University Press, 2004), 163, 200.

161 **"him the word on local doings":** William Grier and Price Cobbs, *Black Rage* (New York: Basic Books, 1968), 88.

161 **145 restaurants, and 70 taverns across the city:** St. Clair Drake and Horace Cayton, *Black Metropolis: A Study of Negro Life in a Northern City* (1945; repr., Chicago: University of Chicago Press, 2015), 438, 461.

162 **"blanket condemnation of police actions":** Harris-Lacewell, *Barbershops, Bibles, and BET*, 198.

162 **"nothing but sit her black ass down":** *Barbershop*, story written by Mark Brown; screenplay written by Mark Brown, Don D. Scott, and Marshall Todd, directed by Tim Story, 2002.

162 **prepared to engage the world outside:** Urban ethnographers have also observed the social processes visible in black barbershops in other protected spaces, including the tavern. The classic study is Elijah Anderson's *A Place on the Corner* (Chicago: University of Chicago Press, 1978). Anderson writes: "Urban taverns and bars, like barbershops, carryouts, and other such establishments, with their adjacent street corners and alleys, serve as important gathering places for people of the 'urban villages' and ghetto areas of the city. Often they are special hangouts for the urban poor and working-class people, serving somewhat as more formal social clubs or domestic circles do for the middle and upper classes" (1).

163 **even reducing violent crime:** The most impressive studies that measure the effects of community organization on local life are Robert Sampson, *Great American City: Chicago and the Enduring Neighborhood Effect* (Chicago: University of Chicago Press, 2012), and Patrick Sharkey, *Uneasy Peace: The Great Crime Decline, the Renewal of City Life, and the Next War on Violence* (New York: W. W. Norton, 2018).

163 **10 percent black by 1990:** Elmhurst-Corona was the site of a remarkable research project led by the City University of New York anthropologist Roger Sanjek. Sanjek and his team of research assistants began studying how community organizations shaped group relations in the multiracial, multilingual neighborhood in the early 1980s. They remained there, conducting fieldwork on everyday ac-

tivities and closely observing what happens in civic associations, churches, neighborhood events, and local political meetings, until 1996. The main findings from the project are reported in Robert Sanjek, *The Future of Us All: Race and Neighborhood Politics in New York City* (Ithaca, NY: Cornell University Press, 1998). My account of community organizations in Elmhurst-Corona draws heavily on this work.

164 **INS would root them out:** Ibid., 72.

165 **"or we won't survive":** Quoted in Roger Sanjek, "Color-Full Before Color Blind: The Emergence of Multiracial Neighborhood Politics in Queens, New York City," *American Anthropologist* 102, no. 4 (2000): 765–66.

165 **doubling their level of representation:** Ibid., 766.

167 **meaningful relationships off the field:** Victor Turner, *The Ritual Process: Structure and Anti-Structure* (1969; repr., New York: Routledge, 2017). For an overview of the anthropology of sport, see Kendall Blanchard, *The Anthropology of Sport* (Westport, CT: Bergin & Garvey, 1995).

167 **a cricket field in Brooklyn plays a starring role:** Joseph O'Neill, *Netherland* (New York: Pantheon, 2008).

168 **"un-Americanness accentuates their singularity":** James Wood, "Beyond a Boundary," *New Yorker,* May 26, 2008.

168 **who's trying to find secure footing:** Ibid.

170 **our social distance narrowed:** For an ethnographic account of similar experiences, see Anderson, *Cosmopolitan Canopy.*

172 **"employed elsewhere in the community":** Liam Delaney and Emily Keaney, "Sport and Social Capital in the United Kingdom: Statistical Evidence from National and International Survey Data," December 2005, http://www.social-capital.net/docs/file/sport%20and%20social%20capital.pdf.

172 **democratize a deeply divided society:** Eric Worby, "The Play of Race in a Field of Urban Desire: Soccer and Spontaneity in Post-apartheid Johannesburg," *Critique of Anthropology* 29, no. 1 (2009): 105–23.

173 **"without this team":** Emmarie Huetteman, "Shooting Shines Light on an Annual Baseball Game and a Bipartisan Pastime," *New York Times,* June 14, 2017.

173 **"and work together again":** See Cass Sunstein, "The Polarization of Extremes," *Chronicle Review,* December 14, 2007. Haidt is

quoted in Sean Illing, "Why Social Media Is Terrible for Multiethnic Democracies," Vox, November 15, 2016, https://www.vox.com/policy-and-politics/2016/11/15/13593670/donald-trump-jonathan-haidt-social-media-polarization-europe-multiculturalism.

174 **cannot be entirely to blame:** Levi Boxell, Matthew Gentzkow, and Jesse Shapiro, "Is the Internet Causing Polarization? Evidence from Demographics," Working Paper, 2014, http://web.stanford.edu/~gentzkow/research/age-polar.pdf.

174 **different education level, ethnic identity, or religious affiliation:** Gina Potarca, "Does the Internet Affect Assortative Mating? Evidence from the U.S. and Germany," *Social Science Research* 61 (2017): 278–97.

175 **to get news from home:** Ivan Watson, Clayton Nagel, and Zeynep Bilginsoy, " 'Facebook Refugees' Chart Escape from Syria on Cell Phones," CNN, September 15, 2015, https://www.cnn.com/2015/09/10/europe/migrant-facebook-refugees/index.html.

175 **with a diverse set of peers:** See Nicole Ellison, Charles Steinfield, and Cliff Lampe, "The Benefits of Facebook 'Friends': Social Capital and College Students' Use of Online Social Network Sites," *Journal of Computer-Mediated Communication* 12, no. 4 (2007): 1143–68, and Min-Woo Kwon, Jonathan D'Angelo, and Douglas McLeod, "Facebook Use and Social Capital: To Bond, to Bridge, or to Escape," *Bulletin of Science, Technology & Society* 33, no. 1–2 (2013): 35–43.

175 **attend traditional support groups:** See Tabor Flickinger, Claire DeBolt, Ava Lena Waldman, George Reynolds, Wendy F. Cohn, Mary Catherine Beach, Karen Ingersoll, and Rebecca Dillingham, "Social Support in a Virtual Community: Analysis of a Clinic-Affiliated Online Support Group for Persons Living with HIV/AIDS," *AIDS and Behavior* 21, no. 11 (2017): 3087–99.

CHAPTER SIX: AHEAD OF THE STORM

182 **rainfall figures were "simply mind-blowing":** Jason Samenow, "Harvey Marks the Most Extreme Rain Event in U.S. History," *Washington Post*, August 29, 2017, https://www.washingtonpost.com/news/capital-weather-gang/wp/2017/08/29/harvey-marks-the-most-extreme-rain-event-in-u-s-history/?utm_term=.94d4e7d3b7ad.

182 **deepened their faith in the community:** Two of my research assistants, the NYU graduate students Kiara Douds (who grew up in
Houston and had friends at Wilcrest) and Delaram Takyar, went to
Houston to report on the collective response to Harvey. They were
at this church meeting, and they spent several days with the Wilcrest Baptist Church congregation observing how it helped those
affected by the storm.

182 **and it didn't happen at random:** "Congregations have long been
hyper-segregated," writes the sociologist Michael Emerson. "As of
2007 (our most recent data with such detail), 85 percent of congregations in the United States were comprised of at least 90 percent
of one group. As of 2010, just 4 percent of all congregations claimed
to have no racial majority." See Michael Emerson, "A New Day
for Multiracial Congregations," *Reflections: A Magazine of Theo-
logical and Ethical Inquiry from Yale Divinity School,* 2013, https://
reflections.yale.edu/article/future-race/new-day-multiracial
-congregations.

183 **a place of cross-racial, multiethnic integration:** Rodney Woo has
written a book that recounts his experience helping Wilcrest become more open and multiracial: *The Color of Church: A Biblical
and Practical Paradigm for Multiracial Churches* (Nashville: B&H
Academic, 2009).

187 **rising for thousands of years:** See Anders Levermann, Peter Clark,
Ben Marzeion, Glenn Milne, David Pollard, Valentina Radic, and
Alexander Robinson, "The Multimillennial Sea-Level Commit-
ment of Global Warming," *Proceedings of the National Academy of
Sciences* 110, no. 34 (2013): 13745–50.

188 **"combined and multiplied by three":** Korie Edwards, Brad Chris-
terson, and Michael Emerson, "Race, Religious Organizations, and
Integration," *Annual Review of Sociology* 39 (2013): 212.

189 **"ever occurring again":** The quotes from Nicole Lurie and Barack
Obama appear in Eric Klinenberg, "Adaptation," *New Yorker,* January 7, 2013.

189 **"the social infrastructure matters, too":** Ibid.

196 **people who watch them:** De Urbanisten explains how the
Water Square works on its website: http://www.urbanisten.nl/wp
/?portfolio=waterplein-benthemplein.

199 **dangerous monsoons and floods:** See Khurshed Alam and Habi-
bur Rahman, "Women in Natural Disasters: A Case Study from

Southern Coastal Region of Bangladesh," *International Journal of Disaster Risk Reduction* 8 (2014): 68–82.

199 **betting on the concept:** David Gelles, "Floating Cities, No Longer Science Fiction, Begin to Take Shape," *New York Times*, November 13, 2017.

201 **Bjarke Ingels and the BIG Group:** See Eric Klinenberg, "Want to Survive Climate Change? You'll Need a Good Community," *Wired*, November 2016, https://www.wired.com/2016/10/klinenberg-trans forming-communities-to-survive-climate-change/.

203 **goal of Living Breakwaters:** Ibid.

205 **flood protection, adaptation, and climate security:** City of New Orleans, *Plan for the 21st Century: New Orleans 2030*, 2010, https://www.nola.gov/city-planning/master-plan/.

206 **its bike-share program:** See Shannon Sims, "Building a Social Scene Around a Bike Path," CityLab, August 1, 2017, https://www.citylab.com/life/2017/08/lafitte-greenway-new-orleans/534735/, and Richard Florida, "Mapping America's Bike Commuters," CityLab, May 19, 2017, https://www.citylab.com/transportation/2017/05/mapping-americas-bike-commuters/526923/.

CONCLUSION: BEFORE WE LIFT THE NEXT SHOVEL

209 **"Are we building the world we all want?":** Mark Zuckerberg, "Building Global Community," Facebook, February 16, 2017, https://www.facebook.com/notes/mark-zuckerberg/building -global-community/10154544292806634/.

210 **"That's who we are":** See Tony Romm, "Trump Campaign Fires Back at Zuckerberg," Politico, April 13, 2016, https://www.politico.com/story/2016/04/mark-zuckerberg-trump-feud-221897, and Seth Fiegerman, "Mark Zuckerberg Criticizes Trump on Immigration," CNN, January 27, 2017, http://money.cnn.com/2017/01/27/technology/zuckerberg-trump-immigration/index.html.

212 **"engagement will go down":** Mark Zuckerberg, Facebook post, January 11, 2018. https://www.facebook.com/zuck/posts/10104413015393571/.

213 **reach their targeted audiences:** Benjamin Elgin and Vernon Silver, "Facebook and Google Helped Anti-Refugee Campaign in Swing States," Bloomberg.com, October 18, 2017, https://www.bloomberg.com/news/articles/2017-10-18/facebook-and-google -helped-anti-refugee-campaign-in-swing-states.

214 **experiencing displacement or gentrification pressures:** See the Urban Displacement Project's map and report at http://www .urbandisplacement.org/map/sf.

215 **remains a food desert:** George Avalos, "Facebook Campus Expansion Includes Offices, Retail, Grocery Store, Housing," *San Jose Mercury News,* July 7, 2017, http://www.mercurynews.com/2017 /07/07/facebook-campus-expansion-includes-offices-retail-grocery -store-housing/.

218 **are "without peer":** Philanthropy Roundtable, "Andrew Carnegie," http://www.philanthropyroundtable.org/almanac/hall_of _fame/andrew_carnegie#a.

218 **"depth of gratitude which I feel":** Andrew Carnegie, *Autobiography of Andrew Carnegie* (Boston: Houghton Mifflin, 1920), 47.

219 **establish Internet connections:** See the press release here: https:// www.gatesfoundation.org/Media-Center/Press-Releases/1997/06 /Bill-and-Melinda-Gates-Establish-Library-Foundation.

219 **just need companionship to get through the day:** Until 2017, when the Stavros Niarchos Foundation gave $55 million to rebuild the circulating library in Midtown, the last major effort to invest in the New York City Public Library was a misguided, massively expensive, and ultimately ill-fated effort to renovate the flagship library, led by elite trustees who, as one former library executive said, "only care about the 42nd Street building" and "don't care about the branches." See Scott Sherman, *Patience and Fortitude: Power, Real Estate, and the Fight to Save a Public Library* (New York: Melville House, 2015), 73.

221 **maintenance on existing facilities:** See the transcript of testimony by Jonathan Bowles before the New York City Council in September 2013: https://nycfuture.org/research/testimony -building-better-libraries.

221 **24 percent drop in staff hours:** In 2014, the city increased public library funds for the first time since 2008, to $144 million, but this is still far below the level of public support that it had offered to libraries in the early 2000s, when it was typically above $200 million per year. See New York City Independent Budget Office, "Library Funding: Subsidies Rebound, Disparities Remain," Fiscal Brief, July 2007, http://www.ibo.nyc.ny.us/iboreports/library spending.pdf.

224 **"reopen a store in the Bronx in the future":** Steven Goodstein, "Barnes & Noble Commits to Bronx Return in 24–36 Months,"

Bronx Times, November 15, 2016, https://www.bxtimes.com /stories/2016/46/46-barnes-2016-11-11-bx.html.

224 **"100 feet away from you":** McDonald is quoted in Elizabeth Segran, "Two Ex-Googlers Want to Make Bodegas and Mom-and-Pop Corner Stores Obsolete," *Fast Company,* September 13, 2017, https://www.fastcompany.com/40466047/two-ex-googlers-want -to-make-bodegas-and-mom-and-pop-corner-stores-obsolete?utm _content=bufferb45ab&utm_medium=social&utm_source= twitter.com&utm_campaign=buffer.

225 **households lacked Internet access:** See Deborah Fallows, "Not Your Mother's Library," *Atlantic,* October 6, 2014, https://www .theatlantic.com/national/archive/2014/10/not-your-mothers -library/381119/, and the report "Internet Connection Data for Cities," Governing.com, http://www.governing.com/gov-data/city -internet-connection-household-adoption-rates-data.html.

226 **all the local branches:** "Voters OK 2.8-mill Columbus Metropolitan Library Levy," *ThisWeek* Community News, November 3, 2010, http://www.thisweeknews.com/article/20101026/news/310269541.

226 **"a thriving community where wisdom prevails":** Columbus Metropolitan Library, "Columbus Metropolitan Library to Eliminate Overdue Fines Beginning Jan. 1, 2017," press release, December 1, 2016, http://www.columbuslibrary.org/press/columbus -metropolitan-library-eliminate-overdue-fines-beginning-jan-1 -2017.

226 **sixty thousand participants in its summer reading groups:** Columbus Metropolitan Library, "Media Fact Sheet," 2017, www .columbuslibrary.org/sites/default/files/uploads/docs/Media%20 Fact%20Sheet_0.pdf.

227 **conceal potential contaminants:** Oliver Milman and Jessica Glenza, "At Least 33 US Cities Used Water Testing 'Cheats' over Lead Concerns," *Guardian,* June 2, 2016, https://www.theguardian.com /environment/2016/jun/02/lead-water-testing-cheats-chicago -boston-philadelphia.

227 **across group lines:** See the Studio Gang description of the Polis Station on its website: http://studiogang.com/project/polis-station/.

232 **organize economy and society:** David Billington, *The Tower and the Bridge: The New Art of Structural Engineering* (Princeton, NJ: Princeton University Press, 1985).

PHOTO CAPTIONS AND CREDITS

1 The Seward Park Library
PHOTO CREDIT: Eric Klinenberg

25 The New Lots Library Bowling Team
PHOTO CREDIT: Eric Klinenberg

55 Community park on remediated empty lot in West Philadelphia
PHOTO CREDIT: Eric Klinenberg

83 Early literacy program at the Seward Park Library
PHOTO CREDIT: Eric Klinenberg

117 Growing Home Urban Farm in Englewood neighborhood, Chicago
PHOTO CREDIT: Andy Collings. Used by permission.

147 Though formally they are sites for competition, athletic fields also
provide common ground.
PHOTO CREDIT: Public domain

177 Volunteers from the Wilcrest Baptist Church who cleaned out the
flooded home of a fellow congregant after Hurricane Harvey
PHOTO CREDIT: Wilcrest Baptist Church. Used by permission.

209 The Stavros Niarchos Foundation Cultural Center. Athens, Greece
PHOTO CREDIT: Stavros Niarchos Foundation. Used by permission.

INDEX

INDEX

ABOUT THE AUTHOR

ERIC KLINENBERG is a professor of sociology and director of the Institute for Public Knowledge at New York University. He also serves as research director for Rebuild by Design, a federal competition that generates innovative infrastructure projects for twenty-first-century challenges. Klinenberg is the coauthor, with Aziz Ansari, of the #1 *New York Times* bestseller *Modern Romance,* and author of the acclaimed books *Going Solo, Heat Wave,* and *Fighting for Air.* He has contributed to *The New Yorker, The New York Times Magazine, Rolling Stone, Wired,* and *This American Life.*

Moisture damage noted 6/17/20 gr